ASIA FALLING

Other BusinessWeek Books

Mastering the Art of Creative Collaboration
Robert Hargrove

TransCompetition
Harvey Robbins and Michael Finley

Conquering Uncertainty
Theodore Modis

The Market Makers
Daniel Spulber

ASIA FALLING

Making sense of the Asian crisis
and its aftermath

CALLUM HENDERSON

 **BusinessWeek Books**

McGRAW-HILL

New York San Francisco Washington, D.C. Auckland Bogotá
Caracas Lisbon London Madrid Mexico City Milan
Montreal New Delhi San Juan Singapore
Sydney Tokyo Toronto

Library of Congress Cataloging-in-Publication Data

Henderson, Callum.
    Asia falling : making sense of the Asian crisis and its
aftermath / Callum Henderson.
        p.   cm.
    Includes bibliographical references.
    ISBN 0-07-028148-3
    1. Foreign exchange rates—Asia.   I. Title.
HG3968.H46   1998
332.4'53'095—dc21   98-16964
                                                    CIP

McGraw-Hill

A Division of The **McGraw·Hill** Companies

    2 3 4 5 6 7 8 9 0   DOC / DOC   9 0 2 1 0 9 8

ISBN 0-07-028148-3

The sponsoring editor for this book was *Jeffrey Krames,* the editing
supervisor was *John M. Morriss,* and the production supervisor
was *Suzanne W. B. Rapcavage.* It was set in Guardi Roman by
North Market Street Graphics.

Printed and bound by R. R. Donnelley & Sons Company.

McGraw-Hill books are available at special quantity discounts to use as
premiums and sales promotions, or for use in corporate training programs.
For more information, please write to the Director of Special Sales,
McGraw-Hill, 11 West 19th Street, New York, NY 10011. Or contact
your local bookstore.

 This book was printed on recycled, acid-free paper containing
a minimum of 50% recycled, de-inked fiber.

To the Memory of my Mother,
God Bless Her and Keep Her,
and to my Father.

Sláinte

Acknowledgments

For those who have occasionally thought about writing a book but not yet done so, I can only issue the following heart-felt warning: It is a soul-destroying, all-encompassing, crushing task. For the five months spent in writing this book—following many months of research—it took almost every minute of every hour of my life, that is, the part of my life outside my normal work activities as a foreign exchange analyst in the markets. Given this situation, my colleagues at Standard & Poor's MMS, throughout Asia, displayed patience and tolerance levels that are quite beyond me. My sincere thanks to them, for their tolerance and generosity, in giving of their time and ideas. I am truly fortunate to work with such people. Particular thanks must go to Meryl Phang, Yolanda Ho, and Tony Ngan from Standard & Poor's MMS in Hong Kong, all experts in their respective fields of analyzing Greater China, as well as David Cohen, Alison Seng, Sani Hamid, and Andy Tan in the Singapore office who specialize in the ASEAN countries, and finally John Lilley, Director of Analytical Operations, Asia, and Ken Ho, Managing Director, Asia, for allowing me the time, particularly in a period of unparalleled market turbulence, to complete the book. In addition, I would also like to express my thanks to Paul Tan and Tony Lim of McGraw-Hill Publishing in Singapore, for their dedication to and faith in this project.

With analysts and dealers depending for their very livelihood on the industry of financial markets, confidentiality is a frequent and understandable necessity. This is particularly the case in Asia, where the need to maintain contacts is paramount and the pressure for "self-censorship" ever-present. As a result, many of the analysts, dealers, fund managers, and central bankers with whom I spoke requested, and received, anonymity. My sincere thanks to them and also to those individuals who felt less inhibited and were happy to be quoted freely. Where I cite the views of individuals (anonymous or otherwise) or published sources, I have made clear and open reference to these. In all other cases, the opinions expressed in the book are my own. All Asian economic data mentioned, unless otherwise referenced, are taken from the economic database of Standard & Poor's MMS, Asia.

70999

Contents

Introduction

"Currency trading is unnecessary, unproductive and immoral!" Dr. Mahathir Mohammed exclaimed in a blistering speech he gave at the Annual Meeting of the IMF and World Bank in Hong Kong. Speaking before the massed ranks of the world's media, international delegates, and government and IMF officials, Dr. Mahathir held his audience on the edge of their seats.

"It should be stopped. It should be made illegal!" he thundered. Railing against foreign funds whose gains "must come from impoverishing others," the Malaysian prime minister, impeccably dressed and with his traditional charisma, lashed out against those who had brought low the Malaysian ringgit, and, in the process, forced Malaysia's stock and bond markets into panicked flight. "Currency traders have become rich—very, very rich," he said, "through making other people poor!"[1]

While the Asian currency crisis was already well under way by then, the events of the IMF meeting, and more specifically the statement by Dr. Mahathir, brought home like nothing before the global resonance of the drama unfolding in Asia.

The comments, made on the evening of Saturday, September 20, 1997, caused an immediate reaction, not least from George Soros. Soros is the founder and head of Soros Fund Management and chief adviser to the Quantum Fund, the largest "hedge fund" in the world. He had come under personal verbal attack from the Malaysian prime minister and seemed to symbolize the speculative forces about which Dr. Mahathir was talking. In a televised briefing the next day, Soros, in a vigorous retort, said the suggestion that currency trading should be banned was so inappropriate it did not deserve serious consideration. He declared, "Interfering with the convertibility of capital at a moment like this is a recipe for disaster. . . . Dr. Mahathir is a menace to his own country."[2]

Deputy Prime Minister and Finance Minister Anwar Ibrahim, while supporting his prime minister, moved swiftly to try to calm the situation and instigate some damage control. He stressed that there were no plans to change the currency trading regime in Malaysia—contrary to the suggestion that currency trading would be limited to trade finance—and said it was time to put an end to this type of acrimonious dispute and get on with sorting out the economy.

It was a brave attempt to calm the situation, but when Malaysian markets opened on Monday, September 22, 1997, traders did not listen to such reassurances. Focusing instead on the Mahathir comments, investors panicked, stunned by what many deemed inflammatory remarks that would only add to already shaky market conditions. Malaysian stocks were hit from the opening bell. On that day the Malaysian composite (stock) index lost 27.34 points, or around 3.5%, declining to 760.50, while in the global currency market the dollar-ringgit (USD-MYR) traded as high as 3.1300.

International investors were just as dismayed as their domestic Malaysian counterparts, indeed probably more so. "After he made those comments, I phoned Boston and told them to get out—totally—while we still could," a U.S. fund manager with a Boston-based mutual fund told me, referring to both stock and bond positions.[3]

Subsequently that week, both the ringgit and the stock market managed to stabilize somewhat, with Anwar doing his best to soothe investor nerves. However, confidence had been severely damaged, and market and economic conditions were to get much worse still. Politicians and bureaucrats the world over, as is their wont, blamed the "speculators" for the Asian currency crisis—and, as a result, the ensuing economic slowdown in Asia. It was all the fault of rich individuals and funds whose sole purpose was to rob from the "poor" to further enrich themselves, if one is to believe this argument. All this brings back fond memories of the equally hysterical reaction of French and German officials to the second ERM (exchange rate mechanism) crisis in August 1993, when in a violent paroxysm of release the markets managed to throw off (but not break) the chains by which they were held—those of the ERM.

Politicians and bureaucrats have a habit of blaming "speculators" when things go badly because they need a convenient scapegoat. It is classic Sun Tzu (or Metternich, or Clausewitz, for that matter) to avert an internal disturbance, create an external diversion. "Speculators" are an easy, amorphous target and usually do not fight back, at least verbally—the obvious exception being Mr. Soros. The speculators themselves scoff at such talk, contenting themselves with their returns on winning trades. Privately, the "macro" hedge funds and other types of speculations base their strategies on traditional fundamentals and technicals. As one hedge fund manager told me pointedly, "We wouldn't make money if the fundamentals were properly aligned. It is precisely because economic and financial policies are out of line (with economic demands of the country concerned) that we are able to take on a currency or an asset market."[4]

Indeed so. Soros himself, in his public musings, has said as much. It is understandable that politicians feel considerable anger and frustration, seeing a currency crisis destroy (temporarily) much of what they have strived so hard to achieve and build. They are rather vigorous in their blame of others—and here I speak generally rather than specifically—because it is their own policies that were at fault. This is not to say that the "market"—however one defines that—is infallible. One could well argue that the ringgit, Thai baht, and Indonesian rupiah all overshot their fundamental levels amid the crisis that hit all the

Asian markets in the summer of 1997. The market is, however, a better arbiter of government policies than the governments themselves.

I will argue that the long-term economic health of the Asian economies was potentially saved, not destroyed, by the forced breaking of the dollar pegs to the regional currencies—potentially, because ASEAN specifically, and Asia as a whole, are at a crossroads. In terms of deregulation the countries have two choices. One is to use the currency crisis as a lesson with which to force through and speed up market and economic liberalization and deregulation. The other is to turn inward, make a critical mistake, and waste years of progress. The risks—and the rewards—are great indeed.

The dollar peg links served a purpose, for years providing the requisite stability to allow foreign direct and portfolio investment to flow into the region and at the same time insulating it from the ravages of inflation—but they had clearly passed their "sell-by" date. Fixed or pegged exchange rate regimes, unless flexible enough to allow for the variations in the economic cycle and unless backed by strong economic fundamentals, will inevitably fail. It may happen sooner, it may happen later, but it will happen eventually.

During the Asian currency crisis, the speculators had a go at the Hong Kong dollar (HKD). To tame the selling demand for the HKD, the Hong Kong Monetary Authority (HKMA) was obliged to intervene in the currency market by selling dollars and in the money market by allowing the overnight borrowing rate to soar as high as 300%. The HKMA's efforts were successful, not just because the HKMA was skillful and determined, but because the HKD was and is presently backed by sound economic fundamentals and a system that matches every U.S. dollar with 7.8 HKD. Steering the economy is a tricky task in the best of times, but especially so within a fixed or pegged exchange rate system. The Hong Kong authorities will have to remain both vigilant and flexible or the speculators will be back.

While the specifics for this book only became clear in early 1997, they sprang from a long-held fascination with a region whose economic successes, while marvelously notable, are but a recent phenomenon, the culmination of emergence from a century of political turbulence, widespread conflict, oppression, and plunder. Witnessing this emergence has been a thrilling experience. In only three decades, Asia achieved a degree of economic transformation and improvement that in Europe and the U.S. took almost a century. Accompanying this, the East Asian "miracle," as the World Bank described it, were several by-products, both positive and negative. The Asian emergence became an economic boom, with all the usual trappings that proliferate in such periods. A new doctrine, one concerning "Asian values," was created to explain the rise of the East—and the anticipated decline of the (decadent) West. Easy answers were sought and, as is usually the case, found. For a time, Asian markets and economies could only go up.

Nothing is ever that simple, however, or permanent, particularly in financial markets. For every boom, there is a bust; for every bubble, a crash. The markets, and thus real economies, are always in a state of flux. And yet, for a time Asia broke—or rather, bent—the rules, experiencing year after year of unheard-of growth. The story, the region, the economies were irresistible—until they were resisted by global market pressures and forces that seemed to explode onto the scene in July 1997 with the devaluation of the Thai baht, but that in reality had been building for several years.

Here in Hong Kong, the subsequent regional market crisis was equated with a *dai foong*—the Cantonese word from which the English "typhoon" originates. Now that the hellish winds of the *dai foong* have abated somewhat, the financial markets have finally managed to grab some time for quiet reflection—not only to review what went before and why, but to predict where we go from here. Such a period of reflection will be all too brief, the pace of change here in Asia being so much faster than elsewhere. And the rapid pace of change applies equally well to the views of many commentators who had typed up Asia well beyond even its prodigious capacity. How quiet now are those who argued that growth rates of 10% or more were natural, unending, almost genetic in Asia. And how quick to judgment are the doomsayers who call an end to the "Pacific century," not because such a title was misplaced in the first place, but because the crisis supposedly marks the end of the Asian miracle. Once again, easy answers have (hastily) been sought and found. Such commentary is not reasoned, economic analysis but a hysterical, knee-jerk reaction. Those easy answers reveal a glaring gap in understanding what has happened. This book, consequently, seeks to fill that gap. As the currency crises of the ERM (September 1992, August 1993), Mexico (December 1994–March 1995) and Asia teach us, financial markets, which pass judgment on economies and governments every day of the year, can be particularly unmerciful and unforgiving to those they deem misaligned. The effects of such crises are real. They are felt on the street by the unemployed and the homeless. Indeed, they are usually felt by those unable to fight back. However, to blame the speculators alone is to mistake a symptom for the disease.

The spectacular growth rates that Asia achieved in the 1980s and 1990s will be difficult, if not impossible, to match in the future, but that is no bad thing. To paraphrase Federal Reserve Board Chairman Alan Greenspan, it is vital to target and achieve sustainable, noninflationary, productivity-oriented growth for the long-term health of an economy. Growth driven chiefly by temporary, cyclical factors such as easy credit, low wage costs, and headline-grabbing, large infrastructure projects is of necessity more vulnerable to a sharp slowdown or even a crash.

Several ASEAN countries will experience sharp slowdowns— a painful process, but better a slowdown than a crash. Thailand and Indonesia are the obvious exceptions. They face the twin curses of an economic crisis and a political system that continues to hang on the very edge of a precipice from which it might not return. To be sure, Thailand's new constitution is a positive step in averting political disaster. IMF officials at the meeting in Hong Kong were quick to acknowledge the speed and dedication with which the Thai authorities were addressing the crisis. Such speed is necessary, for confidence needs to be restored quickly—for the market, the investor, and, not least, the domestic population of Thailand. Equally important, in Korea the election of Kim Dae Jung as president, whatever his individual merits, must result in a major change in the style of government. Such a change is necessary given the appalling credit policies of previous administrations, which have led to the current problems there. The threat exists in Korea also of economic recession—i.e., negative growth, as opposed to merely slower growth.

As for Dr. Mahathir, such bitter recrimination, as his comments implied, is understandable. He and those around him (notably his Deputy Prime Minister and Finance Minister Anwar Ibrahim) have brought Malaysia a long way and deserve much praise and respect—praise and respect that is all too lacking in the West. However, looking ahead, the new priorities, both economic and political, that Asia faces require a lighter touch, greater caution, and serious and significant reform of Asian financial sectors. Chief among those priorities must be to stabilize the economic fundamentals first—trusting in the market to find the appropriate level for the currency and thus letting go of some control. Then, for Asia as a whole, the priority is to transform export-led economies into consumer-driven economies that are less dependent on external demand and founded on strong domestic institutions and markets.

1

The Objective — Growth
at Any Price

THE RISE OF ASIA before its recent stumble is arguably one
of the most important events in world economic history. It
changed and leveled the world's economic playing field, and in
the process uplifted the lives of millions of people in Asia to a
degree never seen before. Productivity, growth, and investment—both foreign and domestic—virtually exploded.

Growth, fueled principally by exports, boomed and, with it,
living standards shot up—granted, from a relatively low base.
For example, between 1980 and 1990 growth of real GNP per
capita in the Republic of Korea was 121.8%. For Taiwan, that
figure was 88.0%. In Hong Kong, real GDP growth per capita in
that period leaped 64.2%, while in Singapore it was 77.5%.
Growth in real earnings has been even more impressive, rising
115.8% in Korea, 102.7% in Taiwan, 60.0% in Hong Kong, and
79.8% in Singapore.[1]

As for national growth levels, the average annual growth rate
for 1980–1991 for Hong Kong, Singapore, Korea, Indonesia,
Thailand, Malaysia, and China together was 7.3%. The Asian
currency crisis of 1997 will certainly have a substantial economic impact this year—Standard & Poor's MMS expect 0%
GDP growth in 1998 for ASEAN (Association of South East
Asian Nations) as a whole—but in one or two years this should

be back to around 5–6%. Compare this growth with that of Western Europe, which is just starting to climb out of economic stagnation, or even with that of the U.S., where economists and policymakers fret about the inflationary consequences of 3%-plus growth.

How did all this come about? After all, it wasn't that long ago that Asia was known more for regional wars and conflicts than it ever was for its economic performance. To see where Asia is going, we need to look at where it has been. We need to examine the fundamental positives behind the region's ascent and also the flaws and faultlines that caused this temporary "stumble."

People have put forth a number of theories to explain Asia's phenomenal economic success of the past three decades, though they are generally split into two camps: those who believe it was largely the result of Asian values and practices (education, the family, teamwork as opposed to individuality, networks) and those who say that it was due to external financial and economic factors—such as currency movements, foreign investment, technology transfers, and so on. While both arguments have merit, to leave it there would be oversimplistic. Amid the controversy at the IMF meeting in Hong Kong between the Malaysian prime minister Dr. Mahathir and Soros, Deputy Prime Minister Anwar Ibrahim responded pointedly to a question regarding Asia's "economic miracle," saying it was no miracle, but sheer hard work.[2]

The Asian success story reflects a unique combination of market- and government-led policies, a balance that doesn't exist in the mature Western nations to the same degree. Key to this success story was prudent macroeconomic management— "getting the basics right," as the World Bank described it in its research report *The East Asian Miracle.*[3]

Asian governments fostered an environment in which private domestic investment could grow rapidly. At the same time, these governments created strong primary and secondary education systems—or, in pure economic terms, "expanded the human capital base"—albeit to varying levels depending on the country. Extraordinarily high levels of domestic savings provided the bedrock for supporting that private investment, but this too did not happen by chance. Governments created the environment in which savings could flourish. Inflation was kept low through prudent monetary policy, while in many cases real interest rates were kept relatively high to attract high levels of domestic savings (Hong Kong and Singapore being notable exceptions). From 1981 to 1990, the gross domestic savings rate (the difference between GDP and total consumption expenditure, private and government) for the newly industrialized economies (NIEs), China, the ASEAN, and India together was an average 30.6% of GDP[4]; this is a stunningly high figure relative to the rest of the developed world, let alone other "developing" regions. In 1996, that average stood at around 32%. This compares with 17.5% for the U.S. and 12% for Western Europe.[5] Note also that the savings rate in Asia remains significantly higher than in Latin America. By as early as 1990, the savings rate of the fast-growing Asian economies was an average of 20 percentage points higher than the LATAM average[6]—though this figure has decreased since, in the wake of LATAM efforts to construct strong government/private pension systems.

So much for savings. Differences also exist in the relative domestic tax burdens. Government expenditure in the NIEs, ASEAN, China, and India averaged around 17% in 1996. One can argue that the U.S. and Europe have far higher absolute GDP levels and therefore this figure somewhat distorts the true picture. The bottom line, however, as Americans and Europeans can tell simply by looking at their tax bills, is that Asians save far more and are taxed less than their U.S. and European counterparts. This has in theory—and has had in practice over the past three decades—profound economic consequences, providing the fuel for sustaining high government and private investment levels and thus the economy itself. Prudent government policies, at both the microlevel and macrolevel, provided the base for these high savings levels. However, these by themselves would not have been enough had the respective Asian governments not attempted to shore up their banking and financial systems through improved supervision, providing their citizens with a safe(r) environment in which to place those savings. In the wake of the Asian currency crisis, one can argue that "improved supervision" had clearly not been sufficient given the asset inflation and credit bubbles that were allowed to develop. However, everything is relative—relative to the first two decades after World War II, Asia made great strides in this area, and the currency crisis should only serve to further these improvements, with the respective central banks likely to be much more stringent on issues such as nonperforming loans (NPLs), capital-adequacy ratios, and reserve requirements going forward than they were in the 1980s and 1990s.

On the agriculture side, while the role of this sector continued to gradually decline as the industrial revolution of Asia progressed, governments sought to maximize what resources they had available by emphasizing productivity and efficiency. They were well aware of the potential of a rural, social, and political backlash if urban and rural development rates were seen as strongly divergent. As well, they were wary of the economic impact from an excessive and too rapid decline in the agricultural base while the industrial base was still growing. As a result, the governments were careful not to overtax the rural and agricultural communities.

So the Asian governments got the "basics right," creating high savings rates, not overtaxing their citizens, and enhancing productivity in the rural and agricultural sector. That again is not the whole story, not by a long shot. While seeking to gradually liberalize and deregulate their economies and financial markets, these same governments also pursued deliberate and carefully targeted interventionist policies within the economies concerned, seeking to promote specific sectors and industries, principally those that were export-oriented. Specific industries, starting with the heavy manufacturing industries, through chemicals and commodity production, and finally to computers and electronics, were subsidized (sometimes on a broad basis, sometimes case by case, depending on the specific government and country concerned). To aid in this process, national development and export/import banks were created to exist alongside the ADB.

In addition, governments sought to invest in sector-specific research, subsidize declining industries, and protect import substitutes in order to maintain the positive trend in the overall trade balance. Finally, channels of communication were developed between industry and the bureaucracy in order to create a more responsive manufacturing base and reduce reaction time to changes in global industrial and economic trends. Government intervention didn't stop with manufacturing. It also penetrated the domestic labor markets, emphasizing flexibility and job creation and thus eliminating or at least reducing potential labor disorder.

This, combined with parallel drives to boost the export sector (and thus the trade balance) and productivity, created the rise in employment and real wage levels. In the more populated Asian countries, worker "supply" is disproportionately high, although declining birth rates will reduce that substantially over the next two decades. However, in the 1980s and 1990s, such was "demand" that the benefits fed directly through to real incomes, which in turn fed back into the savings rate and thus investment—a virtuous cycle. Most notably, with the governments seeking to support the domestic agricultural sectors, there was, at least initially, little price distortion between urban and agricultural growth.

Improvements in Asian domestic fundamentals didn't go unnoticed elsewhere. Asian governments, to varying degrees, pursued policies designed to attract both foreign direct investment (FDI) and portfolio investment and, more notably, foreign technology. With regard to this, many Western commentators, with the usual myopia, have pointed approvingly to rising Western nation FDI into Asia in the 1980s and 1990s. While this was important, Japan has gradually overtaken the West in terms of total FDI into the Asian region and is presently a significantly more important player. In 1977, Japan's FDI stock in Asia was just around $6 billion, about the same as that of the U.S. By 1994, Japan's FDI in Asia had risen to some $74.7 billion, while that of the U.S. to only $45.7 billion.[7] One point to note regarding this is that Japanese manufacturers broadly achieve significantly higher rates of investment relative to production than is generally the case with their Western counterparts (which remain burdened by the demands of a short-term shareholder focus). Japanese manufacturers invest more abroad to create an offshore manufacturing network and service that network with an ever-rising volume of parts and components. This is what happened in the U.S. and it is also what happened in Asia. As Hatch and Yamamura, in their work *Asia in Japan's Embrace,* note, between 1985 and 1993 Asia's trade deficit with Japan exploded, rising from a mere $9.3 billion to some $54.2 billion.[8] This is in direct contrast to the Asian experience with the U.S. and Europe where it was Asia's trade balances that moved sharply into surplus.

Asian governments created an investment-friendly atmosphere via investment subsidies and favorable tax policies. Also, they gradually cut trade tariffs—partly for investment purposes and partly to avoid global criticism about their rising trade surpluses with the West. They sought foreign technology through acquisition, imports, training, and licensing. Here, too, Asia's experiences with the West and with Japan have been radically different. No company is exactly eager to part with manufacturing technology. On the whole, however, Western companies have been more willing to share their technological innovations, in some cases their own cost.

In contrast, Japanese manufacturers are extremely reluctant to part with their technological advantages and advances. In recent years, Japanese manufacturers have entered into a series of ventures and alliances in which they have appeared to give away more on the technological side than they had before. However, in many cases, the technology acquired by the other party was of low value relative to Japanese technological capabilities. Despite this different experience with Japan, Asia as a whole has benefited greatly from FDI and acquisition of foreign technology. Those specific countries, such as India, which in contrast sought, at least initially, to limit or hinder domestic consumption of foreign technology suffered in the process. Finally, in a further attempt to boost the export sector, some Asian governments allowed grad-ual—albeit insufficient—depreciation of their domestic curren-cies, a factor that also accelerated FDI.

The two measures of "success" which Asian governments held up as virtues (almost at the expense of all else) were ex-ports and GDP growth. The results they achieved were as-tounding. As the World Bank report notes, "Since the 1960s, the high performing Asian economies have grown more than twice as fast as the rest of *East Asia,* roughly three times as fast as Latin America and five times faster than sub-Saharan Africa. They also significantly outperformed the industrial economies and the oil-rich Middle East–North Africa region. Between 1960 and 1985, real income per capita increased more than four times in Japan and the Four Tigers and more than doubled in the Southeast Asian NIEs."[9] Tables 1 and 2 clearly demonstrate the degree of success that Asia achieved in terms of GDP and export growth.

Table 1

GDP Growth

(percent per annum)

	Average 1981–1990	1990	1991	1992	1993	1994	1995	96 (S&P MMS)
NIEs	9.8	7.3	7.9	5.9	6.4	7.5	7.6	6.1%
HKG	6.9	3.4	5.1	6.3	6.4	5.4	4.6	4.7%
Korea	12.7	9.5	9.1	5.1	5.8	8.4	9.2	7.1%
Singapore	6.5	8.8	6.7	6.3	10.1	10.1	8.9	7.0%
Taiwan	8.0	5.4	7.6	6.8	6.3	6.5	6.3	5.7%
China	10.4	3.9	9.3	14.2	13.5	11.8	10.2	9.7%
SE Asia	6.4	8.7	7.3	6.6	7.1	7.8	7.9	7.5%
Indonesia	6.0	9.0	8.9	7.2	7.3	7.5	7.6	8.0%
Malaysia	5.2	9.7	8.6	7.8	8.3	9.2	9.3	8.2%
Philippines	1.0	3.0	−0.6	0.3	2.1	4.4	4.8	5.7%
Thailand	7.9	11.2	8.5	8.1	8.3	8.7	8.6	6.4%
South Asia	5.6	5.4	1.7	5.4	4.6	5.8	5.8	5.9%
India	5.6	5.4	0.8	5.1	5.0	6.3	6.2	6.5%

Source: *Asian Development Bank Outlook, 1996 and 1997,* and *Standard & Poor's MMS.*

Table 2
Merchandise Export Growth
(percent per annum)

	1994 Exports (in $ millions)	1990	1991	1992	1993	1994	1995
NIEs	435,967	8.4	14.3	12.3	10.4	15.3	20.6
HKG	151,360	12.3	20.0	21.2	13.1	12.0	16.7
Korea	93,676	2.8	10.2	8.0	7.7	15.7	32.4
Singapore	98,689	19.8	12.1	9.6	15.9	26.8	15.5
Taiwan	92,242	1.4	13.0	6.9	4.5	9.4	20.5
China	102,561	19.2	14.4	18.1	8.8	35.6	23.0
SE Asia	159,785	15.4	16.0	15.3	13.2	19.0	22.8
Indonesia	40,223	16.7	10.5	14.0	8.3	9.9	11.1
Malaysia	56,906	16.3	17.0	18.1	16.1	23.1	26.6
Philippines	13,434	4.7	8.0	11.1	15.8	18.1	28.9
Thailand	44,478	15.0	23.8	13.7	13.4	22.2	24.5
South Asia	41,184	11.6	3.6	7.9	18.4	16.6	17.7
India	26,763	9.0	−1.1	3.3	20.3	17.9	21.1

Source: *Asian Development Bank Outlook 1996 and 1997,* and *Standard & Poor's MMS.*

Asia's success increasingly took on world significance, capturing an ever-growing proportion of real-world economic activity, particularly with regard to trade. From representing only 8% of world exports in 1965, the HPAEs (high-performing Asian economies—Japan, Korea, Hong Kong, Singapore, Taiwan, China, Indonesia, Malaysia, and Thailand) saw their share grow to 13% by 1980 and 18% by 1990.[10]

To recap, they had "the basics right"—high savings rates, relatively low taxation, the creation of strong education systems, high productivity rates in both industry and agriculture, the maintenance of relatively low price pressures to ensure high savings rates, the acquisition of foreign know-how and technology, the creation of an investment-friendly atmosphere, and strategic government intervention in the economy. These were the core factors behind Asia's success. As great as that success was, it did not come without a significant (though not permanent) price. By focusing on headline growth and export figures as the standards of national "success" at the expense of everything else, the foundations of a boom-bust cycle were eventually created—though the "boom" period has admittedly lasted for a remarkably long period. *Growth was seen as the "end" rather than the "means."* Given the impoverished state of Asia after World War II, this emphasis on growth, whatever the cost, is clearly understandable. However, such a disproportionate focus on headline growth figures—almost as a point of national virility—led to financial and political authorities ignoring the quality, and thus the sustainability, of that growth.

As we shall see later, within any boom cycle, growth becomes self-fulfilling for a period—business and individual investment plans are executed based on expectations of high growth and therefore high returns. The greater the expectations, the more the real economic investment. The problem comes, of course, when expectations turn down. It is classic demand and supply theory. The demand side falls off, so the supply side has to adjust. This adjustment is what Japan continues to experience. After the falloff in expectations, investment also experiences a sharp falloff in order to adjust. Usually, it overshoots on the downside—just as much as the upside. Regarding the Asian domestic economies, these high expectations resulted in huge foreign capital inflow as the world's corporations and funds sought to take advantage of and exploit these high returns. This, along with the credit policies of the Asian authorities themselves, helped fuel significant domestic asset bubbles. As long as the budget account was in surplus, so as to fund this implicit large (and growing) current account deficit, there was no immediate problem. Expectations, by themselves, supported what had become somewhat of a pyramid scheme.

Meanwhile, looking at the issue in an international context, developments in the foreign exchange markets were to have a crucial impact on Asia's surging economies—initially from a beneficial point of view and then in a somewhat more negative fashion, culminating in the Asian currency crisis of 1997. Chapter 3 looks at the U.S. dollar and its gyrations in the foreign exchange market in great detail, particularly from the turning point in 1995 when it started to rebound in earnest, but to summarize, here are the key points: The dollar fell like a stone initially after the free floating of exchange rates in 1970–1971 which put an end to the era of fixed exchange rates under the Bretton Woods system. A growing budget deficit—requiring higher interest rates to attract investors to fund it—together with external shocks such as the oil crisis of 1973 and the Iranian Revolution of 1979 led to an eventual reversal in the dollar's direction. It began to soar in earnest during the initial years of the Reagan administration. This was a combination of fiscal profligacy—notably on the defense spending side—and a Federal Reserve seeking to offset this—most notably in the form of the redoubtable Fed chairman Paul Volcker.

While this allowed U.S. corporations to buy abroad at much cheaper rates, it severely hurt U.S. exports and thus the trade balance. Something had to be done, and eventually it was when the Plaza Accord to drive down the dollar's value came into being in 1985. This effort by the central banks and treasury departments of the developed world to force the dollar lower was very successful. Indeed, it was so successful that a subsequent effort to slow the dollar's fall and put a base under it, in the form of the Louvre Accord of 1987, failed miserably. The dollar continued to head lower. U.S. exporters were delighted, as this helped them right at their bottom line. Elsewhere, this also had a profound impact. Asian countries had pegged their currencies to the dollar. With the dollar-yen (USD-JPY) heading lower, they also saw their currencies rise against the dollar. This in turn led to more stable conditions for corporate investment in the form of building or acquiring manufacturing bases in the region. Initially, because of the decline in the dollar's value, Asian (including Japanese) exports to the U.S. and Europe boomed in terms of value (the higher Asian currency value translating into more dollars' worth of exports). The continuing fall in the dollar might have eventually cut into this Asian export boom (as lower dollar value hurt Asian export competitiveness relative to domestic pricing), thus fulfilling what we know as the "J-curve effect," were it not for three crucial factors during that period. The first was the rapid development of a Japanese manufacturing base in Asia, which gradually shifted the focus from solely direct trade between Japan and the West to trade (together with Japanese re-exports) between developing Asia and the West. The second factor was the wage-cost disparity between developing Asia and the more developed states such as Japan. This, together with the falling value of the dollar, allowed developing Asia greater trade competitiveness. Finally, the third factor was Asia's inherent and dynamic ability to adapt quickly to changing price and cost circumstances.

Thus, the weakness of the dollar and the consequent strength and stability of the Asian currencies—with Asian central banks having on occasion to combat "excessive" strength of their currencies—allowed the perfect platform for corporate and eventually portfolio capital inflow to these countries. This added to the domestic investment boom, which was then recycled in the form of ever-rising exports. Again, however, the initial focus—and here I mean in broad rather than specific terms—was quantity, not quality. It is a point that recurs in this book. Although the dollar had a respite at the very start of this decade, tightened monetary policy in Japan to (belatedly) burst its own asset bubble and tame roaring inflationary pressures, together with the spillover from German unification and the ERM crises (September 1992 and July 1993), soon had the greenback heading lower again.

However, the culmination of the U.S. dollar's fall from grace in the first half of this decade was not an international event, but a domestic policy change. On February 13, 1993, U.S. Treasury Secretary Lloyd Bentsen, speaking at a briefing at the National Press Club in Washington, D.C., said that he wanted to see the yen rise against the dollar to better reflect relative economic fundamentals between the U.S. and Japan.[11] The U.S., let us not forget, was just emerging, somewhat slowly, from a painful recession. This was a bombshell to the financial markets. Subsequent further comments to this effect by Bentsen, U.S. Trade Representative Mickey Kantor, the late U.S. Commerce Secretary Ron Brown, and even President Clinton himself added to the weight of selling pressure

which hit the dollar. International investors scrambled to eliminate or at least reduce their exposure to U.S. assets, given what
they presumed was an overt attempt by the U.S. to devalue the
dollar for trade purposes, i.e., to hurt Japanese exports to the U.S.
and force Japan to open up its own markets.

U.S. officials have subsequently said their remarks over the dollar were significantly misinterpreted by reporters and the markets
and that the U.S. never had a policy to devalue the dollar.[12] However, the repeated nature of comments by numerous officials from
various U.S. administration departments—running all the way to
the top—causes one at least some skepticism. My own view is that
the U.S. did have a deliberate policy of devaluation, whatever the
subsequent denials; it was a deliberate attempt to get Japan to the
negotiating table on trade, and it achieved some results (the U.S.–
Japan auto trade accord being a notable example). Subsequently,
when the dollar's fall got out of hand, this policy was quietly
changed—or rather, reversed. This reversal in policy was clearly
evident at the April 1995 G7 Accord to support the dollar. By that
time, the U.S. had a new Treasury secretary, Robert Rubin. Unlike,
Bentsen, who had had no prior grounding in financial markets,
whatever his superb political qualities, Rubin actually came from
the markets. Having made his way up at Goldman Sachs, the prestigious U.S. investment bank, he knew how markets worked and
more importantly what they needed to hear from him and his
subordinates.

The G7 Accord of April 1995 was the first warning signal for
Asia. It shouldn't have been, but it was. Support for the dollar
caused the subsequent reversal of the dollar's fall, which eventually led to a rise of more than 50% against the yen. Asian countries should have let their currencies weaken to reflect this new
set of international market dynamics. And some, such as
Indonesia, did for the most part. On the whole, however, just as
with growth and export figures, strong currencies were seen
almost as status symbols, with the respective Asian governments
and central banks seeking to maintain the previously enjoyed
stability and even strength. This was a mistake. The warning was

not heeded, and the focus remained on GDP, export growth, and currency stability at the very least—and preferably the maintenance of a strong currency. This last ignores the fundamental dynamics of an international capital market system. Given that economies are in a constant state of flux, varying in the time and depths of their business cycles, currencies also must reflect this. That is not to say that a fixed or a pegged currency system does not work of necessity. Such a system can indeed work for a significant period of time—as the Bretton Woods system did so successfully from the end of World War II to 1970–1971—if it is allowed the flexibility to reflect these changes in the real economy. Any attempt to distort the adjustment process by the currency—and thus impinge upon the flexibility of the currency system—can and does have significant economic impact. Governments may not like it, but it has been that way throughout history. Governments can seek to impose managed systems, but unless the fundamentals are sound and unless the system has the flexibility to allow for fundamental changes, it will inevitably fail. So it was with the gold standard, Bretton Woods, the ERM, and the Asian dollar-linked pegs.

Political and financial authorities can also seek to manipulate exchange rates outside of a fixed currency system, where the currency remains shackled by a "managed float" or "crawling peg" system. This also leads to external and internal price distortions—and the inevitable reversal in the currency (usually a collapse) if appropriate economic policy measures are not taken ahead of time. This was the case with Mexico, as we shall see in Chapter 4, a currency crisis that bears more than a passing resemblance to the Asian currency crisis and that also has important lessons for those seeking to extricate themselves or profit from the ongoing events in Asia. In addition, in both the Mexican and Asian crises, there was a further common denominator, one that played on and exacerbated the price-distorting features of pegged currency regimes, and therefore that accelerated and greatly increased the force of the ensuing collapses—the phenomenon of emerging market fever.

2

The Hype—Emerging
Market Fever

IF THE 1980s marked the decade of realpolitik, the cold war, and developed world political and economic dominance, the 1990s have surely seen the rise of a new focus, emerging markets. In the 1980s, while the U.S. and the Soviet Union stared each other down—ICBMs at the ready—many of these markets that were to "emerge" were decidedly unpleasant places to be, ruled overtly or dominated by the military and frequently with appalling human rights records. In the great chess game of the cold war, many were used as pawns (occasionally more important pieces) on the global chessboard. The game changed with the fall of the Berlin Wall and the release of Eastern Europe from imprisonment.

In Latin America, the U.S. no longer had such a need to pursue the Monroe Doctrine to the letter in order to keep the Soviet hordes at bay. Indeed the need to cut the budget deficit required that the U.S. let Latin America get on with it—a relief to both sides undoubtedly. Africa was left to pursue its tribal difficulties without the nefarious encouragement of the "great" powers. And in Asia the espionage war between the U.S., the Soviet Union, and China slowly wound down, all sides allowed to retire gracelessly from the field of battle.

No longer burdened by the need to pursue a conflict that had nothing do with them, emerging countries set about, in their various ways, to open up their political and economic systems. With the economic fundamentals in place thanks to prudent Asian government economic management, domestic and foreign direct investment booming, and Asian exports continuing to soar thanks to stable to firm exchange rates to the dollar, foreign fund managers began to take notice. Many of these will say now that they were investing in Asian emerging markets—and others—in the 1980s, but it was the 1990s when emerging market investment took on the cult status that we now know and love (or not). Can you remember seeing Western fund managers waxing lyrical about the delights of emerging market investment on your TV set in the 1980s? No you cannot. As ever, the figures tell the story—or at least part of it. In 1970, according to the World Bank, portfolio equity investment in developing countries was zero.[1] It was still zero in 1980. By 1985, it had risen to a mere USD100 million. Only in the 1990s did it really start to pick up—some USD3.8 billion in 1990, rising to USD39.5 billion in 1994. In the 1980s, the idea of Western fund managers trawling the bazaars of Marrakesh or visiting mines outside Moscow or plantations in Vietnam would have been regarded as worse than comical. In the 1990s, the financial markets took such concepts for granted.

This process did not start with the fund managers or with portfolio investment. First came official government lending to the developing countries, then commercial bank lending. The latter was rudely interrupted by the Mexican debt crisis of 1982, but after a couple of years it began again, attracted inexorably by the sort of returns that were unavailable in the developed world. With domestic investment booming and the requisite commercial loans available, companies in emerging markets continued to expand, albeit in many cases at the low end of the manufacturing scale. Such was the drive for expansion, however, that more capital was needed. With governments in emerging markets, particularly in Asia, having created an attractive environment for investment through tax concessions and deregulation, foreign direct investment also started to pick up. Initially Western and subsequently Japanese companies started to build factories and plants in the emerging markets, attracted by the potential to make faster and greater returns than were available in their domestic markets.

Table 3 shows the various kinds of investment that have moved into emerging markets over the past 2½ decades, demonstrating the shift from government and commercial lending, to foreign direct investment, and finally to portfolio investment.

Table 3
Total Net Flows to Developing Countries
(by type, in USD billion)

	1970	1975	1980	1985	1990	1991	1992	1993	1994
Official develop. finance	4.6	13.9	24.6	26.6	44.9	48.0	43.0	42.4	44.6
Other official finance	0.8	4.3	10.6	11.2	13.0	13.9	7.3	11.5	9.9
Commercial bank lending	2.3	14.4	33.9	8.5	0.1	3.9	12.8	−2.2	
Bonds	0.0	0.2	2.6	5.6	3.4	12.5	12.9	42.1	
Other private	1.1	3.7	13.4	7.7	11.5	2.1	15.7	5.8	
FDI	2.3	7.5	5.3	11.3	26.7	36.8	47.1	66.6	77.9
Portfolio equity flow	0.0	0.0	0.0	0.1	3.8	7.6	14.2	46.9	39.5
Total	11.0	44.0	90.3	71.1	103.4	124.8	153.0	213.1	227.4

Source: World Bank, *Managing Capital Flows in East Asia.*

In the 1980s, Latin America received the lion's share of FDI, with Mexico at the top of the list, followed by Brazil in second place and Argentina in sixth.[2] Even Colombia received more FDI than Indonesia. By the 1990s, that had changed. China, which had been third overall in the 1980s, led the FDI table of developing country recipients of FDI and by a very long way. Mexico was still high on the list, this time in second place. Malaysia, though, had crept up to third, displacing Brazil for total FDI received, with Indonesia and Thailand now fifth and sixth, respectively. Indeed, the story of the last 15 years of FDI is China. Between 1990 and 1996, China received some USD167 billion in FDI (at 1996 prices).[3] Through the late 1980s and into the 1990s, East Asia grabbed an increasingly large proportion of total FDI in developing countries. In the 1980s, FDI in East Asia was USD1.3 billion, or 10% of net capital flows. By 1993, this figure had spiked to USD36.5 billion, or 50%.[4] Between 1990 and 1996, East Asia received some 3.5% of the region's GNP and 10% of its investment in the form of FDI, the highest rate for any region during that period. Aside from an attractive regulatory environment, companies in the developed world were also drawn by the privatization opportunities that were rapidly becoming available, once again principally in East Asia and the Pacific. In 1995, East Asia accounted for well over half of the FDI to all developing countries—about USD51.132 billion out of USD95.370 billion.

While company executives were salivating over the enormous human capital resources that Asia possessed—hard-working, low-wage-cost labor in abundant supply—which along with tax and export concessions could boost corporate margins by up to 10 percentage points relative to their domestic operating conditions, fund managers began to take notice as well. Two events occurred which accelerated this process. First, in the early 1990s, following the go-go years of the 1980s and then the crash of 1987, the U.S. went into a recession. Consumption fell off a cliff and the banking industry was in deep trouble. Once again it was overexposed, this time to the property market which itself had suddenly discovered oversupply and was heading into one of its steepest corrections in the past fifty years. This was the time of the credit crunch, when people occasionally talked about large banks such as Chase or Citicorp going under, such was the hysteria. While an exceedingly shrewd prince of the Saudi Royal Family picked up Citicorp stock in the low double digits, Federal Reserve Board Chairman Alan Greenspan continued to ease interest rates, more than reversing the previous tightening phase and thus giving a boost to global liquidity. In effect, he bailed out the U.S. banking system, by keeping rates lower for longer than they would otherwise have been. This permitted banks to trade the spread—borrowing at or around the Fed funds rate, which continued to decline, and effectively lending to the government at the long end of the yield curve by buying the long bond. Thus, U.S. banks repaired their balance sheets.

More importantly for the emerging markets, the effects of the credit crunch in the U.S. resulted in lower yields all along the curve. This, together with the rise in global liquidity which the Fed easing caused, resulted in U.S. fund managers looking offshore for higher returns than were available in the domestic markets. U.S. pension funds alone are a USD6 trillion industry. Add to that mutual and hedge funds and investment trusts, and one sees the potential result of even the smallest shift in portfolio allocation. The early 1990s marked the first major shift of U.S. fund investment to offshore markets. The more aggressive funds raised their total offshore weighting to 5–8%.

The second event was the bursting of the Japanese bubble economy—itself a potential warning for the booming East Asian economies. The then Bank of Japan Governor Mieno declared war against asset price inflation, tightening interest rates to crush inflationary pressures. The end result was that he also crushed the economy. Through the 1980s, the Bank of Japan had allowed the asset bubble to continue to inflate, creating in the process some of the most expensive real estate in the history of the planet. Anecdotes abounded—such as the land around the Imperial Palace equaling in value the entire real estate of California or the total Tokyo real estate market equaling the entire U.S. itself. The point is not whether these were true or false. The point is that one could even conceive of such parallels. The giant bubble that the Bank of Japan and the Ministry of Finance had allowed to develop burst, the effects of which are still being felt today. Eventually, the Bank of Japan started to loosen policy again, once convinced that the inflation threat had been vanquished, only to find that a deflationary spiral had been put into effect. The easing accelerated. Meanwhile, the Ministry of Finance, at its usual glacial pace, began to deregulate the Japanese financial system.

The combination of falling yields in the Japanese domestic markets and small steps by the Ministry of Finance to free up the

Japanese institutional investor base, allowing investors greater ability to invest abroad, caused a second "wall of money" to develop (the first occurred in the late 1980s when the Japanese economic boom created excess capital that was then invested abroad, through either bank lending or corporate acquisition). Initially, this flow went to the developed world, more specifically to the U.S. and Western Europe. Increasingly, however, Japanese investors focused on Asia, attracted as their U.S. counterparts were by the amazing growth rates being churned out year after year in countries like Thailand, Malaysia, Indonesia, and Singapore. In 1986, 80% of Japanese equity investments were in the U.S. and 14.4% in Southeast Asia. By 1994, 40% of Japanese equity holdings—USD40 billion—were in Southeast Asia, compared with 38.8% in the U.S.[5]

These two events, along with the dramatic improvement in fundamentals in developing countries, provided the foundation for a wave of portfolio investment that was to reach from Santiago to Bratislava, from Vladivostok to Chiang Mai, Xian, and Java, and back around. Between 1989 and 1992, foreign portfolio investment (FPI) in developing countries increased fivefold, initially focusing on Latin America, but then shifting to Asia. In 1988, foreign investors bought USD2.5 billion of Asian stocks. By 1992, that figure was USD11 billion, and in 1993—the boom year for emerging markets—that figure had risen to USD38.9 billion, of which USD13.4 billion went into Hong Kong and China alone.[6]

With global monetary policy remaining lax, capital continued to pour in, notably to stock markets. Cross-border equity investment flow to emerging markets roared—USD10 billion in 1989, USD22 billion in 1992, rising to USD62 billion in 1993.[7] All this was great news for the Asian markets, but it required deregulation of capital markets in order for it to continue. Asian governments did so, but always with an eye to maintaining control—rather than the big bang approach taken by the UK and the U.S. Indeed, some did not have a stock market at all; the Jakarta Stock Exchange reopened in 1992 after having been closed several times since 1968. Others like Thailand got there a lot earlier, in 1975. Bond markets also saw the result of this focus on emerging markets. By 1993, the total stock of all emerging market country bond issues outstanding was some USD224.2 billion, up from USD19 billion in 1980.

Investment in emerging markets reached a peak—perhaps *the* peak?—in 1993. By then, one out of every three U.S. dollars invested in international stock markets went to the emerging markets. The index of emerging stock markets compiled by the International Finance Corporation rose about 63% in 1993 in U.S. dollar terms. Other emerging market indexes rose 80% or more. By 1994, Asian stock markets made up 6% of total world stock market capitalization, and people were confidently predicting that this would double by the end of the century. Looking at Asian countries individually, China's market capitalization in 1994 was USD44 billion, that of Indonesia USD47 billion, South Korea some USD191.8 billion, and Malaysia USD199.3 billion. The case of Malaysia was particularly notable, or should have been, because its stock market capitalization was equal to over 300% of GDP—substantially higher than anywhere else on the planet, higher than the stock market boom in Japan. There were days when the turnover on the Kuala Lumpur Stock Exchange was higher than that in New York.

Extraordinary returns were to be had. From 1975 to November 1994, the South Korean stock market index rose 1604%, that of Malaysia 1733%, and that of Thailand 1711%. A trust fund for a well-known brokerage in Hong Kong rose 8000% in value from 1971 to 1994. Needless to say, all this had a profound effect on the economies and populations in Asia. In those heady days, if you took a taxi ride anywhere in Hong Kong, the conversation, albeit in somewhat stilted broken English, would inevitably turn to how the Hang Seng was doing (the same is true today, though more likely if your Cantonese is good enough). Every taxi driver, every secretary, every cleaner, road sweeper, bar owner, waitress, and traffic attendant had a position. In 1974, the Hang Seng was 400. By 1994, it was 12,000.

The same kind of frenzy gripped Indonesia and Malaysia, especially the latter where retail investing in the stock market became almost a form of entertainment or social interaction rather than a means to secure financial benefits in one's old age. Fortunes were made; people were elevated beyond their wildest dreams. The news of easy money—if there is such a concept, and whenever you hear it, run the other way—naturally reached the developed world and particularly the U.S. The U.S. mutual fund industry was on a roll in any case. With Greenspan keeping rates low, investment continued to pour into stocks rather than bonds. News that you could get even better returns in emerging markets just added fuel to the fire. I recall vividly the sight in January 1994 (before Greenspan spoiled the party and started to hike interest rates) of the lines of people waiting patiently outside the office of a well-known U.S. mutual fund and brokerage on Broadway, just off Wall Street. Now, U.S. investors are savvy people. But I would bet that many of those in that line had not the slightest clue where the countries they were putting their money into were actually located. Granted, they were no doubt educated on the matter by dutiful brokers, but the point is the same. This was a classic sign of frenzy, of mass speculation at work. In 1993 and early 1994, some mutual funds were taking in USD2–3 million a day, which they then used to invest in the emerging markets.

Somewhere along the way, these lesser developed countries had become developing countries, and then finally emerging markets. Whole industries were created to cover their every facet, from national economic data to local news, to features and analysis of this new phenomenon. Magazines and newspapers sprang up to meet the thirst for knowledge of these foreign parts. A torrent of books appeared, some studious and well thought-out, others less so. All were optimistic, all—in Barton Biggs's immortal words—were "maximum bullish." The Fed tightening cycle, starting on February 4, 1994, and the subsequent Mexican crisis of late 1994–1995 (analyzed in depth in Chapter 4) dented this optimism severely but only for a while. By the end of 1995, with the Mexican stock market up over 50% from its lows, retail investment in emerging markets was back to the levels of 1992. While U.S. retail and institutional investors were particularly fond of investing in Latin America given its geographical proximity, nowhere did this optimism reach such a height as in Asia.

Commentators fueled this process, proclaiming the arrival of a new dawn, a new century, the Pacific century. The sun was rising in the East and across more than just Japan. The more left-thinking intellectuals in the developed world heralded this as the final renunciation of the colonial past and the full and complete victory over the decadent West. Some of the more extreme even went on to pontificate that it was due to inherent Asian superiority. Indeed, there was the implicit—and in some cases explicit—suggestion that while Asia was rising, the West—presumably due to its inherent inferiority and decadence—was falling. Taking a look at the state of the manufacturing industry or property markets on the Eastern seaboard of the U.S. in 1992, one could understand such musings—however erroneous in the final analysis they were.

A second rush of books poured in, focusing more specifically on the rise of Asia, with titles like *Pacific Century, Pacific Destiny, Megatrends Asia,* and *Asia Pacific.* The message was clear: The Asian "miracle" had come, an event momentous in its importance not just for Asia but for the globe. Media commentators, whether on TV, in the newspapers, or over the newswires, were relatively unquestioning, and for a decade there did indeed seem no reason to question. Just as the skyscrapers ascended in Jakarta, Kuala Lumpur, and Singapore, so did the growth and the profits. For a time, in the developed West, it did seem as if the world's growth center was shifting, from the U.S. and Western Europe—fresh from the latter's ERM humiliation—across the Pacific to Asia.

Back in Asia itself, consumption patterns were changing, self-confidence very much on the rise. Companies, both foreign and domestic, which had initially seen Asia only as a low-cost manufacturing platform from which to export to the West, now suddenly took notice of Asian consumers. While the companies had been focusing on exporting to New York, Los Angeles, Paris, London, and Munich, a new, burgeoning middle class had emerged all around them, one dominated by the tight family structures that are prevalent in Asia. This Asian middle class was itself dominated by ethnic Chinese—the Overseas Chinese as they are now known, or the *hua qu* in Cantonese. More specifically, the *hua qu* of Asia were the *nanyang hua qu*—ethnic Chinese of the "southern Ocean." A group about 60 million strong, with estimated assets of over USD2 trillion, the *hua qu,* be it in Bangkok, Jakarta, Kuala Lumpur, Singapore, Taipei, or Hong Kong, were the emergent economic power. If these Overseas Chinese lived in one country, its GDP would exceed that of mainland China itself. In Indonesia, the *hua qu*—or *hua chiao* in putonghua, or Mandarin—made up only 4% of the population, yet they dominated business. In Thailand, they were around 10%—and completely dominant in Bangkok. Such wealth caused luxury product retailers—whether in fashion or cars—to target the East. Just as had been the case earlier with Japan, anecdotes, whether true or not, abounded. In one month, BMW sold more cars in Shanghai than it had ever done in its history. By 1996, there were more Rolls-Royces per capita in Hong Kong than in any other country. A casual walk along Chater Road, in Central Hong Kong, resplendent as it is with the likes of Dior and Ferragamo and Bally, shows how Asian consumers are growing increasingly accustomed to the (very) good life.

With domestic consumption on the rise within Asia, it was not long before inflationary signals started to pick up. Inflation is basically caused by excessive demand over supply. Limited residential and commercial property space (particularly the case in Hong Kong), an increasingly rich middle class, and strong demand from all sectors of society to better themselves caused an explosion in real estate prices. By 1996, the most expensive real estate to be found on the globe was not in the centers of New York, Tokyo, or London, but in Bombay (now Mumbai). Shanghai and Hong Kong were ranked fourth and fifth. Indeed, by 1996, such had been the rise in asset prices—and thus loss of competitiveness—in Hong Kong that it had caused most of the local manufacturing base to move to Guangdong province in China, where hourly wage costs were one-eighth of those in Hong Kong. Foreign companies also began to look more favorably on Kuala Lumpur and Jakarta, and even Singapore, though the latter would quickly eliminate its price advantage over Hong Kong for a time.

The Western media, for the most part, treated such ruthless price competitiveness as a further sign of Asian dominance. Just as it had heralded the Japanese century in the late 1980s and early 1990s—while the bubble was in fact bursting—in the process making alarmist calls of the inevitable decline and decay of the West (particularly the U.S.) and the rise of Japan, so it did with North and South East Asia.

The rise of Asia thus went from being a joyous and momentous event to a threat not only to Western dominance but to Western survival. As Asians manufactured more with decreasing cost and worked even harder, it was inevitable that thousands of Westerners would lose their jobs given that Western companies would not be able to compete. Needless to say, corporate elements within the U.S. and Europe fed on such alarmist ideas for their own purposes. In most of these examinations of Asia, there was a recurring theme—the rise of the East and the consequent decline of the West, a zero-sum game. There were a few notable exceptions, but for the most part the Asian phenomenon was seen in such extreme terms—first an unparalleled land of opportunity, the new frontier, and then the economic equivalent of Japan in the 1930s.

Along with the rise of Asian consumption came a change in Asia's beliefs and self-confidence. Part of this can be explained by Asia's colonial past. There remains, quite understandably, a deep sense of bitterness, humiliation, and injustice at the subjugation of parts of Asia by the West. In the case of what Japan did to Asia in the 1930s and 1940s, there is outright hatred—just ask any Korean what he or she thinks of Japan. And so there was a need, in some cases unconscious and in others quite conscious, to reverse this by proclaiming Asian superiority, thus offsetting the previous sense of inferiority.

In part also, the Asian media mimicked their Western counterparts. When the West was in the initial process of proclaiming the rise of Asia, domestic media in Asia and even some teachers and university lecturers began also to take up the idea that Asian—and more specifically, Chinese—success was due to the fact that they were Asians. A school of thought developed which sought to explain Asian success by examining the social and philosophical aspects of Asian society and attributing these as being the foundations of not only Asia's success but the West's decline. Thus, Asian commentators also followed their Western counterparts in seeing Asia and the West as a zero-sum game. Asia, so the argument ran, was dominated by strong family units, respect and obedience for authority, and a desire for cooperation rather than individualism (for this, read "decadent Western" individualism). In sum, Asian capitalism was characterized as a state of neo-Confucianist harmony, whereas Westerners were the modern equivalent of the Vandals and the Visigoths sacking Rome.

With this kind of snake-oil scholarship, there is no harm done as long as no one actually believes it. The trouble was—and is—that major figures in Asian society became both proclaimers and believers. In business, the most dangerous thing for a businessperson to believe is his own press releases, because inevitably they are sparing or at least convenient with the truth. For politicians, it is even more dangerous potentially—though eminently more natural. Asian values and even a particularly Asian sense of human rights were advanced as the way by which Asia as a whole was progressing. Asian business and political leaders themselves started to proclaim the arrival of the Asian century, based on the economic premise that stratospheric growth would go on for ever.

In the real world of economics, such proclamations of Asian superiority, whether by Asians or Westerners, can do—and did—considerable harm because they distort the overall picture. Both sides were happy to criticize the West, but remarkably inhibited at criticizing the East. There was a sense that criticism was not warranted because Asia was different and different rules applied.

Media coverage and in some cases superficial coverage by investment banks gave retail investors the veneer of legitimacy to throw money at emerging markets. Institutional investors were persuaded not only to stay but to continue to raise their weightings in the region, this despite increasingly disappointing results.

While 1993 was the year of years for emerging markets, the early part of 1994 and 1995 were a disaster in relative terms, particularly for Asian stock markets. "Watch, wait and pray for money from abroad" was how *Business Week* summed up the sentiment in Asian stock markets at the end of 1995.[8] Most Asian equity markets had barely moved, while Taiwan had dropped over 30%. Only Hong Kong had shown any resilience, rising 20% on the year—this after a fall of 45% in 1994 amid the slump in property prices, with bank and property stocks (72% of the Hang Seng index) getting hit particularly hard due to this. Meanwhile, the DJIA and the S&P 500 indexes, after a downturn in 1994 due to the Fed tightening cycle and the resultant meltdown in Treasuries, continued to rally. Despite this, many fund managers held on, lured by the headline economic growth numbers and past returns. Fund manager surveys in the U.S. and UK in early 1996 showed that most were still bullish on Asia. Indeed, in 1996, events seemed to prove them right. In the first half of the year, Asian stock markets boomed, led by Shanghai which rose 85%, Manila up 27%, Taipei up 26.5%, and Bombay up 22.5%.

Despite this, actual earnings per share were relatively disappointing, but with those kinds of stock market returns, no one cared. Indeed, such unpleasantness was entirely forgotten toward the end of 1996, with further opportunities emerging. The Russian stock market had risen 350% that year as investors supposedly "re-rated" Russian assets. Prior to this, the Argentinean stock market had rallied 440% in 1991. Faced with such returns, fund managers and even retail investors were willing to put up with a lot. They would have to, but not for a while.

While the market continued to focus on Asian growth (at any price), certain economic fundamentals were starting to deteriorate. The most notable was the balance of payments current account. Boosted initially by large imports of capital goods, first for manufacturing and then for the so-called megaprojects seen in the likes of Malaysia and Indonesia, the current account balance of several Asian countries was put further into deficit as a result of the rise of portfolio investment into Asia. When the Mexican crisis occurred, these current account deficits were in the spotlight. For 1995, Malaysia had a current account deficit of 9.0%, Thailand 8.1%, and Indonesia 3.4%. For a brief period, Asian markets came under pressure in the wake of the Mexican collapse. However, commentators were quick to point out that Asian countries, unlike Mexico, had borrowed prudently and cautiously. Indeed many had budget surpluses and thus were able to finance their current account deficits.

The domestic investment rate, spurred on by government efforts to modernize the economy, continued to exceed the domestic savings rate. In other words, these countries were still dependent on foreign capital despite the highest savings rates in the world. Asian markets eventually shook off the Mexican jitters and moved higher, at varying speeds. The riots in Indonesia in July 1996 were a further wake-up call, but Western fund managers who sold Indonesia did so because of the specifics, not the regional picture. A look at the latter, and more specifically the authoritarian nature of many Asian governments relative to the West, could have caused a different evaluation. The lesson should have been, however, that beneath the surface of superficial stability in the Asian region lay undercurrents of political just as much as economic instability.

Meanwhile, as the domestic long-term fundamentals deteriorated and domestic warnings were given off—and ignored—the global financial markets themselves sounded a global warning. It was to have profound resonance for Asia—the recovery from 1995 in the value of the dollar, and the consequent loss of Asian trade competitiveness.

3

The Warning — Dollar-Yen Rebounds

THE PLAZA ACCORD OF 1985 was a major external catalyst for the subsequent Asian export boom because it caused a disproportionately large fall in the dollar-yen (USD-JPY) relative to the dollar rates against the Asian currencies (not including Japan's). This boosted Asian trade competitiveness at the expense of Japan. The dollar bottomed out in mid-1988 and for a brief period started to move higher again. However, this was to prove temporary and with the USD-JPY weighed down by the burden of Japan's ever-increasing trade surplus and the dollar-mark (USD-DEM) pressured in 1992 and 1993 by the ERM crises that caused the deutsche mark to soar, Asian exporters remained relaxed (unlike their Japanese counterparts, which set about furiously restructuring themselves to become competitive at these new low rates).

Indeed, for the Asian corporate sector, and for Western companies exporting from Asia back to the West, there was even better news to come. In November 1992, Bill Clinton was elected president of the United States, defeating George Bush. While Bush's attempts to focus on Clinton's character were easily dismissed, Bush's grasp of geopolitical strategy was undeniable—hardly surprising in a former director of the Central Intelligence Agency. Clinton was unencumbered by such experience, running on a platform of putting Americans back to work and turning around the U.S. economy. As part of this, he promised to right the wrongs of previous administrations, specifically in the realm of trade. In this endeavor, he had two devoted supporters, Lloyd Bentsen, a veteran of Capitol Hill, and Mickey Kantor, a Los Angeles lawyer who ran Clinton's campaign. The former was a polished, Washington sophisticate, made legendary by his demolition of Dan Quayle in the vice presidential televised debate; the latter was a bruising negotiator who gave no ground. Bentsen was made treasury secretary, while Kantor was appointed to the post of U.S. trade representative (USTR).

Clinton was elected on a domestic platform that had overtones of the kind of splendid isolationism from which the U.S. occasionally suffers. This official emphasis was quickly changed, however; and with Mickey Kantor at the helm of the USTR Department, Clinton focused on promoting global free trade— that is, promoting the interests of U.S. exporters and the U.S. economy. The campaign phrase, "It's the economy, stupid," was thus extended to represent the global, rather than just the U.S., economy, though the interest of the two were synonymous, at least in U.S. official eyes. In January 1993, Clinton was sworn into office and vowed to take a new approach with Japan, emphasizing trade. American workers should not have to tolerate closed Japanese markets, which in the end cost them their jobs. The U.S. produced the finest products in the world and deserved the same degree of access to Japan as Japan was able to achieve in U.S. markets. In the real world, there is no such thing as perfectly fair trade, only variations of moderately fair, scaling down to completely closed. Among these, the U.S. is only relatively fair, though the protectionist elements in Congress think even this is too much.

In the first half of 1993, as the U.S. economy began to pick up, imports from Asia caused the U.S. trade deficit to balloon out again. This in turn caused the USD-JPY to fall further. Meanwhile, the U.S. introduced its new dollar policy on February 13, 1993, when Treasury Secretary Lloyd Bentsen stated that he would like to see the yen rise against the dollar to better reflect the prevailing fundamentals, notably those regarding the widening U.S.-Japan trade deficit. For a second, there was a stunned silence as reporters grappled with the implications of Bentsen's comments, and then they ran for the phones. The USD-JPY had been heading lower anyway due to the fundamentals, but here was the U.S. overtly advocating USD-JPY weakness. The dollar's decline and the yen's rise accelerated through the first half of 1993, just in time for Clinton's summit with Japanese Prime Minister Miyazawa in July. With the dollar going "the right way" in terms of making U.S. exports to Japan more competitive and Japanese exports to the U.S. less so, Clinton had a stronger position with which to press for deregulation and openness in Japan. As a result of the talks, Clinton walked away with a "framework" with which to begin bilateral negotiations to set numerical targets for U.S. exports to Japan. At least that was what it meant to the U.S. side. To Japan's Ministry of International Trade and Industry (MITI) and Ministry of Finance, it meant more of the same—all talk and no action. However, those in the MITI and Ministry of Finance who thought they had again succeeded in derailing a U.S. effort to open up Japan did not take into account Mickey Kantor. Kantor was just warming to his task and was in no mood to shirk trade confrontation with Japan or anyone else.

The following month, two events occurred that were bombshells to the financial markets. First, in the midst of its worst recession since the 1950s, following the bursting of the asset price bubble in 1989–1991, Japan elected its first non-Liberal Democratic Party prime minister in four decades in the person of Morihiro Hosokawa of the Japan New Party. Accustomed to the Liberal Democratic Party winning every election in memory, markets were stunned. In Japan itself, business leaders and the media quickly called for the new Hosokawa government to stimulate and deregulate the domestic economy and lead Japan out of mounting recession. The leading financial daily newspaper, the *Nihon Keizai Shimbun,* declared that to fulfill its historic mission the Hosokawa government should deliver responsible and accountable economic policy that leads Japan out of recession and reduces in the process its trade and current account surpluses. Needless to say, such sentiments were very close to Mickey Kantor's heart.

The second event was that the USD-JPY came within a whisker of cracking the 100 level, trading at 100.35 on August 17, 1993, the lowest level since the war, before heavy intervention by the Bank of Japan resulted in a rebound. There was even talk of the yen being re-denominated, causing Japanese printing stocks to rally, though such spurious talk was quickly rebuffed. On January 5, 1994, when the USD-JPY was trying to rally, Bentsen effectively stopped that dead in its tracks. He said that Japan should stop weakening the yen or trying to export its way out of recession and that the yen should be a strong currency given the fundamentals of a large and rising Japanese trade surplus. The USD-JPY had hit 113.20 just prior to those comments, and thereafter 113.20 became known as the "Bentsen ceiling." The USD-JPY started to head down again.

Meanwhile, with signs of inflation finally picking up again in the U.S. economy, Greenspan pulled the trigger on February 4, 1994, hiking the Fed funds target rate 25 basis points to 3.25%. Faced with the double whammy of an administration that seemed to be actively devaluing its currency and a central bank that appeared to be behind the curve in tightening monetary policy, foreign investors fled the U.S. asset markets, the dollar plunge accelerated, and the world witnessed the biggest Treasury market meltdown ever seen.

In the U.S. Treasury itself, a fierce battle was brewing between the "hawks," who wanted to see the dollar sink further in order to force Japan to the trade bargaining table, and the "doves," who warned of the potentially catastrophic effects on U.S. interest rates and thus the economy of a continuing collapse in the dollar. Needless to say, Kantor and the rest of the USTR Department supported the hawks. European political and financial leaders, notably Bundesbank President Hans Tietmeyer, themselves faced with the results of a plunging dollar in the form of a roaring deutsche mark, began a chorus of criticism of the U.S., saying the U.S.'s apparent policy of benign neglect was irresponsible and threatened the global financial system if it was continued. The pressure built until finally the doves won out. In mid-1994, the Treasury changed its tune. Bentsen came out and said that the U.S. was not trying to devalue the dollar, and the New York Fed desk intervened to support the greenback.

That was not the end of the dollar's woes. With the U.S.-Japan trade deficit continuing to widen and foreign investors continuing to hammer U.S. assets as signs of inflation picked up, increasing the impression that the Fed was late in tightening, both the USD-DEM and the USD-JPY continued to head lower. As far as Asia, with the exception of Japan, was concerned, this was a godsend. The NIEs (Hong Kong, South Korea, Singapore, and Taiwan) had export growth in 1993 averaging 10.4% Y/Y. By 1994, that was up to 15.2%.[1] China, benefiting additionally from the devaluation of the renminbi in 1994, saw export growth of 8.8% in 1993, followed by 35.6% in 1994. For Southeast Asia as a whole, the respective figures were 13.2% and 19.0%.[2]

Toward the end of 1994, three events proved important in putting a long-term base under the dollar. First, the Federal Reserve hiked the Fed funds rate 75 basis points to 5.50%. Second, a fiscally hawkish Republican Party, led by that bastion of fiscal prudence Newt Gingrich, swept the congressional elections in the same month. Finally, in December, Bentsen resigned as treasury secretary. Even then, the dollar had not hit bottom, but the first steps had been taken which would put an end to the long-term dollar decline from 1985. For one thing, Robert Rubin, the new Secretary of the Treasury, was a very different phenomenon from Bentsen. A partner at Goldman Sachs and a veteran of the markets himself, he had come from the market and knew how it worked. Before he was made treasury secretary, he was the head of Clinton's National Economic Council. There he ruled firmly but by consensus, seeking to avoid the sort of head-on confrontations that both Bentsen and Kantor appeared to favor and that not unnaturally worried foreign investors. Rubin's main challenge was to restore market confidence in the Clinton administration.

Rubin's challenge was substantial. With the dollar having dropped like a stone in 1994 and investors fleeing the U.S., the dollar was increasingly no longer seen as a safe haven. This was a marked turnaround in sentiment from the late 1980s and even the early 1990s when the dollar roared on any sign of tension, let alone conflict. A key characteristic of a safe haven currency has to be liquidity. Granted, the U.S. markets were—and are—the most liquid in the world. But in years past when the dollar was not only *a* safe haven but *the* safe haven, investors had little choice of liquid markets and as a result usually parked their money in the U.S. markets in times of crisis. The financial market deregulation that had taken place in the U.S., Europe, and even Japan in the 1980s and early 1990s meant, however, that by the end of 1994 investors had a wide choice of deep and liquid markets. The most obvious one was the deutsche mark, although both the Swiss franc and the yen also benefited occasionally from safe haven flows.

A second factor in safe haven status is the net financial position of the country. The U.S., previously the world's largest creditor, was now its largest debtor, thanks to the combined fiscal profligacy of the Reagan administration and the Democratic Congress during the 1980s. Indeed, if one looked at the U.S. in purely economic terms at the end of 1994, regarding its huge current account and budget deficits, the U.S. was a basket case. In times of crisis, when the issue of safe haven is most relevant, investors usually repatriate capital flows. Given the large relative degree of foreign investment in the U.S., this meant substantial net outflows.

A third factor is the issue of market confidence in the country's authorities. While market confidence in the Fed had been boosted—or rather saved—by the November 15 rate hike, confidence in the administration remained exceedingly low. The Clinton administration had finally ceased its overt jawboning of the dollar, yet it continued to posture on trade issues in full knowledge of the likely effects.

Last, there is the issue of geographical proximity. The deutsche mark, which also gained from the Bundesbank's ultrahawkish reputation, was clearly the anchor of the ERM and thus gained whenever there were political or economic concerns within the mechanism. In Japan's case, its rising budget deficit was offset by its equally rising current account surplus. Regarding the Americas, the irony was that the dollar could have gained limited new safe haven status as it was perceived as the safe haven within NAFTA (Northern American Free Trade Area)—the lesser of three evils. It *could* have gained, but Rubin's appointment quickly became a baptism of fire when the Mexican currency crisis broke on the world stage. The Mexican crisis will be examined in detail in the next chapter, but suffice it to say that it played an important role, first in formulating U.S. Treasury policy under Rubin and second, in projecting Rubin's own image to the markets.

While President Clinton acted with surprising decisiveness to bring together a bailout package for Mexico, Rubin, with his measured yet scalpel-sharp tones, was equally decisive in his attempts to calm the markets. That was not to say he met with immediate success. With the U.S. promising Mexico aid from the Treasury's Exchange Stabilization Fund, the market took the view that this might damage the U.S.'s ability to defend the dollar itself. In addition, in such volatile conditions, some feared that the Bank of Mexico drawdown from the facility, and thus the selling of dollars for pesos to repay debt, would cause the dollar to plunge further. It was a bit like the chicken and the egg scenario—which came first? The New York, Tokyo, and London foreign exchange desks sold the dollar to get out of dollar positions because they thought it would fall. But because of their selling, it did fall. Meanwhile, the U.S. trade situation had not improved at all, with Kantor threatening dire repercussions if Japan did not come to the bargaining table to open up its markets. Indeed, Kantor said he was prepared to "jump over the precipice" if necessary—a reference to his willingness to start a trade war against Japan if needed to force Japan to open up its markets to U.S. goods. Kantor's specific target was Japan's auto trade surplus with the U.S., which made up over 60% of the total trade surplus with the U.S.

Finally, the Federal Reserve wasn't playing ball. Having hiked the Fed funds target rate 75 basis points in November, it hiked it a further 50 basis points to 6.00% at the January 31–February 1 meeting of the Federal Open Market Committee (FOMC). This was good news for the dollar, at least initially. Given the tightening seen in 1994 (250 basis points), the U.S. economy was, however, showing the first signs of responding to Greenspan's more hawkish monetary policy, amid a barrage of vehement criticism from Congress that Greenspan was effectively robbing the poor. Housing data, retail sales, and nonfarm payrolls started to slow to what the Fed saw as "more sustainable levels." Following the February 1 hike, the market began to take the view that that was it; there would be no more tightening. This was great news for the Treasury market. Of course, by that time any news that wasn't appalling was seen as good news, such was the despondency on bond desks on Wall Street after the debacle of 1994. It was horrendous news, however, for the dollar. The market had built its expectations for 1995 on still wider interest rate differentials, with the dollar seen boosted by the combination of further rate hikes from the Fed and steady policy from the Bundesbank—with the added hope that the Bank of Japan might ease further. With the Fed now seen on hold, that abruptly took away the dollar's interest rate support, not in absolute nominal yield terms but with regard to interest rate trends.

The dollar continued to plunge against all the major currencies. At the Bundesbank's fortresslike headquarters in Frankfurt, the heads of the German central bank viewed this development with deep concern and even a sense of outrage.[3] Bundesbank members were angry that the U.S. continued to give only tacit verbal support to the dollar, while at the same time continuing to bash Japan on trade matters. The result was the continuing collapse of the dollar around the globe. This was of particular concern to the Bundesbank because a sharply lower USD-DEM rate was deflationary to the German economy. It also caused the deutsche mark to shoot higher against Germany's European Union (EU) partner currencies, severely hurting German exports and thus growth. The Bundesbank was further irritated by higher than expected domestic wage settlements between German employers and trade unions. The market began to turn to the view that the Bundesbank might actually hike, given this and the rising producer price trend seen in early 1995.

As for Japan, it was experiencing a further period of *endaka*— or yen strengthening. Having finally cracked the 100 level in October 1994—causing roars in dealing rooms around the world—the USD-JPY had rallied back through there into 1995, following the November 15, 1994 Fed tightening and the Republican election to Congress on a promise to balance the budget (which thus made U.S. Treasuries more attractive). With the dollar turning down again across the board, the USD-JPY started to fall back. The Kobe earthquake on January 17 seemed the last straw. With scores of dead and injured, the quake further dampened economic expectations for Japan, causing economists to revise down their GDP projections. *Endaka* was shaking the Japanese economy to its foundations. The economy was already in deep recession and deflation was rampant, as evidenced by falling property, producer, manufacturing, and retail prices. And so the surging yen was the worst news possible for Japan, since it threatened the only sector in the Japanese economy which was showing any signs of health—exports. Acutely aware of the threat of further USD-JPY losses to their own balance sheets, Japanese exporters (automakers, electronics, semiconductor, and heavy manufacturing companies) sold a flood of dollars on any dollar rally, accelerating the fall.

This was further exacerbated when range binary option knockouts were triggered, forcing Japanese banks and corporates to hastily rehedge by selling yet more dollars and thus adding to the deluge. Range binaries were a relatively new phenomenon, a type of exotic option that allowed the "investor" to buy a vanilla currency call or put with double-reverse knockouts. If the spot rate did not hit the barriers during the specified maturity of the option, the investor received a multiple (in some cases 10:1) of the initial premium paid out for the option. Needless to say, with Japanese corporate earnings stagnant at home and getting hit abroad due to the rising yen, these were popular with corporate treasuries as a way of making up some of the lost ground. Range binaries are, however, not well suited to periods of extreme volatility, as the knockouts are more likely to be triggered during these times. This is good news for the bank that sold them in the first place, but not for the investor that bought them. Naturally, hindsight is 20-20, but in retrospect these were effectively leveraged short volatility positions that were just ripe for being blown out of the water given the extreme volatility that was being seen in the spot markets. The victims included not only the Japanese companies that had bought them, but also some of the hedge funds that were convinced that the dollar had hit bottom already. Rumors circulated in the market that George Soros's Quantum Fund had lost some USD600 million on USD-JPY trades alone. Indeed, Soros reportedly said he thought range binaries should be banned and likened them to crack cocaine.

Back in the U.S., the dollar's collapse became a frenzy of selling by mid-February after several Federal Reserve officials reinforced the perception through comments to the media that the Fed was done with tightening. This culminated in Alan Greenspan's Humphrey-Hawkins testimony on February 22 in which the Fed chairman said "there may come a time when we hold our policy stance unchanged, or even ease, despite adverse price data should we see signs that underlying forces are acting ultimately to reduce inflationary pressures."[4] For portfolio managers who had held onto long-dollar positions, whether directly in the foreign exchange market or through the U.S. stock and bond markets, this was the last straw. They started dumping their positions rather than just hedging them. In addition, the Japanese year-end on March 31 was fast approaching. In 1994, this had caused a precipitous decline in the USD-JPY as Japanese companies and banks sought to repatriate dollars—and other currencies—back into yen ahead of their book closing for the fiscal year.

The selling reached a crescendo as wave after wave of dollars were sold into the market. On the morning of Thursday, March 2, it reached what many—erroneously—thought was the peak. When New York desks walked in, the USD-JPY was just above 96.50. By midday, New York time, the dollar had fallen below

Y95. The USD-DEM had fared even worse, plunging 3 pfennigs to DEM1.4350. For the U.S. authorities, enough was enough. Rubin, Greenspan, and the FOMC's Foreign Currency Subcommittee met and decided that the market was in free fall, that the dollar was now seen as a one-way bet, and that two-way risk had to be restored.

That afternoon, the New York Fed foreign exchange desk, the operational arm of the Treasury's Exchange Stabilization Fund, together with the Treasury's own foreign exchange desk, intervened in the market. Located on the seventh floor of the gray fortress that is the Federal Reserve Bank of New York in downtown Manhattan, the Fed desk is a hexagonal table around which the chief dealer and his dealers sit, each with a flag in front of him to represent the currency he covers. For the dealing arm of the most feared and respected central bank in the world, it is a remarkably small and stark room. The way the desk intervenes is that the Fed dollar-yen or dollar-mark trader will call a bank on the bank's "Fed phone"—a secure telephone line that the Fed connects to the various banks it deals with, for either intervention or its usual commercial business. When the Fed phone rings, all those at the bank dealing desk instantly snap round. It could be intervention, or it could be commercial—operations for other central banks around the world or for its own investments—there is no way to know. The Fed trader will ask for a price, usually on USD10 million, though it can be larger, and then immediately execute the trade. There is no warning.

That afternoon, when bank desks were called around New York and asked repeatedly, "Price on more?" they knew they were in for a fight. That day alone, the Fed bought up USD300 million for deutsche marks and another USD300 million for yen.[5] It was not enough. With the fundamentals, both political and economic, seemingly pointing down for the dollar, proprietary desks, hedge funds, and other short-term speculators just used the Fed buying as a target to sell into. The USD-DEM and USD-JPY closed the New York session only fractionally above the initial intervention levels, at DEM1.4410 and Y95.15. The

Fed desk regularly holds teleconferences with the foreign exchange desks of the other major central banks of the world, such as the Bank of England, the Bundesbank, the Swiss National Bank, and the Bank of Japan. That night, it got the agreement from 13 other central banks, the Bank of Japan, and most European central banks to intervene to support the dollar. U.S. Treasury Secretary Rubin added his weight to the effort, highlighting official concern over the dollar's fall, saying, "A strong dollar is in our national interest. That is why we have acted in the markets in concert with others. The Administration is continuing its work on strengthening economic fundamentals including bringing down the budget deficit further."[6] For good measure, the Fed desk bought a further USD450 million for marks and USD370 million for yen that Friday.

Still it was not enough. The dollar selling continued. While Rubin's comments regarding the budget deficit were sincere, the market remained skeptical because the balanced budget proposal had been rejected. Indeed, there was talk at that time—as incredible as it seems—of the U.S. defaulting on its debt, though such talk was quickly squashed by Rubin. The markets needed to see a determined response from the G7 as a whole and the U.S. in particular; they needed to see a change in macroeconomic policies; they needed to see actions rather than just words. Initially they got more words—the following week, and from none other than Greenspan himself. The Fed chairman, speaking before the House Budget Committee, said the dollar's fall was both "unwelcome" and "troublesome" because it added to the threat of imported inflation given the persistent strength within the U.S. economy. Dollar comments from Alan Greenspan are rare indeed. When he makes them, the markets sit up. Those together with further dollar-positive comments by Rubin caused the dollar to stabilize somewhat, even though it was just temporary. However, without changes in G3 monetary and/or fiscal policies, and with the U.S. current account deficit (a further warning for others with large current account deficits) remaining the major drag on the dollar and with the market continuing to focus on capital repatriation by Japanese institutions ahead of the fiscal year-end, the dollar continued lower through the end of March. This was not helped by continued steady policy by the Fed at the March 28 FOMC meeting. No end seemed in sight.

By this time, the market was in fact trading largely on the perception of repatriation to Japan rather than the actuality. Given the extent of the fall in the USD-JPY through March 28 (13%), most Japanese companies and financial institutions had already repatriated everything they needed to. Indeed, they had been the ones that had been primarily responsible for the extent and speed of the dollar's plunge, though speculators had subsequently sold on the back of their flows. A group of institutions that did remain heavy sellers of dollars at that point were Asian central banks. Controlling about USD400 billion in foreign exchange reserves (excluding Japan), the Asian central banks had quietly become an increasingly important factor in the foreign exchange market as they sought to recycle these reserves, the result of a decade of export-led growth. The fall in the USD-JPY was of more than passing interest to them because it caused some to look at changing their reserve ratios more in favor of the yen; at the time the average dollar-denominated percentage of reserves of the combined reserves of China, Hong Kong, Indonesia, Malaysia, Singapore, Thailand, Taiwan, South Korea, and the Philippines was around 70%. Yen-denominated reserves made up an average of around 20%, with the remainder shared by several other currencies including sterling, the Swiss franc, and the deutsche mark. Purely from an investment point of view, the continuing fall in the dollar began to make dollar-denominated assets look less attractive. Several Asian central banks began to trim their dollar ratio of assets in favor of the yen, with desks citing the central banks of Taiwan, Indonesia, Thailand, and China. A couple actually began open speculative positions against the dollar on the USD-DEM and USD-JPY, acting through intermediaries in New York and Asia.[7] Needless to say, such activity—which was noted by the Federal Reserve Bank of New York in its quarterly review of foreign exchange activity—did not go down well at the U.S. Treasury, or indeed at the Bank of Japan. Certain Asian central banks, such as Bank Indonesia, had a rather more pressing need for yen, however, as a relatively high percentage of their foreign debt was denominated in yen. For Indonesia, this figure was around 40%. From the end of 1994 through the end of March 1995, Indonesia's debt servicing costs rose by around 10% annualized due to the rise of the yen.

However, while Asian central banks fretted about the currency denomination ratios of their reserves or debt servicing burdens, Asian exporters were delighted, particularly those that competed head-on with Japanese exporters for the markets of the U.S. and Europe; and none were more delighted than the Korean chaebol who faced their toughest competitors in their major industries such as automobiles, heavy manufacturing, petrochemicals, and semiconductors. With the USD-JPY plummeting relative to the USD-KRW (the dollar versus the Korean War), Korean exporters had the price edge they needed to stay ahead—temporarily—of their Japanese trading rivals. It was also a positive, because the yen easing against the won lowered the costs of yen-denominated imports into Korea from Japan, a crucial part of Korea's export machine.

The first real policy change came shortly after the FOMC meeting of March 28, and not from the Fed, but from the Bundesbank. At its March 30 regular central council meeting, the Bundesbank stunned the market by cutting its discount rate 50 basis points to 4.0% and its repo rate 35 basis points to 4.50%. The following day, the Bank of Japan allowed its unsecured call rate to fall to a historical low of 1.75%. The first building blocks of the needed policy changes that the markets had been looking for were being put into place. Two legs of the G3 had done their part, though the market was still looking for more from them as well. Now, it was up to the U.S. to give the market what it wanted, tighter monetary and fiscal policy to offset the twin current account and budget deficits. The market was fast losing patience and ahead of such changes started to sell the dollar again, with the USD-JPY ending the quarter at a fraction above 86, yet another postwar low.

In March, the Fed desk had received a bruising from the markets; the intervention had not been seen by many participants as effective, not just because the dollar ended the day lower than when the desk intervened, but because market sentiment had not been changed. New York Fed Executive Vice President Peter Fisher explained it this way: "Sterilized intervention can be useful in countering short-term trends which become self-justifying. The Federal Reserve is trying to establish communication through the process of intervention, trying to send a message. It is not so important if the dollar ends that day above where we intervened. It is important that there is a sentiment change, if the message has got through."[8]

The message had not got through, and so the Fed was determined to give it another hefty push. On Monday, April 3, in the Tokyo session, the Fed desk intervened again, buying USD-JPY. The Bank of Japan by that stage was also intervening, almost continuously; in March alone it bought around USD15.5 billion. The desk intervened again in New York, this time buying more heavily both the USD-DEM and USD-JPY. Then again on Wednesday, the Fed desk intervened once more. By doing so, it broke one of its cardinal rules. According to Fisher, the Fed desk prefers to intervene (to support the dollar) when it knows the market is short dollars and can therefore catch the market by surprise and force a short squeeze.[9] Yet the Fed had little choice. The market was disappointed that Greenspan had not hiked the rate at the March 28 FOMC meeting and was still not convinced that the U.S. Treasury had changed its tune in now wanting a strong dollar, as Bob Rubin continued to publicly insist. Privately, Treasury officials were concerned at the ongoing plunge in the dollar and made every effort to persuade the market, through meetings with bank chief dealers in New York, that they were serious about wanting the dollar to stabilize.

To Rubin, there was no alternative but to emphasize that the U.S. administration was focused on improving U.S. economic fundamentals, particularly with regard to the budget deficit; that the Treasury was in favor of a strong dollar; and that it believed the dollar would eventually right itself as it came back into line with those fundamentals. Meanwhile, he had the G7 meeting to attend that month. If ever agreement was needed on stabilizing the dollar, it was now. The markets had little expectation for the G7 meeting of April 1995. In the end, however, it was to prove momentous—indeed, Rubin's "finest hour." The G7 foreign exchange communiqué from the meeting noted that there were major misalignments in exchange rates and that exchange rates should reflect economic fundamentals, and it called for an "orderly reversal" of the dollar's decline, correcting such misalignments. The G3 authorities did not expect an immediate reversal, but they at least hoped for greater stabilization.

Meanwhile, the Bank of Japan, despite criticism at home, cut the discount rate 75 basis points to 1.00%. Markets always overshoot, and this time was no different. On April 19, 1995, the market was at its frenzied peak, a cacophony of screaming in dealing rooms around the world as the USD-JPY cracked the 80 level and the USD-DEM hit 1.3438. Though the market had no idea at the time, those were the cyclical lows. The Fed, Bundesbank, and Bank of Japan came in again, first that day, then again on May 31, this time much more aggressively. While this was going on, U.S. Trade Representative Kantor was threatening Japanese automakers with 100% sanctions on 13 luxury car models, with June 28 being the final deadline for acquiescence to U.S. market-opening demands. Meanwhile, the Treasury, led by Rubin himself and Larry Summers, soon to be the new deputy treasury secretary, continued to talk up the dollar. The "message," at least from the Fed and the Treasury, was clear: The U.S. was not prepared to sacrifice the value of the dollar for the purpose of a reduced trade deficit. Meanwhile, well past the eleventh hour, Kantor and MITI's Ryutaro Hashimoto reached a compromise agreement on opening up Japan to U.S. car dealerships and auto parts, saving the world in the process from a potentially catastrophic protectionist spiral.

It was just what the Treasury needed. On July 7 and then again on August 2, the Fed desk caught the market napping, in the process extracting some measure of revenge for the drubbing it had taken in its previous interventions that year. On August 2, the desk came in at 8:06 a.m. New York time, just as New York dealers were coming out of their morning meeting. It asked for a price from a Japanese bank with the USD-JPY at 90.20 and immediately bought dollars. At the same time, all the other Fed traders, not just the USD-JPY trader, were calling up other banks and asking for prices. The Fed bought again, at 90.55, then at 90.95, and again at 91.05. The Treasury followed up the intervention with a statement, saying that it was in line with the April and June G7 communiqués, calling for an orderly reversal of the dollar's decline in 1993–1995. Finally, the desk intervened again on August 1995, the last time it was to need to do so again.

As Peter Fisher put it, the market had finally got the message. Two-way risk had been established. Yet the interventions of July 7 and August 2 were different from those before. They were designed to specifically put a floor under the dollar and push it higher, rather than was the case in March, April, and May when the Fed was simply trying to calm and stabilize an extremely disorderly market. One way to gauge this is to look at a market indicator that the Fed desk itself watches quite closely—option risk reversals. Put in market terminology, these are the differences in implied volatilities between the same "delta"—the measure of the change in the value of the option relative to the change in the price of the underlying—of put and call options. They are thus a measurement of both prevailing sentiment and anticipation. The benchmark risk reversal is usually the 1-month 25 delta. Prior to the July 7 and August 2 interventions, every Fed intervention occurred when the 1-month 25 delta risk reversal was over 2.0 in favor of yen calls (that is, the difference between the implied volatility on a 25 delta yen call was 2.0 vols or higher above that of the same delta yen put). Just before the Fed desk came in on July 7, the yen risk reversal was still in favor of the yen call (0.9/1.3), but had been trading lower all week and was well below the 2.0 level. In the case of the August 2 intervention, the risk reversal had actually moved in favor of yen puts beforehand and was 1.0/1.5 before the desk came in. Thus, the market was already favoring the dollar when the Fed intervened—and the Fed knew it. The U.S. Treasury and Fed were effectively saying that they wanted the orderly reversal of the dollar's decline accelerated, that they wanted the dollar to go higher rather than just for it to stop falling. Fisher has said the Fed does not target dollar levels, but clearly these two interventions showed that the Fed and Treasury were not satisfied with existing levels at the time and wanted the dollar to rise. This was further confirmed by the August 15 intervention, which was designed to breach the 94.00 technical level, trend-line resistance from the April 1990 peak of 160.35. On September 8, the Bank of Japan cut its discount rate to 0.50%. For dollar bears it was the last straw. The dollar had found its bottom and was set to rebound.

From the April low through the end of the year, the USD-JPY rebounded 29.6% to around 103.50. In Asia, little heed was paid to this. Asian exporters had had a stellar year, as reflected in corporate earnings and national merchandise export growth. For 1995, the NIEs as a whole had 20.6% Y/Y export growth, a level not seen before in the 1990s.[10] Individually, Hong Kong saw a 16.7% rise in exports, the highest rate since 1992, while Korean exports leaped 32.4% as Korean companies gleefully snatched market share away from their Japanese competitors due to the high value of the yen relative to the Korean won. Taiwan's export growth in 1995 was also the highest it had seen in the decade, up 20.5%. As for Southeast Asia, as a whole it averaged annual export growth of 22.8%, with Malaysia, the Philippines, and Thailand all experiencing 20%-plus growth in exports. The good times were here to stay, and they were getting better by the day, or so it seemed.

For corporate Japan, and particularly for those companies that focused principally on exports, *endaka* had been a disaster. Initially, Japanese exports had risen in value as the yen rose because in value terms the yen worth of exports increased in dollar terms. However, this also increased the price of Japanese goods relative to those in the domestic markets of the U.S. and Europe. Thus, Japanese export volumes to those places began to fall as they lost out to cheaper goods from within the U.S. and Europe and also to Asian exports. Eventually, this was translated into a lower Japanese trade surplus and thus a lower current account surplus.

The overall Japanese trade surplus peaked at USD144 billion in the year to March 1994 and then started heading lower. As for the U.S.-Japan bilateral trade deficit, this also peaked in 1994, at USD65.67 billion, heading down to USD59.28 billion in 1995 and USD47.68 billion in 1996. The relationship involving the delay between a change in the exchange rate and the consequent change in the trade balance is called the J-curve. The length of the J-curve—the delay period—can vary with exchange rates, and it can also vary with different manufacturing products, some being less sensitive to changes in exchange rate value than others. In the past decade or so, the USD-JPY J-curve period has usually been around two years. Thus, in this case, theoretically the USD-JPY can be heading down for two years before the Japanese trade balance is materially affected. In practice, this was indeed the case as the above data show.

Japanese manufacturers of products from cars to semiconductors and chemicals began to lose market share. From 1992 to 1995, the market share for Japanese automakers in the U.S. fell from 26% to 22% despite major efforts by Japanese companies to take the hit on their margins rather than by hiking prices of cars they sold in the U.S. There was bad news at home in Japan as well; foreign companies were slowly eating into their domestic share, as a result of both trade agreements with the U.S. and the fall in the USD-JPY, which made foreign imports much cheaper despite the best efforts of the Japanese ministries to keep them out of Japanese markets altogether. From 1986 to 1995, foreign market share of Japan's own semiconductor market rose from 8.6% to 26%.

Japan Inc., in the form of the *Keidanren,* the Japanese business association and lobby, had to respond. Amid Western calls for Japanese companies to cut workers Western style and "reengineer," Japanese companies responded in particularly Japanese style. First, there was a focused shift of manufacturing capacity overseas, since the fall in the USD-JPY made manufacturing in Japan even more expensive than it already was. Japanese companies sought to expand manufacturing capacity in the U.S. and more importantly throughout Asia. Second, instead of just firing workers en masse, they sought to shift perceived "excess" workers to less frontline positions. To fire them would have undermined the social cohesion of the firms and thus the country; that is how it is seen in Japan. The Japanese employment system is based on three principles: lifetime employment, cooperation between company unions and management, and seniority pay. Other ways to cut costs were sought—Japanese companies, unencumbered by the need to provide any significant dividend income to their shareholders, devote a far higher average percentage of research and development to revenues and profit than most of their Western counterparts. While this can be a short-term negative in terms of total costs, it is undoubtedly a long-term positive in terms of new product development.

At the manufacturing level, Japanese companies tried to become competitive despite the burdens placed on them by *endaka,* in stark contrast to their counterparts in Asia—or the U.S. or Europe for that matter. Meanwhile, the high yen also caused structural changes in the Japanese economy, either despite the best efforts of the various ministries or because of them. Retailing is a case in point. The Japanese retail system has for years, either deliberately or not, dampened domestic consumption rates relative to the normal levels experienced in developed Western nations. Between 1991 and 1995, consumption needed no encouragement from the system itself to fall. Total department store sales declined for four straight years in Tokyo and Osaka resulting from the effects of the bursting asset price bubble felt in the real economy. This caused a notable change in Japanese consumption patterns, a fact that the Ministry of Finance itself has acknowledged. For the first time in memory, Japanese consumers became price-conscious. This benefited those few Western retailers that had bothered to set up in Tokyo. Since they focused more on price, they saw their sales boom. Once again, Japan Inc. sought to restructure to adapt to this new environment.

As a whole, Japanese businesses were able to do so because of the two major advantages within the Japanese economy: extremely high productivity and the best technology in the world. Take the auto industry as an example. In 1995, the Japanese auto industry employed a mere 514,000 workers, as against 1.996 million in the U.S.[11] In the JD Power auto survey in the U.S., year after year, Japanese cars are voted the best in the world. How is this achieved? Because Japan Inc. invests three times as much in each of its workers and the surrounding technology as the U.S.—and considerably more than is the case in Europe, where investment is truly pitiful. Take another example, the somewhat unfashionable tobacco industry. In 1991, at the height of Japan's recession, Japan Tobacco, then a government-owned monopoly, produced 286 billion cigarettes that year with only 19,100 workers. By comparison, U.S. tobacco manufacturers produced 695 billion with 61,691 workers—a ratio of 15 to 1 versus only 11 to 1 in the U.S.[12]

On the technology side, Japan has developed the best wealth of technology in the world. Pick almost any leading manufactured brand in the U.S. and Europe and you will find that major components of it are made in Japan—and only made in Japan because no one knows how to copy them. Japan has invested sufficient capital to develop technology in numerous manufacturing fields which, by its uniqueness, creates "natural monopolies." Japan Inc., unlike the West, has done everything it can to hold onto technological information. It is happy to copy the West's best-kept "secrets" but loath to give up anything itself. Indeed, to many Japanese company officials, it is quite baffling why Western companies give away such information, but they are happy to receive it nonetheless. In the electronics industry alone, Japan has such natural monopolies, in flat panel displays, laser diodes, compact disk players and CD-ROM drives (and in the future, DD players), supercomputers, capacitors, laser printers, computer data-reading heads, nickel hydride batteries, semiconductors, and hot wall oxidation and diffusion furnaces which are crucial in the making of semiconductors.[13] Other Japanese natural monopolies can be found in cameras, musical instruments, robotics, and avionics.

Such natural monopolies distort and change the duration of the J-curve and indeed by themselves make Japanese corporate earnings in the areas they are found less sensitive to the effects of the USD-JPY than would otherwise be so, or for that matter than would be experienced by their competitors. They do not eliminate foreign exchange risk—nothing does—but they limit it. Which brings us back once more to the issue of intra-Asian competition. In the initial Japanese boom period of 1960–1980, Japanese manufacturers (and this is a grand generalization, open to justifiable rebuke, but for that, it should stand the test of time) focused on capacity generation, on quantity rather than quality. Needless to say, this is no longer the case. In the years 1985–1988, thanks to the Plaza Agreement and the failed Louvre Agreement of 1987, and again in 1993–1995, Asian exporters, who were gradually moving up the manufacturing ladder in terms of complexity and added value (but not fast enough), were in effect given price advantage. While some were wise enough to plow such profits back into investment in technology in order to climb further up the ladder, many, which were family-oriented firms, reaped the short-term gains. Those same companies are now reaping the whirlwind. The years 1993–1995 were a gift to Asia, with the exception of Japan, to boost its technological capacity rather than its gross manufacturing capacity, to invest for the future, for a rainy day. The rebound in the USD-JPY should have been a warning to spur this movement for techno-logical innovation and improvement. It was ignored.

Meanwhile, the U.S. continued to support a strong dollar in 1996. With the German recovery much weaker than expected and even threatening to go back into recession, while Japan's recovery was feeble at best—and soon to peak out in the first quarter of calendar 1997—the G3 were content as a whole to push the dollar higher. For the U.S., with industrial capacity stretched to its limit and labor market conditions continuing to tighten, a strong dollar was an effective way of capping any threat of imported inflation—the strong dollar boosting imports at cheaper prices, thus dampening overall prices. To those who are skeptical about the effect of trade on the U.S. economy, trade makes up only 13% of GDP, but it has been steadily rising for the past five years, ever since Clinton became president in fact. This will continue to rise, barring any protectionist backlash on Capitol Hill.

The strong dollar reduced the need for Federal Reserve tightening in 1996, thus keeping market interest rates lower and keeping the economy strong; this was extremely important in light of the upcoming November 1996 election. Ahead of that event, and in the wake of the China-Taiwan military tensions in February 1996, which reinforced to the U.S. the crucial nature of its security alliance with Japan, trade tensions between the U.S. and Japan eased significantly. Indeed, U.S. officials, basking in the glow of the then ongoing fall in the U.S.-Japan trade deficit, were positively effusive in their praise for Japan. This was not to say that Japan had not deregulated and opened up markets (a little), nor to say that the U.S.-Japan auto accord of 1995 had not produced any results (albeit marginal). Yet the degree of praise and the extent of change in the U.S. rhetoric left one suspicious. Even the American Automobile Manufacturers Association, the ultimate U.S. trade hawk, was remarkably silent in the run up to the U.S. presidential election. On April 20, 1996, Mickey Kantor, who had been promoted to the post of commerce secretary with the passing of the late Ron Brown, said that Japan was "playing fairer" on trade. The stronger dollar had economic benefits for the U.S., but allowing it to rise was also very much a political decision by the White House, just as forcing it lower in 1993 had been. So the dollar continued to rise. From January to June 1996, the USD-DEM rose 6.1%, while the USD-JPY rose 4.5%. In the whole of 1996, they rose 7.5% and 11.8%, respectively. Thus, from the April low to the end of 1996, the USD-JPY had risen 41.4%. For any Asian exporters who were listening, this was a screaming alarm bell. Few listened, and fewer still did anything about it.

Meanwhile, back in Washington, Greenspan and his colleagues had been taking a fresh look at the U.S. economy. The sharp tightening in 1994 and early 1995 had been necessary to tame rising inflationary pressures. Inflation hawk that he is, the last thing Greenspan wanted was for the economy to have what pundits termed a "hard landing" due to excessively high interest rates. By July 1995, Greenspan was easing monetary policy once more, by 25 basis points, at the July 6 FOMC meeting and then a further 25 basis points at the December 19 FOMC meeting. In 1996, he cut, for the last time, 25 basis points at the January 31 FOMC meeting (before reversing that last move, hiking 25 basis points at the March 25 FOMC meeting). When the Fed eases monetary policy, it has a significant impact in boosting global, not just U.S., liquidity. Along with easier policy by the Bundesbank in 1995 and rock-bottom rates in Japan, this was a major supportive factor for global asset markets, but especially for U.S. asset markets given the strength of the U.S. economy. In mid-to-late 1995, 1996, and the first half of 1997, the DJIA and S&P 500 stock index soared so high, they were almost in orbit. Treasuries also produced stellar returns, with the virtuous combination of huge capital gains and high real yields as inflationary pressures continued to fall through the end of 1996 and into 1997. Domestic U.S. retail and institutional investors were the major driving force behind the gains in U.S. stock markets. However, foreign investors were a major factor behind the gains in the Treasury market, in the process financing the U.S. budget and current account deficits. Foreign institutional investors were also heavy buyers of U.S. Treasuries, particularly from Japan.

Having been burned in the 1993–1995 collapse of the dollar, which hammered their holdings of dollar-denominated assets, and no doubt feeling a keen sense of betrayal at the tactics of the U.S. government—the U.S. would have gone bankrupt a long time ago had it not been for Japanese investors financing the U.S. budget deficit—the Japanese institutional investor base was understandably reluctant to invest again in U.S. assets in 1995.

Japan's Ministry of Finance is housed in a drab six-floor building in the Kasumigaseki district of Tokyo. Despite the uninspiring appearance of its headquarters, it is the pinnacle of administrative power in Japan. Indeed, it is the center of power in Japan as a whole. Within it, many factional battles are fought, but all aspire to the common goal of leading the country forward. Through strategic leaks to the local and foreign press, the Ministry of Finance in 1995 let it be known that there was a battle within it between those who wanted to open up the economy and financial markets in Japan and those who wanted to maintain the "old way." Such a suggestion was complete rubbish, but extremely convenient for its purposes. For in mid-1995, there appeared an individual—contrary to the Ministry of Finance tradition of team over the one—who seemed to represent the drive for modernization, of both the Ministry of Finance itself and Japan as a whole. He was Eisuke Sakakibara, director general of the Ministry of Finance's International Finance Bureau. On August 2, 1995, just as the Fed and the Bank of Japan were intervening, Sakakibara-san announced the loosening of restrictions on foreign currency investments by Japanese life insurers. Japanese life insurers have around USD18 trillion worth in assets. At the time, their policies guaranteed a return of around 4 to 5%; yet with the Nikkei 225 remaining weak, given the bearish economic outlook due to the strong yen and the JGB (Japanese Government Bond) market only yielding a maximum 3%, they had to invest offshore.

The Ministry of Finance, through the public personage of Sakakibara, allowed them greater access to do so. They were not slow about taking up the opportunity. By August 16, the USD-JPY was back above 98, helped of course by the intervention the previous day, but also by the sheer weight of dollar buying—mostly for U.S. Treasuries—by Japanese life insurers. Sakakibara even went on the record as saying that if he were a Japanese investor, he would borrow in yen and buy dollars. Going into 1996, the dollar had turned around for good, at least in this cycle, and Sakakibara was to become known, both in Japan and in the global financial markets, as the man who had turned around the yen, "Mr. Yen." In reality, the Ministry of Finance as a whole was delighted because once again the weakening yen allowed Japan to export its way out of recession, and this is precisely what it set about doing.

With both the U.S. and Japan pushing for a higher dollar, and thus implicitly—and sometimes explicitly—a weaker yen, Japan Inc. began to grab back the market share it had lost to its Asian counterparts. With the USD-JPY up some 55% from its low by May 1997, the yen had effectively been devalued. To counter this threat, Asian governments and central banks should have pushed their own currencies lower against the dollar, while Asian companies should have cut costs and restructured—as their Japanese counterparts had done—to reflect an increasingly competitive trading environment. Neither side did so. Meanwhile, Asian export growth started to fall dramatically. The NIEs saw export growth fall to a measly 4.8% Y/Y in 1996, down from 21% in 1995.[14] Among these, the worst affected was South Korea, whose export growth plunged from 32% to 4.1%. With little quality advantage over Japanese manufactured products and with their price advantage having been severely reduced or in many cases more than wiped out, in market after market the *chaebol* were being picked off by the *Kaisha* of Japan.

In Southeast Asia, the picture was just as grim. Malaysian export growth fell from 26% to a pitiful 4.0% in 1995 and Indonesia's edged down from 13% to 8.8%. In Thailand, exports collapsed, rising only 0.1% for the whole of 1996 compared with 25% the previous year. Even China, which had devalued the yuan some 35% in 1994, saw export growth plunge from 25% to only 1.5%.[15]

The result was also predictable—rising current account deficits. Southeast Asia as a whole had a total current account deficit in 1995 of some USD33.534 billion. In 1996, this rose to USD36.473 billion. Individually, Indonesia's current account deficit rose to USD8.900 billion from 7.023 billion, that of the Philippines to USD3.538 billion from USD2.514 billion, and Thailand's to USD14.545 billion from 13.555 billion.[16] Even more important than these figures was the rise in Asian current account deficits as a percentage of GDP. Combined with shrinking budget surpluses, this reflected a reduced ability to pay for those widening current account deficits. This was particularly the case in ASEAN, where most notably Thailand's budget surplus as a percentage of GDP shrank from 3.0% in 1995 to 0.9% in 1996, while its current account deficit to GDP was roughly flat at a huge 8.0%. Korea's current account deficit more than doubled from 2.0% to 4.8%, while at the same time its budget surplus shrank from 0.6% of GDP to 0.3%.

While the USD-JPY continued to rise and Asian export growth slowed significantly, Asian wage growth continued to outpace productivity—a "double whammy" as far as trade competitiveness was concerned. Faced with rising current account deficits in Asia, Asian governments had varying responses, none of them constructive. South Korea and Thailand, instead of solving the fundamental problems within their own manufacturing bases, decided to try to tinker with imports, creating official campaigns to dissuade citizens from buying luxury product imports. The Malaysian prime minister hinted at imposing import controls on "nonessential" imported goods.[17] Instead of such tinkering, and with growth still booming, Asian authorities should have sought to dampen domestic demand through the tightening of both monetary and fiscal policy. The former might have led initially to currency strength against the dollar and increased short-term foreign capital inflow, but would have imposed tighter and stricter credit allocation. The latter would have helped shore up government budget defenses against the crisis to come—and could have certainly made the effects of the crisis less painful, if not averted it. Both would have gone a long way to restoring competitiveness. As it was, faced with massive foreign debt burdens and with excessive monetary growth and the shrinking ability to finance that imbalance through budget surpluses, such inadequate policies encouraged speculators to attack a number of currencies, notably the Thai baht. The Indonesian rupiah also came under the speculators' collective eye, further pressured as it was as a result of the riots in Jakarta in July 1996.

A few voices, including Standard & Poor's MMS and *Business Week,* warned of the dangers of such large current account deficits, saying that over the long term these were unsustainable. Unfortunately, such voices in 1996 were all but drowned out, such was the mood at the time with Asian stock and bond markets rallying in line with global asset markets and foreign capital flow starting to come back in earnest. A bevy of statistics was set forth to defend the case that this time was different—that Asia was not Mexico—ranging from a superficial outlook of Asia's budget surpluses, to foreign reserve to short-term debt cover, to import cover, both of the last being relatively high in Asia. However, such indicators are subject to short-term capital; if short-term capital leaves, foreign reserves fall of necessity, both because of central bank efforts to defend the currency and because such capital has left and thus is no longer translatable into reserves.

Much more important for the long-term health of an economy are manageable current account deficits—and more preferably surpluses—combined with healthy budget surpluses. Hong Kong is a case in point where this is true, though it has other fundamental weaknesses such as an overvalued property market, which will inevitably be corrected. National authorities also have to let markets work and not distort market signals by imposing inappropriate exchange rate or interest rate systems. A number of economists said the fall in 1996 was purely cyclical and due to a downturn in demand in the U.S. and Europe, principally in electronics and electronic components upon which many Asian countries are largely dependent for their export growth. Such analysis did not take account of the rebound of the USD-JPY and the consequent rebound of Japan Inc. and Japanese exports.

The fall in Asian exports was not merely cyclical. It was, and is, structural against both a domestic and an international setting. On the domestic front, Asian exporters increasingly became uncompetitive, on a wage/productivity basis and an exchange rate basis, and did not do enough—or indeed anything—to reverse this. On the international front, Japanese exporters were let back in the game and started to make inroads on their competitors in Asia. In addition, the previous fall in the USD-JPY, which had forced Japanese manufacturing capacity offshore, had accelerated the drive of Japan Inc. to manufacture in Asia rather than in Japan itself; while Asian wages were increasingly uncompetitive relative to Asian productivity, they were extremely competitive relative to Japanese domestic wages. Thus, Asian exporters were hit from two fronts: a tougher exchange rate environment that allowed Japanese exporters as a whole back in the game, and Japanese manufacturers competing with them in their own backyards for the right to export to the U.S. and Europe.

Because of the rise of the USD-JPY, while dollar exchange rates stayed relatively stable against Asian currencies due to the pegged exchange rate systems, the yen gradually fell against the Asian currencies from April 1995 to early 1997. The JPY-THB, for instance, fell 22% in that period. Weak Japanese domestic demand and the overappreciation of Asian currencies, relative to their deteriorating economic fundamentals, combined to cause an explosion of Japan's trade surplus with Asia. The end was near. This was unsustainable. Asian countries had ignored a number of domestic and international economic warnings. Left at that, they could have still turned the situation around in time, if only they had remembered one last warning, a precedent in fact—Mexico.

4

The Precedent — Mexico

WHILE ASIAN AUTHORITIES did little or nothing to take account of the rising dollar and the effect that might have on their export sectors, they also did their best to ignore an event that should have served as a clear warning of the potential excesses that can build as a result of rapidly changing dynamics within a developing economy—the Mexican currency crisis.

That event, which began with the December 20, 1994 widening of the Mexican peso band and then its abandonment two days later, was in fact seen as a major nuisance rather than a warning, causing fallout across the world's financial markets, including Asia. Commentators at the time were swift to point out that Asia was different. The market concerns about current account deficits in certain Asian countries, caused by the focus on Mexico's huge hole in its own current account balance, were not valid given the tight fiscal policies that Asia kept to, strong fundamentals and growth potential. Irritated by the volatility in their domestic markets as a result of the Mexican crisis, Asian authorities were all too happy to support such a view.

The Asian currency crisis was predated by the collapse of the Bretton Woods system, the volatility of the European monetary "Snake" system, the ERM crises of 1992 and 1993, and several other smaller periods of extreme volatility. More than any, however, it was predated by Mexico. The Mexican currency crisis of

December 1994–March 1995 (with the real economic after-effects lasting for the whole of 1995) was the precedent—a country with a very significant current account deficit, a country that up until early 1994 ran a very tight fiscal ship, and a country that attracted massive foreign capital inflow and foreign direct investment. All these things could have been said of many of the ASEAN countries that were subsequently humiliated and forced to devalue their currencies.

Such an observation raises the tempting idea that the Asian currency crisis (and perhaps also the Mexican crisis?) was due purely to what economists call "exogenous shock"—that is, an external event that traumatizes and alters significantly (for the worse) the prevailing domestic fundamentals. Such temptation should be avoided. This is not to say that external factors did not play a significant part in both crises. Rather, it is to stress that domestic considerations were equally if not more responsible and that to seek out external factors in the first place is merely the age-old practice of looking for a convenient scapegoat—a satisfying but delusional activity.

It is thus instructive to examine in detail the Mexican currency crisis, the impact it had on the Mexican economy and other Latin American currencies and economies, the warning that was not heeded, the lessons that might have been learned but were not, and those lessons from it that are still available.

Memory in the financial markets is a very short-term concept. Dealers sitting at their desks, screaming in the phone, are bombarded with a wealth of data and news, the likes of which has never before been experienced by humanity. News items are used and discarded at frightening speed. Even in the real economy this is also the case. Those who said Asia was different were also the kind who forgot what Mexico was like before the crisis, when confidence was not high but stratospheric, when Mexican and international authorities talked confidently of Mexico having finally achieved the status of a first-world nation—in those glory days after the signing of the North American Free Trade Agreement in November 1993. Treated as a pariah after it defaulted on its debt in 1982, Mexico was, in the early 1990s, feted as an example of how fundamentals could be brought back into line after wandering so long in the wilderness (both politically and economically). NAFTA did not mark the birth of this optimism, but its culmination, its fulfillment. Mexico tapped the international capital markets with confidence and provided an investment-friendly environment for direct and portfolio investors alike.

Although it was in progress before, Mexico's turnaround began in earnest with the stabilization program implemented by the government in December 1987. After the 1982 debt crisis, the peso was in free fall as the authorities sought to restore at least some semblance of trade competitiveness in order to meet creditor demands, and inflation exploded. By 1987, inflation was running at an annual rate of over 160%. The need for drastic reform and stabilization was clear, and a stabilization program was forced through. The main elements included tight fiscal policy (broadening the tax base, reducing marginal tax rates, and increasing tax compliance, as well as spending cuts), major external debt restructuring (which helped to lower interest payments via the first implementation of the Brady plan), and major structural reforms, including privatization and trade liberalization. Key to the structural reforms was the *Pacto*—the agreement between the government, unions, and the business community to all move in the same direction on issues such as trade and business conditions.

Along with tight fiscal policy, the Bank of Mexico kept monetary policy tight in order to squeeze inflationary pressures out of the system. In addition to keeping interest rates high, the Mexican peso was also used to dampen prices. From March to December 1988, it was fixed to the dollar, and then allowed to depreciate for the next three years at a limited and preannounced rate. The Bank of Mexico created an intervention band in November 1991. The floor of the dollar-peso (USD-MXP) intervention band was kept constant, while the ceiling fell from less than 1.5% by January 1992 to 9% at the end of 1993.

Despite the problems that were to develop later on, the 1987 stabilization program had excellent initial results: Real GDP recovered to an average of 3.5% during the period 1989–1992 from a meager 0.5–1.0% in 1985–1988, while inflation collapsed to a mere 12% by 1992, hitting single digits in early 1993. Foreign portfolio flow started to return, and with it the Bank of Mexico's foreign reserves recovered sharply—to USD25.5 billion by the end of 1993 compared with only USD6.5 billion at the end of 1989).[1] Fueled by rising domestic and foreign investment, whether through portfolio or FDI, private consumption boomed.

As Table 4 shows, Mexico made significant progress during the period 1987–1993.

Table 4

Mexican Economic Performance, 1987–1993

	1987	1988	1989	1990	1991	1992	1993
Real GDP	1.7	1.2	3.5	4.5	3.6	2.8	0.6
Net saving (%/GDP)	21.6	18.2	18.5	18.7	17.6	16.0	14.1
Real effect foreign exchange rate, 1980 = 100	56.3	73.1	73.3	77.4	85.9	93.3	99.3
28-d cetes (annual rate)	122.0	52.3	40.6	26.0	16.7	16.9	11.8

Source: Bank of Mexico, Mexican Ministry of Finance, *Standard & Poor's MMS.*

There were two interlinked problems, however, on the economic side. First, the consumer boom in Mexico, principally in Mexico City itself, sucked in imports. Import growth during that period averaged over 20% a year, outpacing non–oil export growth, which was around 15%. This was a commendable result by any standards, but the resulting imbalance led to a sharp deterioration in the overall Mexican trade account. Second, this was exacerbated by the appreciation of the real effective exchange rate, which hurt export growth relative to imports. In addition, foreign portfolio into the country continued to grow—a double-edged sword for a developing economy. This, together with the worsening trade situation, caused a significant deterioration in Mexico's current account deficit, which rose from USD2.9 billion in 1987 to some USD23.4 billion in 1993. By 1994, that figure was a deficit of USD29.5 billion—or about 8% of GDP. At the same time, domestic private savings fell from around 22% to 13% by 1994, confirming Mexico's reliance on offshore capital to fund that current account deficit.

Current account deficits do not of necessity cause financial crisis or collapse. The U.S. has had a pronounced current account deficit for the last decade without any realistic suggestion of such an event. In the U.S.'s case, of course, it has been bankrolled by the central banks of the world and Japanese life insurers and pension funds. In Mexico, the current account deficit was financed mostly by U.S. portfolio flow (which led to the capital account balance achieving a surplus of USD30.5 billion in 1993) and tight fiscal policy. Eventually, a very large current account deficit is unsustainable. As the World Bank pointed out in a subsequent analysis of the crisis, Mexico's 8% current account deficit would have eventually required that the country devote 100% of its GNP just to pay the interest and dividends to foreign investors in Mexican securities.[2] That said, current account deficits can remain sizable for a time—as proved to be the case in the U.S. and also Asia—without serious damage to the economy. There are two conditions to this: that no exogenous shocks occur which severely damage investor confidence—and thus the ability to finance the current account deficit—and that the currency be allowed or even encouraged to weaken in order to offset the implicit imbalance within the trade and current accounts. In the case of Mexico, neither of these conditions occurred.

On the first count, Mexico suffered a series of domestic political shocks in 1994 which were to severely damage investor confidence, starting with the Chiapas rebellion in January 1994. While the reforms of the government of President Carlos Salinas de Gortari, who held power from 1988 to 1994, undoubtedly provided real economic benefits to major sections of the population, they also left behind a significant portion who saw no benefit whatsoever. According to the World Bank, the level of poverty in Mexico during the mid-to-late 1980s was 27.5%. In the 1990s, this had only fallen to 25.9%.[3] The level of what the World Bank defined as "extreme poverty" actually rose during that period, from 7.7% in the mid-to-late 1980s to 8.2% in the 1990s. A considerable proportion of those who were extremely poor were the indigenous Indian peoples rather than ethnic Spaniards, and they lived for the most part in the southernmost state in Mexico, Chiapas.

On New Year's Day of 1994, as the new year was greeted by the ringing of bells and clinking glasses, in San Cristobal de las Casas, in Chiapas, masked gunmen quietly took control of the town. Their leader, who was to become famous around the world, let alone in Mexico, was Subcommandante Marcos. The gunmen, mostly native Indians and calling themselves the EZLN (Zapatista Army of National Liberation), declared war against the Mexican Federal Army. Named after the Nahua Indian Emiliano Zapata who rose up in rebellion—and was executed by the government in April 1919—the Zapatistas said they were the product of 500 years of struggle by the Indian peoples in Mexico. They called for a series of basic rights: work, land, shelter, bread, health, education, democracy, liberty, peace, independence, and justice.[4]

The initial reaction by the Mexican government was to officially play down the troubles. Small acts of criminal activity had been noted in Chiapas, but these were being swiftly dealt with by the local authorities and order restored. The reality was that infantry units of the Mexican Federal Army were immediately dispatched. Whether or not they were told to take the gloves off, the results were bloody. Arriving somewhat late on the scene, in terms of covering social discontent that had been simmering for centuries, the world's press began to suddenly take notice. International investors were alarmed, but Salinas and his officials did their best to soothe investor nerves. The problems were local, isolated, and easily contained and dealt with. They would have no impact whatsoever on Mexico's economy, and any disturbance in the Mexican asset markets would quickly pass. The peso, for its part, would never be allowed to fall. Most, lured by the high yields on Mexican T-bills and good past returns on stocks, were satisfied by such reassurances. Some, however, were not and took some profit or at least hedged part of their outstanding position. One U.S. fund manager took a private jet down to Chiapas, spent a week touring its towns and speaking to the people, took the jet back to California, and sold the fund's entire holding in Mexico. Such foresight was rare, however. Most allowed themselves to be persuaded to stay, a decision that was to prove costly for many.

Despite this, the Mexican stock market's reaction to these events was certainly not favorable, with domestic investors, more than foreigners, selling down the bolsa by some 10% or so in the first two weeks of the year. The declaration of a cease-fire by President Salinas on January 12 calmed the markets for a time. However, more bad news was to come and from an entirely unexpected source.

The PRI, the Institutional Revolutionary Party, has ruled Mexico unchecked since 1929, the longest political reign of any single political party. Its domination has been total, winning all eleven of the presidential contests from 1929 on. 1994 was expected to yield more of the same. Carlos Salinas could not, according to the constitution, rule for another term, so he had picked a successor, Luis Donaldo Colosio. A protégé of Salinas, Colosio was expected to win the August 1994 election with ease and carry on the process of economic reform that Salinas had done so much to initiate. The war in Chiapas, however brief, had been an unpleasant distraction and a major embarrassment privately with the U.S. looking on. Colosio sought to go on the campaign trail, taking the focus away from that unpleasantness and back to the progress that Mexico had made and the election to come. The last campaign stop Colosio made, on March 23, 1994, was to Tijuana, a tacky boomtown near the U.S.-Mexican border. That evening, after speaking at a town meeting, Colosio was assassinated as he was leaving. Because he was seen as an ardent reformer in the mold of his mentor Salinas, Colosio's assassination was first blamed on the old guard of the PRI. Whatever the case, the loss of Colosio was a massive one for Salinas and a further embarrassment for Mexico. The idea of first-world nation status was slipping fast. Salinas declared March 24 a day of mourning and the markets were closed that day as a sign of respect.

Subsequently, after much soul-searching, the political scene quieted down. A new successor had been found, Ernesto Zedillo Ponce de Leon, a Yale scholar who was part of the new technocratic elite that Salinas had developed. With the U.S. looking on, Zedillo was clearly the acceptable face of the PRI, someone with whom the U.S. "could do business." The August 21 elections went ahead as planned with the predictable result—a Zedillo win by a landslide. U.S. observers said that it was one of the cleanest elections in memory in Mexico, but there is not the slightest doubt that vote rigging took place on a large scale. Still, in a seemingly unstable time, Zedillo was the voice of moderation, of modernization, and above all of stability. He would have won anyway. With the election out of the way and Zedillo in power, the PRI seemed back on track, and with it the return of a greater degree of investor confidence. It was a false calm, however. The following month, in September 1994, PRI Secretary General Jose Francisco Ruiz Massieu was assassinated—a further demonstration of the internal conflicts within the PRI itself and the country as a whole. Elements within the Clinton administration were concerned that the Mexican government, now headed by Zedillo, could be losing control and more specifically that a clear and determined effort was being made to stop the progress of economic and political reform within Mexico. Such concerns were not without justification. The reform process, which Zedillo was subsequently to extend far beyond anyone's expectations, was under attack. Too many vested interests had too much to lose if it continued.

Trouble was brewing with the economy too. Despite the still healthy levels of portfolio flows into Mexican asset markets, economic growth had stalled in 1993, with real GDP falling to 0.6% from 2.8% in 1992. In order to offset this, the government looked at relaxing the fiscal side—which had been relatively austere in the early 1990s—a touch. Meanwhile, the current account deficit continued to widen, and the ability to finance it was becoming increasingly stretched, ever-more dependent on foreign capital inflow. This situation was clearly exacerbated by the Fed tightening process that had begun on February 4, 1994. A weakening of the Mexican peso, the MXP, was clearly needed to offset these economic imbalances. In September 1994, the same month as the assassination of Massieu, the World Bank actually put out a report warning that Mexico was becoming excessively dependent on foreign capital inflow. This dependency made it vulnerable, particularly in light of the falling savings rate and productivity gains that were insufficient to offset the loss of trade competitiveness brought about by the real appreciation of the peso.

There were two further problems: In the run up to the August election, the monetary base had expanded, unchecked at a rapid pace. While the Bank of Mexico significantly increased the supply of *tesobono* (dollar-indexed debt instruments) to the market before the election as a way of helping to convince the markets that it was serious about not allowing the peso to devalue, at the same time it was restricting the supply of *cetes,* thus keeping domestic interest rates artificially low. The suspicion was that the Bank of Mexico had been told to inflate the economy as part of the government's strategy of ensuring a PRI victory. Currencies, like anything else, respond to demand and supply fundamentals. Such creation of "supply" inevitably leads to lower demand. In addition, the market had the suspicion—only a suspicion because data were not released on a timely basis—that the Bank of Mexico's foreign reserves were declining at an alarming rate, pulled down by the burdens of having to finance the current account deficit. Subsequently, the markets would find out that, indeed, this had been the case. Foreign reserves that had been USD25.5 billion at the start of 1994 and USD28.25 billion on March 23, the date of the Colosio assassination, fell by some USD11 billion in April alone and peso cetes rates doubled. The USD-MXP, which had an official ceiling annual appreciation band limit of 4%, promptly hit the top of the band, forcing the Bank of Mexico to intervene. With foreign reserves falling at such a rate, the authorities needed other measures to help them support their currency—which, little did they know, was just starting a decline that would soon become a fully fledged collapse. Mexico's NAFTA partners lent it a short-term credit line, and the Bank of Mexico allowed market interest rates to rise to squeeze out speculators who were just starting to attack the currency.

For a while, these tactics worked in calming down the markets and restoring some degree of stability to the embattled peso. From April to November 1994, foreign reserves at the Bank of

Mexico were relatively steady, at around USD16–17 billion. However, shortly after the inauguration of Zedillo, the assassination of Massieu took place. Then Chiapas erupted into conflict once again. International fund managers were starting to get twitchy and with good reason. With export growth dwindling, import growth still high, and the government taking a more relaxed view on fiscal policy, the Bank of Mexico was effectively forced to finance their exit—or hedging—from the Mexican asset markets through sales of its foreign reserves. By mid-December, reserves had fallen to just above USD10 billion. With long-term investor confidence plummeting, the short-term "speculators" began to attack the peso in earnest. Volumes began to pick up, in both the spot and options markets. MXP options were very illiquid up to that point, but for a brief period before the culmination of the Mexican peso crisis they saw a sharp pickup as funds went long volatility by buying MXP puts on the view the Mexican authorities would be forced to let the peso band go. The authorities vigorously denied any such suggestion—as is always the case with such crises—and some Wall Street analysts were equally assertive in saying that there was no way Mexico would devalue the peso. But the pressure continued to build inexorably. On December 19, one U.S. house alone executed a proprietary buy order for 200 USD-MXP, buying 200 million U.S. dollars and selling pesos. At the time, it was a huge order for that exchange rate, causing the Mexican foreign exchange and asset markets to shudder in its wake. The tension in dealing rooms around the world became electric, the volume of noise a roar.

Still there were many who said Mexico would hold fast to its promises, that Mexico had left behind the policies of devaluation and would maintain the value and stability of the peso whatever it took. Such calls ignored the fundamentals. Mexico was fast running out of money. The sheer weight of portfolio selling by foreign funds, desperate to get out while they could, simply could not be withstood. On December 20, Mexico stunned the world by announcing the intervention band ceiling was widened by 15%. Instead of reducing the pressure, it accelerated it. The flood of selling became a tidal wave. Immediately, the USD-MXP hit the new ceiling. The Bank of Mexico tried bravely to stop the inevitable by intervening repeatedly, losing a further USD4 billion in reserves. Reserves were down to USD6 billion, and that could be gone in a single day.

On December 22, 1994, the peso was allowed to float. For those who had held out to the last, believing in the promises of the Mexican authorities, believing that the peso would be held, it was the bitterest of lessons—and for some of their clients even worse. One U.S. investment bank on the morning of December 21 had organized a quick teleconference to outline bargains within the Mexican asset markets as a result of the initial widening of the band ceiling.

Needless to say, the bolsa and the Mexican bond markets— peso- and dollar-denominated—were in free fall. As for the peso itself, the extent of its collapse was breathtaking. In the first week of December alone, the USD-MXP rose 41.6% in dollar terms, from 3.46 to 4.90. By the second week, the dollar was up a total 63.3% to 5.65. After the devaluation and free floating of the peso, the rise in the USD-MXP not only continued but accelerated. By February 1995, the USD-MXP was trading at 6.55, up 89.3% from the first week of December. The following month, those figures were 7.68 and 122.0%. In total, in peso terms, the Mexican peso lost 55.95% of its value in the December-to-March move, falling from USD0.2890 to 0.1302.

A predictable peso exchange rate had been at the heart of the reforms of former President Salinas. It had provided the bedrock for foreign portfolio and direct investment. With the peso having been floated and investor confidence having fallen off a cliff, market interest rates continued to rise sharply in terms of both the peso and the dollar. With foreign reserves at the Bank of Mexico having fallen so low, and given the more relaxed budget policy, Mexico faced the prospect of an old nightmare coming back to haunt it—that of defaulting on its debt. In particular, many series of the *tesbono* were to come due in the first quarter, and with the Bank of Mexico's reserves all but gone, there appeared little way of paying them back. Mexico needed immediate international help.

The International Monetary Fund gave immediate initial financial backing to Mexico, but more was needed. On January 3,

1995, Zedillo gave a televised address to the nation. The country would have to undergo a year of sacrifices. The budget would have to be tightened drastically. This did not go down well with ordinary Mexicans. Meanwhile, the phone lines between Mexico City and Washington, D.C., were extremely busy. President Clinton was trying to bring together a USD40 billion loan-guarantee package in order to prop up the Mexican peso and its extremely fragile financial system. On January 30, House Minority Leader Richard Gephardt phoned the president to tell him bad news: Congress would not pass the loan-guarantee plan. U.S. administration officials worked long into the night to come up with an alternative. By 5 a.m. the next morning they finally got what they wanted when the IMF agreed to put in an extra USD10 billion on top of the USD7.8 billion it had already pledged.[5] The total aid package to Mexico came to USD49.8 billion—USD 20 billion from the U.S. Treasury Department's Exchange Stabilization Fund in the form of loans with terms of up to 10 years, USD6 billion from the Federal Reserve in short-term loans, USD10 billion from other major industrial nations in short-term loans via the Bank of International Settlements, USD1 billion from Canada, USD1 billion from other LATAM nations, and the extra USD10 billion from the IMF on top of the original USD7.8 billion. Clinton, with his usual sense of timing and drama—and undoubted sincerity—said, "The risks of inaction are greater than the risks of decisive action. It is the right thing to do." The action was indeed decisive, surprising the markets in the process. The U.S. had put its full backing behind Mexico. The U.S. would not let Mexico collapse, but there were conditions. Mexico had to cut the budget sharply, slow credit growth, and increase the privatization drive, all with the aim to boost the national bottom line. U.S. loan guarantees were to be backed by oil export revenues to be held by the New York Federal Reserve as collateral.

Despite this initial stabilization, the effects of the Mexican crisis continued to ripple through the world's financial markets. If the Treasury was to use the ESF—normally used for intervention on the dollar itself—to help prop up Mexico, did that mean the U.S. was no longer as able to defend its own currency? Also, did that mean that the full USD20 billion would be sold for peso? Such was the hysteria, however justifiable, of the time. As a result, while the peso finally managed to stabilize and the Mexican authorities paid off the initial series of maturing *tesobonos,* the dollar itself came under attack. Granted, Mexico was not the only reason for it, but it was a significant consideration. Despite repeated statements by the U.S. Treasury Department that the dollar was not at all affected by the use of the ESF to support Mexico and that the U.S. comfortably had sufficient reserves for its needs, the dollar continued to head lower. Indeed, during those first months of 1995, the inverted graph of the USD-MXP and the graph of the USD-DEM looked remarkably similar, with the former soaring until March while the latter plummeted.

Meanwhile, Mexico sought to bring about long-term stability through a further major stabilization program. On March 9, the government of Zedillo announced an extremely severe list of stabilization measures. They included an increase in VAT from 10% to 15%, adjustment in prices of public-sector goods, reduction in the level of public spending (the fiscal measures were aimed at achieving a budget surplus of 4.4% of GDP), increased bank supervision, higher capital requirements and loan loss reserves, a removal of the ceiling for foreign ownership, and an increase in real spending on social and rural programs of 2% in order to calm social tensions.[6] The stabilization program worked. By June, the stock market and the peso had fully stabilized. Mexico continued to pay off maturing *tesobonos,* while the Bank of Mexico sought to crush inflationary pressures, contracting the monetary base through punitive interest rates. Demand for imports collapsed, helping the Mexican trade and current accounts right themselves. Stabilization was achieved, but at a considerable price. The country was forced into a deep recession, thousands were put out of work, and wages fell. The turndown in the economy and the resulting effects caused more demonstrations against the government and a crime wave in the major cities of Mexico. Muggings, kidnappings, and bank robberies soared. Mexican government–backed unions canceled the traditional May Day parade, but some 60,000 union workers still thronged the main plaza in Mexico City to protest the surge in unemployment caused by the crisis.

Despite these nefarious side effects, Mexico, with international backing led decisively by the U.S., did manage to turn the situation around and provide a sound base for stability and future growth. GDP fell 0.8% in the first quarter, 10.5% in the second quarter, and 8.1% in the third quarter. However, by the first quarter of 1996 it was almost back to flat (–0.4%), and from there it managed strong, healthy growth, supported by rebounds in almost all economic sectors—agriculture remaining somewhat sluggish until the second quarter of 1997. Overall GDP for the second quarter of 1997 was an impressive 8.8%. Even allowing for a greater number of working days, it still expanded at a rate of 7.7% Y/Y, boosted by higher trade surpluses and industrial activity. With the trade surplus rebounding, the budget strongly in surplus, and foreign capital flow gradually returning, the Bank of Mexico was able to restore greater normality to its foreign reserve situation through a variety of means, as Table 5 shows.

Table 5
Bank of Mexico Reserves
(in USD Billion)

	Net international assets	Pemex inflow	Debt servicing	Dollar puts
Q4, 95	−0.04	1.2	3.8	0
Q1, 96	+1.74	1.7	2.3	0
Q2, 96	2.67	1.8	2.2	0
Q3, 96	3.95	2.2	1.8	0.31
Q4, 96	6.31	3.1	1.2	0.29
Q1, 97	10.68	2.2	1.3	0.98

Source: Standard & Poor's *MMS.*

Net international assets were included by the Bank of Mexico in its weekly balance sheet as of the start of 1996, representing pure reserves held by the bank to the extent that short-term liabilities (six months or less) and IMF money are not included. At the start of 1996, net international assets were negative, meaning that the sum of IMF money and short-term liabilities was greater than gross reserves. By June 1997, net international assets stood at around USD13.5 billion. Freed from its duty to defend the peso—the Bank of Mexico last intervened on the peso in late 1995—the central bank was able to effectively stanch what had been the principle cause of outflows from its foreign reserves. In addition, with Mexico restructuring its debt, thus lowering its interest payment costs, debt servicing also fell. Looking at inflows into reserves, the number one factor was inflows from Pemex, the national oil and petrochemical company, helped by the rally in the price of oil. The Bank of Mexico also held monthly auctions of dollar put options, a further source of revenue for the reserve balance. Drawing this ugly chapter in Mexican financial history to a close, Mexico paid back its debts to the U.S., as Table 6 details.

Table 6
U.S. Aid to Mexico
(in USD Billion)

| | Regular Swaps | | | |
	Fed	ESF	Medium-Term Funds	ESF
Dec. 31, 94	0	0	Dec. 31, 94	0
Jan. 11, 95	0.250	0.250	Mar. 14, 95	3.000
Jan. 13, 95	0.250	0.250	Apr. 19, 95	3.000
Feb. 2, 95	1.000	1.000	May 19, 95	2.000
Mar. 14, 95	−0.500	−0.500	Jul. 5, 95	2.500
Nov. 1, 95	−0.350	−0.350	Jul. 25, 96	−7.000
Jan. 29, 96	−0.650	−0.650	Jan. 15, 97	−3.500
Total	0	0	Total debt	0

Source: Standard & Poor's *MMS.*

During 1996, the Mexican peso fell only 1.96% against the dollar. By 1997, even such modest weakness had reversed, and from January to mid-October, the peso had actually appreciated 1.86% against the dollar; this was a further demonstration of how far Mexico had come from the days of crisis in early 1994.

Mexico continues to tap aggressively the international capital markets, both to refinance existing debt and to develop its name with new investor bases. With the economy now back on track, it is clear that the crisis has had important social and political effects as well. The continued privatization of Mexican industry, Pemex notwithstanding, has eroded the PRI's patronage system and done much to cut the links that bound business and the workforce to the PRI. Led by President Zedillo himself—quite a revolutionary by PRI standards—there is greater and wider demand for cleaning up corruption and increasing transparency. Prior to the crisis, the Mexican polity was characterized by bureaucratic capriciousness at the top and local corruption at the bottom. The move to greater openness is causing radical changes in the way the country is run at the grassroots level. At the 1996 PRI convention, the party decided to no longer choose technocrats who have not been elected by the people for the office of governor or president. Zedillo himself is a technocrat, and the decision takes away much leverage that previous presidents wielded in choosing their successor. The PRI remains torn by internal power struggles, but for the long-run health and prosperity of Mexico this is no bad thing. Equally, the resurgent opposition, in the form of the PAN and PRD Parties, which now controls the key budget committee, is also healthy. There are never guarantees, but a strong opposition is one way of guarding against political and economic excesses. Someone has to be there to blow the whistle on those who commit unwise and costly acts. The presidential election in the year 2000 is now no longer such a sure win for the PRI.

Zedillo still faces major opposition from within his own PRI party, specifically from the old guard, the "dinosaurs" as they are known. The latter, fearful of the rise of the PAN and even the PRD, are pushing for a spending binge in order to win voters back. The problem, however, is that small fiscal deficits have a habit of turning into larger ones. Zedillo should reject such a fiscally irresponsible line. Thankfully, the Bank of Mexico has made clear its own view that sound fiscal policy is the only option.

So much for the Mexican currency crisis. It happened because the authorities allowed imbalances to develop in the economy and did not allow the currency to offset this by falling. It also happened because the authorities were content to accept foreign capital inflow, failing in the process to further develop their domestic institutional investor base. What lessons can be learned from the crisis? Clearly, the first one is that the current account deficit is a key economic indicator that cannot be allowed to get out of line. Over the long term, a current account deficit exceeding 3.0–3.5% is unsustainable unless matched by corresponding budget surpluses. Even in this case, the required fiscal austerity would in the end be rejected, one way or another, given its social consequences. Second, both the amount and the composition of capital flow are extremely important. Short-term flows—dominated by portfolio flow—are of necessity extremely sensitive to changes in the market and political dynamics of a country. They cannot be depended upon over the long term to finance the current account deficit. Significant fiscal improvements have to be made and/or measures have to be taken which encourage and boost longer-term investment, such as FDI. Third, productivity—as Fed Chairman Greenspan continually reminds us—is a key aspect of the economy. It is crucial for an economy to continually strive to achieve productivity gains, both to offset potential inflationary influences and to secure and enhance trade competitiveness. Fourth, the maturity structure and currency denomination are just as important as the total outstanding indebtedness of a country. Fifth, strong domestic political and economic institutions are a prerequisite for the long-term growth of a country.

The Mexican crisis provides substantial evidence of the inherent dangers of trying to use the exchange rate as a stabilization device for the economy. Inevitably, the exchange rate and the economy get out of line with each other. In the case of pegged exchange rate systems, this usually entails real effective exchange rate appreciation and thus overvaluation of the nominal exchange rate. In the continuing battle between the state and the market—a battle that has lasted for a millennia—the state is losing out, but it is not giving in easily (as indeed the drive for EMU confirms). The move from fixed exchange rate systems to pegged systems represented a compromise in the evolution of the transfer of power. Pegged exchange rates, as was the case with the Mexican peso, are usually kept within a defined band or around a specified level. In the case of Mexico—and as we shall see, Indonesia—this was a crawling peg system, whereby the currency was allowed to depreciate within the band at a defined rate. The official line on pegged exchange rates has been that they have the benefits of being both fixed and flexible. As long as they work, the authorities can sit on the sidelines. And when a market disturbance occurs, the authorities can coordinate to restore equilibrium.

Economic history, sad to say, is littered with such self-delusion. With the liberalization of capital flows in the major financial centers of the world, the balance between the authorities and private capital flow has swung sharply in favor of the latter. In such an environment, the emphasis on pegged exchange rates must be on flexibility. A pegged system has initial attractions for investors since it provides (initial) stability. This brings in sizable portfolio flow. Down the chain, the central bank must be on the other side of these transactions, buying currency (most likely dollars) against its own local one. That local currency it sells into the market in order to buy the dollars increases domestic credit and money supply, which if left unchecked could be inflationary. Thus, the central bank seeks to "sterilize" this increase by draining liquidity through money market operations. However, local money market instruments are of necessity likely to yield more than the developed offshore market (such as the Treasury yield curve) with the result that even more portfolio flow will be attracted in—a vicious circle.

None of this is good for the central bank's reserves, so at some stage it will stop sterilizing capital inflow. This inevitably leads to a surge of liquidity in the system as portfolio flow continues to be attracted, boosting domestic demand and eventually inflation. The initial exchange rate impact is that the local currency appreciates, exacerbating the country's trade competitiveness. This is, of course, exactly what happened in the case of Mexico, but Mexico is by no means alone. I would argue that in this modern world with liberalized private capital flow and relatively free markets, the pegged exchange rate system is itself the problem. The system is flawed. It was not designed to combat a fully free market, and inevitably it will be overrun, whatever the determination of the authorities, whichever the country, unless—and here is the caveat—the authorities are flexible and quick enough to react to projected changes in the economy by increasing the flexibility of the peg at appropriate times.

This last may sound wonderful, but it has rarely, if ever, been achieved. What usually happens, as was the case with Mexico, is that the authorities dig their heels in and seek to defend to the last an overvalued peg—memories come to mind of the UK government's futile attempt to defend the sterling exchange rate within the ERM in September 1992. The only way to effectively combat capital flow with a pegged exchange rate system is to contract the monetary base. However, the real economic consequences of this will eventually be politically and socially unacceptable. In the end, the costs of a pegged exchange rate system in this new world of "animal spirits"—as Keynes termed speculative flows—eventually far outweigh any benefits it originally had. A free-floating exchange rate system is the only answer.

In the case of Mexico, the imbalances that the pegged exchange rate system caused were further exacerbated by specific liberalization of the Mexican domestic financial sector, boosting the overexpansion of credit growth. Mexican banks were happy to supply large amounts of credit, counting on the government to bail their depositors and them out if anything went wrong. In the end, the government had to provide a bailout—presumably fearful of the social costs if it failed to do so—with some estimates of the cost of this bailout to the Mexican economy put at 10% of GNP. The total cost of the Mexican currency crisis to the Mexican economy has been about 15% of GNP.

A final point to make with regard to the Mexican crisis, one particularly important when we examine Thailand in the next chapter, is the issue of "contagion." This is the ripple effect of crisis in one country spreading to others. It has been argued that the (unsound) macroeconomic background is solely responsible for the initial crisis and the subsequent ripple effect in other countries. However, such a suggestion does not stand up to detailed analysis. Mexico, we can say with the benefit of hindsight, was ripe for a financial crisis (as was Thailand). But the subsequent ripple effect in other LATAM countries resulting from Mexico's woes, which became known as the "Tequila crisis," did not necessarily have the same fundamental grounding.

Mexico had a current account deficit of 8% of GDP, and yet Argentina, whose current account deficit was under 0.5% of GDP, also came under pressure as a result of the Mexican crisis. At the time, and still to this day, Argentina had a currency board system; the Argentinean peso was pegged to the dollar at 1:1 whereby every peso in the system was matched with one dollar in reserves. Argentina had several macroeconomic advantages over Mexico. Its current account deficit was substantially lower than Mexico's. Also it had sound and credible economic and political leadership that not only had carried Argentina out of the misery of the previous military dictatorships but had succeeded in crushing inflation to more manageable levels. The Central Bank of Argentina's reserves remained at a high level considering its increased flexibility in coping with any market disturbance. Furthermore, government debt was not concentrated in short-term maturities, thus avoiding the debt financing problems that the Bank of Mexico had to face. Finally its structural reforms were at an advanced stage, both socially and economically. Yet, despite all this, the market, for a brief time, took on the Argentinean peso and its asset markets. The result was that the central bank was forced to retaliate, allowing interest rates to rise, thus causing a recession. One can argue quite justifiably that Argentina did not deserve such a fate. Happily, the Argentinean economy was able to climb back up from this turndown and is presently enjoying strong growth. There have been those economic commentators who argue, subsequent to the Mexican example, that a lack of economic information is a key aspect of a developing crisis. This was not the case, however, in Argentina or in Thailand.

There are, I would say, three stages of "contagion." In the initial stage, during and following the crisis in a specific country such as Mexico, neighboring countries or currencies get hit because it is believed that their trade competitiveness will be hurt by the devaluation in the crisis country. In the case of Mexico, this certainly played a part in the dollar's subsequent fall given the importance of Mexican trade to the U.S. economy. A country that has sound fundamentals can suddenly find its currency under attack because the crisis country has been forced by market pressure to devalue against it, as well as the dollar. This brings to mind the example of Brazil and even Chile, where fundamentals were very strong and yet their currencies got hit for a time.

The second stage takes place when market forces become more selective—consciously looking to take on those other countries, either within the specific region or even outside it, whose economies might have systemic weaknesses such as weak banking systems, vulnerability of the financial and property sectors to higher interest rates, and low levels of foreign reserves at the central bank. Prior to the crisis, these systemic weaknesses did not matter because they were financed by portfolio flow, attracted by high rates of return.

The third stage occurs at the height of market hysteria. Currencies get hit just because they are *there*, despite the fact that they bear no economic similarity to the crisis currency. Ultimately, contagion will subside and the currencies of those countries affected will right themselves if the authorities take appropriate policy actions: engaging in limited but decisive foreign exchange intervention, allowing interest rates to rise, and publicly emphasizing that fundamentals are sound. This was indeed the case in the LATAM region. However, if the market discovers subsequently that fundamentals were after all not that sound in currencies affected by contagion, the recovery period will be that much longer.

The experience of the Mexican currency crisis reaffirmed the need for sound and compatible macroeconomic policies. It also showed the importance of developing strong domestic political and economic institutions, particularly the domestic institutional investor base, so as not to be overly dependent on foreign capital. In addition, it demonstrated the inherent weakness of the pegged exchange rate system in this new world of ours, which travels at light speed, where fundamentals can decay undetected for a time and where the pegged system actually encourages that, given attractive yields in the domestic market relative to the developed world.

5

The Catalyst — Thailand

AT A RECENT CONFERENCE in Hong Kong which coincided with the IMF and World Bank meeting, a Mexican Finance Ministry official was asked to comment on the Asian currency crisis and what effect or relevance it might have on Latin America. The official, without even the slightest trace of irony, said Mexico in particular and Latin America as a whole did not face the fundamental problems that several Asian countries were presently suffering from—such is the duration of memory in the financial markets!

Beside him were a row of senior LATAM central bankers who nodded sagely at his comment, as if the Mexican currency crisis had never happened and such unpleasantness was a purely new and Asian phenomenon. Granted, Mexico's financial and economic recovery, following the crisis of 1994–1995, has been truly impressive. However, such implied forgetfulness is dangerous, for it allows the possibility of renewed complacency and thus of reoccurrence. If, in a few years, you hear an Asian official saying the same kind of thing about the next Latin American crisis (for there is likely to be one), that is probably as good a sell signal as any retail investor is likely to get—on Asia, not on Latin America.

Like Mexico, the Thailand crisis happened amid a drive for first-world status. Like Mexico, Thailand's path, from the early

1980s, toward that goal was influenced by both internal and external events. It is a story even more colorful—not to say dangerous—than its Latin counterpart. It includes an army coup, rapid industrialization from a predominantly agrarian base over so short a period of time that it put even its ASEAN neighbors to shame, dirty elections (including the murder of political canvassers), the fall in the USD-JPY which supposedly changed forever (it seemed at the time) Thailand's competitive edge, a political system that was rotten through and through, a communist insurgency, and a war against the opium traffickers (not a convincing one at that). Above all, however, it is a story of money, heaps of it, of untrammeled greed, of a city once courtly and refined, turned into a modern-day Sodom and Gomorrah, choking both literally and metaphorically on its excesses.

While the conditions for crisis in other ASEAN countries were already developing in the 1990s, it was in Thailand where these conditions, this festering and decay of sound economic fundamentals, culminated and climaxed. An economy can decay for years if left alone. For it to collapse into crisis, it needs a catalyst, either internal or external. The fundamentals of the ASEAN region of nations, while buoyant on the surface, had been decaying in that way for the past five years. Thailand was that catalyst. In Thailand, all the individual economic weaknesses of its ASEAN neighbors seemed to come together. Thailand, by that time, was nothing if not *the* definition of excess. Yet, in order to know how and why Thailand failed and where it is likely to go from here, we have to look at how it succeeded in the first place—for it did succeed gloriously for a time.

The Thai economic "miracle," if we can call it that, had its initial roots in the late 1950s, when the government made a deliberate and concerted push to expand agricultural production, not only for domestic consumption but for export. Siam had always been a major trading nation in Asia, led by the king and the Thai bureaucratic elite. This trade was largely agrarian based; Thai rice, for instance, dominated the Asian market (excluding Japan). In the late 1950s, the government sought to expand production through a combination of government and private enterprises. It expanded irrigation systems and created investment incentives for the private sector to found crop export companies, sugar mills and factories, rubber plantations, and fish farms.[1] This combination of government and private enterprise had impressive results: From the late 1950s through the 1980s, land under cultivation tripled, and crop exports rose at a cumulative rate of 12% a year.[2] This provided the bedrock for the economic boom that was to come.

In the 1960s and 1970s, the Thai economy was further boosted by U.S. economic aid during the years of the Vietnam War. After the U.S. withdrawal, it was assumed by many economists that Thai growth would collapse. In reality, the U.S. continued to provide Thailand with aid after the fall of Saigon in 1975, and particularly after the Vietnamese invasion of Cambodia. The level of financial and military aid was significantly lower than during the war, however, and the Thai economy did indeed start to slow. Furthermore, Thailand was not helped by the oil shocks that occurred, first in 1973, then in 1979 with the Iranian Revolution, and finally with the Iran-Iraq War, as they caused its foreign debt burden to rise.

The period 1984–1985 was the turning point for Thailand. On the domestic side, inflation was picking up, while simultaneously the country was going into recession as exports collapsed (a familiar story?). Banks teetered on the brink of collapse. This unpleasant combination resulted in the devaluation of the baht by some 15% in November 1984, and the subsequent repegging of it to the dollar.

On the international side, the Plaza Agreement had profound and specific consequences for Thailand. The general collapse in the dollar, as we have seen before, resulted in an Asian export boom. This was particularly the case in Thailand. Its history as a trading nation and its low-wage structure gave it a competitive edge even over the likes of Malaysia and Indonesia, which had begun their industrialization phase earlier. Thai businesses had for some time been pressing the government to focus its energies more on promoting manufacturing rather than agriculture since agricultural growth had already peaked. The recession finally persuaded the government to do so. With the collapse in the USD-JPY, the refocusing on Thai manufacturing capacity, and the large supply of low-wage labor, Thailand suddenly became supercompetitive. To accelerate this, the Thai government provided investment incentives for Western and Japanese manufacturers to set up bases in Thailand. During the Japanese asset boom of the late 1980s, the Japanese had a need to export excess capital. They became the biggest lenders to Thailand in both private and public form, surpassing the U.S. even before the decade was over.

Needless to say, with such high-octane fuel pumped into the Thai economic engine, Thailand Inc. screamed off the starting grid. From 1985 to 1996, Thailand averaged GDP growth of just under 8% a year. In that period, GDP per capita more than doubled, while manufacturing employment rose from around 7% to around 15%. Thai entrepreneurs were quick to take advantage of the more business-friendly conditions. While many had prospered even during the period of overt military dictatorship from the end of the war to 1973, the Thai government's refocusing on promoting business was a heaven-sent opportunity and businesspeople were not slow to take advantage of it. It had been that way for hundreds of years. Thai business was dominated by ethnic Chinese, mostly peoples from Swatow in Kwantung Province. The *Chu ch'iao* (in Cantonese), speaking predominantly the *Hoklo* dialect, were and are a fiercely mercantilist people who initially came to Thailand in the 17th century. This process was accelerated by the victory of the Communists in the Chinese Civil War and the setting up of the People's Republic of China in 1949. While Thai peasants stayed on the land, this migrant community of *Chu ch'iao* quickly dominated the cities, notably Bangkok itself.

Unlike in Malaysia or Indonesia, the ethnic Chinese in Thailand were not persecuted or discriminated against. Thailand had never been colonized and therefore did not need to face the consequent strains of decolonization and nationalism. Indeed, apart from a brief period after the war when the Thai armed forces tried to expropriate wealth from the ethnic Chinese—which the latter easily deflected—the *Chu ch'iao* have lived in remarkable harmony in Thailand, blending into the fabric of urban society. While their domination in the Thai economy is not total, it is a significant presence; nowhere is it more so than in finance, where many leading banking families trace their origins back to Chinese ancestry.

For Thai businessmen, whether ethnic Thai or Chinese, the key was to build connections with the bureaucracy. With both domestic and foreign investment on the rise and the Thai government quick to create a stock market for raising capital, the capital to expand was freely available. Going into the 1990s, Thailand eased restrictions on commercial banks and deregulated interest rates in an effort to become a regional financial center, and the finance industry exploded. At one point, it was just a license to print money. On the securities side, getting a trading permit was a relatively simple affair, and with incomes on the rise, dabbling in the stock market became a social pastime. The Thai stock market quickly developed the reputation of being fast, furious, and dangerous—but extremely profitable if you got your timing right.

By 1995, the Stock Exchange of Thailand had more exchange members per billion dollars of market capitalization than anywhere else in the world. On the lending side, the infusion of investment, together with a national savings rate of around 34% of GDP and rapid monetary growth, fueled an asset price boom, much as it had done earlier in Japan. The property market soared into the stratosphere; the sentiment was one of ever-rising property prices and supply trying to catch up. Bangkok became a boomtown. On the surface it was a sea of cranes, half-constructed buildings, and ring-road factories that greet one on approach from Don Muang Airport. Beneath it was heaving with the results of new money—not least of them, flashy cars in the thousands. The new business elite of Bangkok was born, mobile phone in hand, dapperly dressed, driving a Mercedes, and eating at only the finest establishments.

A new middle class was created around this elite circle, one that had aspirations beyond those of prior generations, for financial betterment and security. This new middle class focused not on Thailand's rural past, but on an industrial and modern future. Meanwhile, the Thai government sought to further improve the bureaucracy by developing it into a technocratic elite. The government created financial institutions to support and nurture the boom, such as the Thai Securities and Exchange Commission and the Board of Investment, but none more important than the Bank of Thailand. However, while the technocrats were providing the financial infrastructure for the boom, education, training, and the political system itself were sadly lacking, a problem that would come back to haunt Thailand repeatedly.

In regard to infrastructure, the immediate images that come to mind are of clogged roads in Bangkok, choking with traffic. Education is just as important as transportation, if not more so, to the long-term health of the economy. In the late 1980s when the boom took hold, the Thai education system was woefully lacking in its ability to cope. It had, after all, been built to produce government technocrats rather than engineers, computer technicians, or businesspeople. In the end, Thailand and the foreign companies that had invested there found the workers they needed through a patchwork effort that included training workers on the job, hiring workers from abroad, and getting skilled Thai workers to teach the less skilled. Also, with the agricultural industry slowing, a million people migrated from the poor northeast—called Isarn—to and around Bangkok.

This lack of educational infrastructure was to prove costly. Initial attempts were made to send Thais to European and U.S. universities, instead of developing Thailand's own educational system further. This could have been beneficial if the newly Westernized and educated Thai university students had then returned home—but by no means all of them did. Thailand was also lacking in democratic political infrastructure. Up until 1973, it had been used to military dictatorship. In 1973 the dictatorship was overthrown by democratic protest, but then the new government itself was overthrown by a revitalized armed forces that now sought to merge their dominance with some semblance of popular representation. The new military government allowed a constitution and a parliament, with General Prem being prime minister from 1976 to 1984. The events of 1984–1985 were a shock to the political as well as the economic system. With the shackles on Thai business loosened, the military could do no less with political power. Gradually, the new political parties took over control of the various ministries and ultimately the premiership itself. The government of Chatichai Choonhavan (nicknamed Cha Cha) was characterized by two aspects: the acceleration of the economic boom and massive corruption. In fact, the corruption reached a level where even the Thai military—itself no slouch in dipping its nose in the trough—had had enough. In February 1991, the army took to the streets and threw out the civilian government.

In most countries such a development would be met with alarm—not to say, a rush to the airport. The initial reaction in Thailand was muted. After all, the Thai people had seen it all before. While business prospered immensely during the years 1988–1991, few mourned the passing of the Chatichai government given how rotten it had been. The military coup did fit badly, however, with Thailand's self-image as a modernizing state. And more importantly, it caused a sharp downturn in tourism, a key industry in Thailand. The military blamed the need for a coup on stamping out corruption, and most people thought it would restore confidence and then leave. It was only when the realization dawned that the army was planning to stay in power for the long haul that organized social protest took hold. On May 20, 1992, after three days and nights of street violence between the army and crowds of demonstrators, King Bhumibol intervened. He spoke on television of the concerns of the people. General Suchinda, who had taken the premiership, resigned and prostrated himself before the king. The army went back to its barracks.

On the economic side, growth had been heading downhill in 1991 and 1992. Having been 11.2% in 1990, it "fell" to 8.5% in 1991 and then to 8.1% in 1992. This could have been a further reason for the popular move to take power back from the military. By this time, Thais had grown accustomed to exceptionally high standards of growth and improvement, and many were not prepared to see this slowing down, let alone return to the bad old days of the 1960s and 1970s. Many within the crowds who protested against the military were businesspeople. For the army, it was effectively its last grasp at power—perhaps—leaving the Thai technocratic and business elites now free rein to get on with continuing to push the economy forward.

Unfortunately, even without the domination of the military, Thai politicians were just as able to get in the way of sound economic progress—especially if to do so benefited themselves. The new elections of late 1992 saw Chuan Leepkai, head of the Democratic Party, become prime minister; he was the first person to do so in Thailand who had not come from either the bureaucracy or the military. Hopes were high initially. A lawyer by training, Leepkai focused on accelerating the modernization of Thailand and restoring domestic and international confidence after the coup. However, given the Thai electoral system, he was dependent on other parties to form a government coalition. Because he was bogged down by factional politics, his efforts to improve the economy did not exactly come to a halt but were greatly slowed. Particularly notable was Leepkai's inability to cure the Bangkok transport system problems. Frustrated by this lack of success, elements of Leepkai's support began to dissipate or move away. Some leading figures formed other parties, while those who had sought to depose him all along closed in for the kill.

In July 1995, the Chart Thai Party was elected back to power with 92 seats out of a total of 391 seats, leaving the Democrats in second place with some 86. By convention, the party with the largest number of seats gets first crack at forming a coalition government. This was no problem. The makings of the coalition had already been organized long before the election took place. Banharn Silpa-archa of the Chart Thai was appointed prime minister. Businesspeople as a whole were not pleased. Banharn was a provincial as opposed to a city politician. Indeed, the Chart Thai itself as a party had very little support in Bangkok, instead finding its popular base in the countryside and particularly in the poor northeast. Some were fearful of a return to the money-grabbing politics of 1988–1991, while others hoped the coalition parties would push for a fresh start, focusing on the economy rather than their own wallets. Those hopes were to be cruelly dashed.

Chuan Leepkai's government had in the end proved ineffective in coping with many of Thailand's economic needs, notably its infrastructure, but at least it had been committed to reform. The Banharn government represented old-style politics, exemplified by his appointment of several members of the disgraced Chatichai government. Even by the usual low standards of Thai politics, it was exceptionally incompetent, not to say venal. In the end, it lasted only about sixteen months, an unfit, bloated long-distance runner who, while falling well short of the tape, was tripped up by one of his own teammates. In little more than a year in office, the Banharn government was faced with numerous accusations of pork barrel politics. This was rather ironic since that was the norm rather than the exception in Thai politics. Scandals included the debacle of the Bangkok Bank of Commerce and finally the accusation in August 1996 by the justice minister that Banharn's government had accepted some USD90 million in bribes in exchange for licenses to operate banks. This led to key coalition member Thaksin Shinawatra, of the Palang Dharma Party, leaving the coalition.

The Bangkok Bank of Commerce scandal stunned even the most cynical of Thailand watchers. At a May 1996 parliamentary debate, it was revealed by the opposition that the Bangkok Bank of Commerce, Thailand's ninth largest bank, had 47% of its total assets, some THB78 billion (USD3 billion) as bad loans, much of which had been lent to associates of the president of the bank. The Thai Finance Ministry was forced to take control of the bank. This was a severe blow to the reputation of the Bank of Thailand, which up until then had enjoyed one of the best reputations in the region for prudent policy management. The Bangkok Bank of Commerce scandal had happened right under the noses of the Bank of Thailand, and the Bank of Thailand had said nothing—resulting in the theory proffered by some that the Bank of Thailand had been gagged. Others looked within the bank itself, accusing the then governor of the Bank of Thailand, Vijit Supinit, of political partisanship and financial carelessness. Supinit resigned, and on July 9, Rerngchai Marakanond, a veteran Bank of Thailand employee, took over as governor. For a time confidence was at least partly restored, though the effects of the Bangkok Bank of Commerce scandal continued to resound in the press and the financial community.

With the government stumbling from one scandal to another, any efforts to right itself and propel Thailand forward were dealt a harsh blow in September when Moody's Investors Service, a credit rating agency, downgraded Thailand's short-term debt. Not that this was not fully justified, for Thai national finances were by that time clearly deteriorating. Finally, amid growing cross-party criticism against the government, Banharn faced a three-day no-confidence debate in parliament. It was then that he was tripped up by one of his own coalition members. After a grilling from the opposition, in which widespread corruption and mismanagement were alleged and even his personal family origin questioned (that he was allegedly born in China rather than in Thailand and thus had no right to be the Thai prime minister), the trap, which had been long in the making, closed on Banharn and his government.

Defense Minister Chavalit Yongchaiyudh, head of the New Aspiration Party which had fifty-seven seats in the parliament, said he would back Banharn in the no-confidence vote only if Banharn stepped down as prime minister. Banharn vacillated but eventually announced on September 21 that he would resign within seven days. During that week, there was the usual fierce political bargaining in an attempt to choose his successor as prime minister. Unable to do so, and having won the confidence vote, Banharn made his last contributions—some would say his only ones—as prime minister by announcing his resignation and then promptly dissolving parliament, calling for new elections on Sunday, November 17.

Despite this last-ditch effort by Banharn to stop Chavalit from becoming prime minister, the latter had been preparing for this day for some time and was not about to let power slip from his grasp at the final moment. A retired army general, he had a natural power base in the army. His New Aspiration Party had also built up strong support in the poor northeast of the country, the area of Isarn, which represented one-third of the seats in parliament. Finally, he had formed an alliance with the Chatichai leader of the Chart Pattana Party and former prime minister from 1988 to 1991. Such was the revulsion of the Thai people at the record of the Banharn government that they would have voted for anyone by that stage to get him out. Just the same, the November 1996 election was one of the dirtiest in memory. Vote-rigging was blatant; the cost of vote buying was estimated to be as much as THB20 billion. And there were actual shootings of political canvassers. Grenades were thrown at family homes, and cars were raked with AK47 fire.[3] Isarn was where much of the vote buying and shootings took place. The election was, predictably, given the Banharn government's record, a disaster for the Chart Thai, whose number of seats collapsed from ninety-two to a mere thirty-nine. Chart Pattana, under Chatichai, came in with fifty-three seats. Chavalit's New Aspiration Party just squeezed past the Democratic Party to win by two, with 125 seats. As head of the party with the largest number of seats, Chavalit got to form the coalition government and became prime minister.

The stock market's reaction to this development was disbelief followed by horror. The SET (Stock Exchange of Thailand Index), which had fallen 30% during the Banharn government, had rallied some 5% on the news of his resignation and the call for new elections. Chavalit's ascendancy to the premiership represented a return to the old-style politics rather than a move forward. The SET plunged. Bangkok voters were not amused either. While the countryside voted in large numbers for the New Aspiration Party, the cities, and especially Bangkok, voted for Leepkai's Democratic Party. It was the party that had promoted itself as being honest and as having a respected economic team that could fix the economy. Ignoring the initial market reaction to his victory, Chavalit sought first to reassure—he would appoint a "dream team" to oversee the economy. While he handled such important matters as defense, foreign policy, and the like, the technocrats, the experts, would be allowed to run the economy. In practice, he got on with the much more serious business of ensuring that his main coalition partner was Chatichai's Chart Pattana and of handing out cabinet posts to his favored.

While the Thai politicians fiddled, the economy burned. This was a tragedy because the 1990s had promised so much. For the first five years, the picture could not have looked rosier—at least on the surface. Initially, despite the political connivance and incompetence, the economy continued to motor along at a startling rate. GDP growth reached a headline-worthy 8.1% even in 1992, the year of the coup. And GDP grew 8.3% in 1993, 8.9% in 1994, and 8.6% in 1995. The GDP per capita growth rate had traced a similar path, slowing from 10% in 1990 to 7% in 1991 and 6.9% in 1992, and then starting to pick up again—6.9% in 1993, and 7.5% in 1994 and 1995. Savings remained extremely robust, with gross domestic savings as a percentage of GDP averaging 34.8% in the period 1990–1995. In the tradition of a trading nation, exports continued to be a major factor in driving growth, averaging 18.8% for 1990–1995, ending that period at 24.7%. The budget was healthy, averaging a surplus of 3.2% of GDP, 2.9% for 1995. Thais, who were used to a mediocre political system and a rural and thus pedestrian growth, were justly proud that Thailand Inc. was one of the fastest-growing countries in the world from 1985 to 1995. Unfortunately, if left unchecked, pride—in any country—can most assuredly lead to a fall. No Western country has been immune, and many an "emerging" country has fallen foul of it long before Thailand.

On the surface, all was well, a boomtime and a boomtown. Beneath it, however, lurked hidden dangers, dangers that few, at least initially, either saw or warned about. Most notably, exports fell off a cliff in 1996. Many respected investment analysts were at a loss to explain this, some citing the comfortable excuse that it was simply a cyclical downturn following several years of extremely high growth. At first, such an explanation did seem plausible. Logic itself suggested that it is unsustainable to continue to experience year-on-year export growth of almost 20% over an extended period of time, given the likelihood of a change in the global economic cycle and therefore a change (downturn) in demand for those exports.

By the end of the first half of 1996, however, the picture was becoming a little clearer. Something very strange was going on. Thai exports had not just slipped back; they had collapsed, achieving only 4% growth in the first half. The full-year report painted an equally bleak picture. 1996 exports were up a mere 0.1%, a stunning result compared with almost 25% in 1995. There were declines across the board. A severe downturn in the world electronics market had bitten hard into demand for Thai computer and electronics exports. Making up some 11.7% of total exports in 1996, compared with 6% in 1991, this sector was particularly important in Thailand's admirable, though laboriously slow, drive to boost production and export of higher-added-value manufactured products. Export growth of electronics as a whole fell to 12% from 29% the prior year. Within this, computer parts held up relatively well with 27% growth relative to 41%, but integrated circuits plunged to only 1% growth from 28%. Even exports of consumer electronics, usually a safe haven, fell by two-thirds.

There was worse news. Thailand's footwear and textile industries, usually a strong backstop in troubled times and former lead export earners for the country, had become a disaster area. With Thai labor costs rising as a result of the general improvement in living standards, footwear manufacturers had begun to put their factories elsewhere, given the relatively thin margins available. Southern China, Vietnam, Pakistan, and even Bangladesh became more favored, due to their large wage-cost advantage over Thailand. A worker in a Guangdong footwear factory was likely to be paid one-third of what he or she could get in Thailand. In 1996, Thai footwear exports actually fell by some 40%, given this new, lower-cost competition. Textiles, another previous bulwark of the Thai economy, also experienced severe trouble, while garment exports fell 22%. Imports had not risen strongly—a mere 4% in 1996—but this was still substantially higher than export growth.

It led to yet another increase in the overall Thailand trade deficit at just over USD10.5 billion, up from USD8 billion the previous year. This, in turn, worsened the current account deficit, which rose to about USD14.5 billion, up from USD13.6 billion. As a percentage of GDP, it actually fell in 1996 to 8.0%—the same level Mexico had in 1994—from 8.3% in 1995. While this obviously was a concern, it would not have led to (justifiable) panic had it not been for severe deterioration in another part of the Thai economy, the budget balance. Thailand had enjoyed a decade of strong and stable fiscal surpluses. That happy situation disappeared when the Thai authorities stunned the markets by announcing a shock budget deficit of 1.1% of GDP for the last quarter of FY1996 due to revenue shortfalls.

In other words, more money was leaving Thailand than was coming in and Thailand no longer had a fiscal surplus to finance its burgeoning current account deficit. This was a familiar if bitter story to Mexicans in the first months of 1995. Looking further at the fiscal side, Thailand's total foreign debt, which had been a mere USD30 billion odd in 1991, continued to climb, rising to almost USD80 billion by the end of 1996. Adding up the total of the current account deficit, debt service costs, and foreign direct investment, Thailand had the heaviest external funding requirement in Asia.

A further negative as far as Thailand's trade competitiveness was that the USD-JPY continued to rise through 1995 and 1996 and the USD-THB stayed relatively steady because of the peg. Thus Thailand's real effective exchange rate had appreciated markedly. Using the year 1990 as 100, the Thai baht's REER had risen from 98.6 in 1991 to 110.7 in 1995.[4] By 1996, it was around 113. This was a double negative, hurting export competitiveness while attracting imports. Finally, linked to its rising current account deficit, there was Thailand's economic Achilles' heel—its dependency on foreign investment. Despite a national savings rate of around 35% of GDP, Thailand was still forced to seek funding from abroad since its domestic investment rate was over 40%. The latter rate had been boosted due to the Thai government's grandiose economic plans as a result of continued heavy inflows of foreign capital and FDI. This funding shortage led back into Thailand's rising external debt, a vicious circle. The situation was far from being just a question of cyclical export downturn—itself a fallacy because Thailand suffered a structural lack of competitiveness due to lack of highly skilled workers, low productivity growth relative to wage-cost increases, and a low level of high-tech, value-added exports. The problems were structural and potentially life threatening to the country as a whole.

A huge current account deficit, a worsening fiscal situation, overdependence on foreign capital, and rising debt, particularly short-term debt—the seeds of Thailand's devaluation had been sown, just as they had in Mexico. Unlike Mexico, though, Thailand's situation was not worsened by overconsumption, although the money supply growth had been running at inflationary levels. Instead, Thailand, like a number of Asian countries, suffered from overinvestment relative to its savings rate; despite the fact that the savings rate was exceptionally high, it was not adequate to fully fund investment needs—investment in low-return, low-productivity projects. Those who had been looking for trouble in Asia in 1996 (and few were, though many proclaimed to in 1997 after the fact) could have done worse than to look for the following: an overvalued real effective exchange rate, rapid monetary growth relative to interest rate settings, weakening exports and weakening domestic demand—and thus an inability to defend the exchange rate for any length of time through interest rates—overdependence on offshore finance, and of course a widening current account deficit. In sum, there was too much liberalization of the financial market apparatus and too little liberalization of the domestic institutional apparatus to cope with this new environment—thus creating excessive foreign dependency.

A key root of the problem had been the BIBF, the Bangkok International Banking Facility. This facility had been designed to boost Thailand's image as a regional financial center, where banks could borrow in U.S. dollars at cheaper interest rates than available domestically in Thailand and then lend onshore to Thai customers, arbitraging the spread. Some economists have argued that this would have been fully successful if Thailand had freed the baht or made the peg system more flexible. But until early 1996 this would have had the likely result of boosting rather than weakening the baht, given strong inflow of both FDI and portfolio capital. Any facility that creates easy money will of necessity be abused, the BIBF being no different. By the end of 1995, BIBF liabilities were over a quarter of Thailand's total GDP. While this might not of itself have added fuel to the fire, such financing was used unproductively, leading to ever-diminishing returns, the results of which were all too visible for any visitor to Bangkok.

Indeed, the worsening Thai situation was in fact much more visible than mere data or economic theory, whatever their merits. A brief trip to Bangkok would have told the average fund manager what he or she needed to know—the city was a sea of oversupply. Thailand was in a state of denial, and had been for some time. Despite the forest of cranes and the ocean of buildings, many of which not a single person or office occupied, property developers continued to build, and lenders—who should have known better but were lulled by the wealth of their past returns—continued to lend. Even with the relatively high nominal interest rates the Bank of Thailand needed to maintain in order to protect the baht and finance the current account deficit through capital inflow, Thailand continued to build. Those past returns protected the developers and their lenders for a time. However, time was fast running out, those margins getting doubly squeezed by rising costs from interest rates and falling returns due to the belated realization that a property glut had been created. As Tarrin Nimmanhaeminda, the Thai finance minister from 1992 to 1994, said: "We're walking a tightrope."[5] And the tightrope was starting to tremble and shake, making the journey even more perilous. In Bangkok alone, in 1996, about 600,000 square meters of office space came on the market, with 900,000 square meters planned for 1997 and 1.3 million for 1998. About 80% of the 1997 supply was already under construction in the first quarter of 1996.[6]

The Thai propensity for face-saving and avoidance of conflict—such as confronting debtors on time—might have added to the problem, but the principles behind the property glut were the same as had been found at the start of the decade in the more developed countries, notably the U.S. and the UK—too much supply and falling demand. It was a classic case of elementary economic fundamentals, but if economic history teaches us two things it is that (1) markets never learn from their mistakes (partly because the twenty-eight-year-old who gets fired for making the mistake is replaced by a twenty-two-year-old with no experience and more importantly no history) and (2) in the passionate throes of economic excess, fundamentals are forgotten entirely. Under Thai regulation, which certainly added to the problem, Thai banks could continue to book interest on a loan without classifying that loan as problematic. Indeed, the attitude of the banks and the politicians—those regulators who expressed concerns being told to keep their mouths shut—appeared to be that the good times would stay, that problems were unpleasant but certainly temporary. Temporary? Only if the market turned back up, but it was going in the opposite direction, having peaked two years before. By 1996, Bangkok had some 350,000 housing units. This was not a temporary phenomenon, and it was of more than passing interest to Bangkok's plethora of finance companies, many of which had an average 30% loan exposure to the property sector. There was also no need for an economist to say that Bangkok had an oversupply of cars, relative to the available transport systems, or that Bangkok lacked the necessary underground and overground rail and road systems to siphon off much of that excess demand.

The combination of factors—Thai exporters facing increasingly hard times selling their goods, the current account deficit widening, the fiscal surplus shrinking, Moody's downgrading Thai short-term debt, the property market slumping, and Bangkok increasingly becoming an eyesore—was like throwing buckets of shark bait into the sea. Eventually a dorsal fin would appear, slicing through the water, attracted by the scent of blood.

First one dorsal fin, then another, and another. The scent of a distressed and bleeding animal—the Thai economy—had attracted the attention of the hedge funds as early as March 1996. At that point, one of the well-known hedge funds out of New York charged the carcass and took a bite—selling baht short for 400 million dollars on March 8 in the forward market. Spot USD-THB was trading 25.20/40, remaining within the specified 2-satang range set by the Bank of Thailand. It briefly jumped before being protested by the central bank via money market operations. The six-month forward shot out to the right, but gradually came back in as Thai exporters were happy to "give the points back"—sell dollars forward at a higher rate. The bearish fundamentals were appearing in the data, but the market remained in solid mood despite the SET losses that continued to follow—a legacy of the Banharn government. The hedge fund, which had borrowed in yen and then swapped into baht to cover its short baht position in the forward, quietly legged out—buying yen to cover the borrowing cost and selling dollars for the forward position. Most market watchers thought it had been a simple sell order in spot USD-JPY which happened to catch the interbank market long dollars on an otherwise quiet Friday. The hedge fund watched and waited. The animal continued to bleed in the water. There was plenty of time, no need to rush.

Toward the end of 1996, a few brave souls in the domestic financial community started to question the viability of the basket system and thus of the peg. Offshore, such voices were more widespread. In a November 29 report in Standard & Poor's MMS, MMS's Thailand economist Alison Seng argued that both a widening of the range band and a change in the basket made perfect fundamental sense given the already apparent slowdown in Thai domestic demand and the collapse in exports.[7] It was suspected that the Bank of Thailand had already lowered the dollar weighting of the basket to 80% from 85%, with the yen rising to 15% given the ongoing fall in the yen against the baht and the consequent rise in volume of Japanese exports to Thailand. Indeed, Nakrong Akransee, the subsequent commerce minister and part of Chavelit's dream team, aimed at sorting out Thailand's economic woes and had hinted as much, saying there could be a change in the baht's basket in mid-1997.

While the sharks began to circle—wide circles at first, but getting ever closer to their prey—the Thai government was determined to put a brave face on the matters at hand. The property market was clearly experiencing a downturn, but the necessary resources would be brought to bear to ensure that property companies, and thus finance companies, did not go under. On January 10, 1997, a THB70 billion rescue fund was set up for this purpose, an impressive sum if one ignored the fact that total outstanding property loans amounted to well over THB600 billion. At the most conservative estimate, and least credulous, if 10% of those loans were bad, the entire rescue fund would be gone almost instantly.

The November monthly current account deficit had shown a fall to THB21.7 billion from 30.2 billion in October, the fifth consecutive narrowing in the current account monthly balance and the lowest level since September 1995. However, this had been due not to export growth but to a collapse in imports as domestic demand slowed. Exports were still falling, and this was confirmed in December when the deficit rebounded. Then on January 27, the government made the announcement that it had experienced a fiscal deficit during the fourth quarter of 1996 after nine consecutive quarters of fiscal surplus and six years of strong full-year surpluses.

The pressures on the baht continued to mount. The first Thai corporate default on a Euroconvertible bond occurred in late January when Somprasong Land & Development PCL defaulted on a USD3.1 million interest payment of a USD80 million issue. This was only the beginning. On the following Tuesday, January 30, the baht started to come under attack in earnest, initially from domestic interests, amid rumors that Thailand's largest finance company, Finance One, was in trouble. The company denied the rumors, but it quickly became clear that they were based in fact. Finance One collapsed. The shock effect of that event was considerable. Created by Pin Chakkaphak in the boom years, Finance One was a classic bull market vehicle and had even become a predatory company, seeking out acquisitions. In 1996, it had tried to buy, through a hostile takeover, Thai Danu Bank, the country's twelfth largest bank. Finance One's subsequent humiliation was completed when it was forced on February 28 to merge into Thai Danu. Funds of all sorts, not just the hedge funds, started to take a much more detailed look at the finance companies and their leveraged exposure to the property sector. Thailand, it was found, had developed a mountain of corporate debt, with loans by banks and finance companies equal to almost 150% of GDP. By the end of 1996, the authorities had discovered that over 14% of total finance company loans, totaling around THB155 billion, were considered nonperforming.

Meanwhile, the baht was coming under increasing attack, forcing the Bank of Thailand to take countermeasures. For the past ten years, the USD-THB had traded between 24.5 and 25.5, surviving six prime ministers, a military coup, the Gulf War, and the Mexican crisis. Every morning at 8:30 a.m., the Bank of Thailand desk had fixed the USD-THB exchange rate, allowing local banks to buy and sell dollars and baht within a 2-satang-range band from the mid-rate. The stability of the system had attracted billions in foreign capital, some of it for FDI purposes, some for investment in Thai stocks and bonds, and some just for the interest rate—swapping dollars or other currency into baht and earning the higher Thai market interest rates that were priced off the discount rate at 10.50%. Now the system and the credibility of the Thai economy and the Thai authorities were threatened. The Bank of Thailand resolved to fight such volatility with everything it had—and it had considerable resources at hand. At the end of December, the Bank of Thailand had some USD38.7 billion in foreign exchange reserves, almost double those of the Bank of Mexico in 1994. It could also, if needed, allow market interest rates to rise sharply, draining liquidity from the system in order to squeeze speculator borrowing positions. Going into the end of the month, USD-THB was trading just shy of the 26 level. The Bank of Thailand counterattacked, allowing the overnight borrowing rate to more than double, forcing baht sellers to retreat, albeit temporarily.

In the first week of February, the Bank of Thailand had some bad news. A noted U.S. investment bank brought out a report, removing all its buy and market outperformer recommendations on Thai banks and saying that while it did not think the baht was fundamentally undervalued, there were rising baht devaluation risks over the next six months. The attitude of the authorities toward reports that expressed concern at the state of the economy and its finances and that raised the prospect of a baht devaluation was that such reports were alarmist and based on inaccuracies. Privately, the Bank of Thailand wanted to make the peg system much more flexible sooner rather than later, given the worsening economic situation; however, that was politically unacceptable. The politicians had decided that the peg would become more flexible only when the economy and exports had rebounded, perhaps toward the middle to the end of 1997. This was, however, leading the cart before the horse. In light of the seriousness of the situation, the peg system had to be made more flexible immediately and major fiscal measures needed to be taken to shore up Thailand's crumbling finances. This had to be coupled with equally immediate measures to tighten the fiscal side.

In that regard at least, one man was determined to avert disaster—Amnuay Viravan, the finance minister. A former executive chairman of Bangkok Bank, Amnuay had practical experience in business and the markets, a crucial advantage over many of his cabinet colleagues. Anxious to turn the fiscal situation around, he proposed a delay to THB50 billion of defense spending for the fiscal year 1996–1997 in January and again in fiscal 1997–1998. He slashed infrastructure spending. Total proposed budget cuts were around 6% of the national budget. There were positive steps, but by this time the market had tasted blood. It was too little, too late. More bad news, depressing Thai market sentiment, was to come, making Amnuay's task even harder and indeed making success all but impossible. On Friday, February 14,

Moody's was again on the newswires, reviewing Thailand's A2 long-term foreign currency rating for possible downgrade due to concerns over the soundness of Thailand's financial sector. The announcement was a body blow to Thailand's medium-term chances of turning the situation around—but more immediately to the stock market and the baht. It caused widespread panic selling by Thai domestic and foreign investors alike, causing the SET to lose some 5% on the day, with the USD-THB breaching the 26 level for the first time in ten years.

The timing could not possibly have been worse. Despite fading market confidence, Thailand was getting ready to issue a USD500 million Yankee bond, with Amnuay having announced that he would be conducting a road show in Hong Kong the following week to "tell the Thailand story." A grim-faced Amnuay, asked about the impact of the Moody's review for downgrade, said, "Under the current circumstances, it does not augur well for Thailand."[8] Indeed not, though he received some temporary support when Standard & Poor's Ratings said it had no current plans to downgrade Thailand, repeating the view that Thailand was financially strong enough to weather its problems.

In the end, Thailand was forced to pay wider spreads on its ten-year Yankee—90 basis points over Treasuries compared with 80—when the issue finally came out on April 11. Before that, general market confidence had been further hit when the SET shut down trading of bank and finance stocks on March 3, the first time in its history it had done so. For investors, there was no way to get out. When the exchange finally opened again, the SET index went into free fall as investors bolted while they had the opportunity, closing the week at 695, the lowest level in over four years. In April the market took a breather, allowing the authorities a valuable but all too brief period to take stock and figure out a way of saving simultaneously the baht, the economy, the finance companies, and the property companies. It was, of course, an impossible task. Thailand did its Yankee issue and then went about trying to shore up its defenses once more, bracing itself for the next attack. On April 9, Moody's downgraded

Thailand to A3 from A2, but since this had been expected, the reaction was muted.

Meanwhile, the economy continued to burn furiously. Thai exports had rallied 5.1% Y/Y in January, but then fell back in February, declining 5.0%. Exports then picked up again in March and April, rising 4.8% and 5.3%, but it was too late for individual reports to turn around market sentiment.[9] The process whereby the baht peg was going to be blown apart and the currency massively devalued was already set in motion. It was now just a matter of execution—of closing in on the carcass. The Thai authorities had few options left, apart from giving up and letting the peg go immediately. Increasingly, there was a feeling of inevitability about the situation—and one of anticipation in the market. But the Bank of Thailand, whatever the constraints imposed on it by the government in the prior two years, was not prepared to give up without a fight.

It would need to fight. On Monday, May 12, the market was ready. The week beforehand, traders in Singapore had begun to hear from their sales desks that some of Thailand's most prominent companies were hedging their exposure to the baht. Major importers who needed dollars anyway to pay for those imports, but usually only hedged out to two to three months, were suddenly buying dollars forward in six-month and out, the presumption being they wanted to lock in dollar rates now while they could on the expectation that the dollar would soon rise against the baht, thus hurting their costs. Thai exporters who usually would have translated spot dollar receivables immediately and hedged future delivery by selling dollars forward were suddenly nowhere to be seen. Many of them apparently wanted to stay in dollars. In other words, Thailand Inc. was betting that the baht would come under attack and that even if the attack were not fully successful, it would push the USD-THB markedly higher. Proprietary desks pricked up their ears at this, noting also that high interest rates would add to the Thai economic slowdown. While Amnuay had said Thailand was prepared to accept slower growth during the road shows for the Thailand Yankee bond issue, there had to be a pain threshold beyond which even he was not prepared to go. Also, the same high rates would add to the woes of Thailand's property companies, putting even more pressure on Thai finance companies. Just as the use of high interest rates in 1992 in a brave but foolhardy attempt to defend sterling within the ERM had failed, high interest rates to defend the baht were simply not sustainable over a long period of time.

That was the theory as the speculators saw it, and it made perfect sense. Many, however, did not count on the sheer determination of the Bank of Thailand. To reach even this stage was a humiliation. The Bank of Thailand desk was determined to hammer those who dared to threaten the peg system that had lasted so long and brought so much benefit to Thailand. The bank could not choose the time or the place of battle, but could certainly alter the conditions of battle and the consequent risks involved—enough to cause such pain, it hoped, that the speculators, those who were able to leave the battlefield, would limp home, never to return. On Tuesday, May 14, it looked like the Bank of Thailand would lose the battle—and quickly. Money market rates continued to rise, but the speculators, and many Thai corporates, continued to hammer the baht, causing the USD-THB to soar as high as 26.60. The battle would be short and sweet, at least the speculators thought so. The next day, on Wednesday, the Bank of Thailand sprung the first part of its trap.

First off, it let the overnight borrowing rate climb to 25%. Then, in a very public display of Asian solidarity, the Hong Kong Monetary Authority and the Monetary Authority of Singapore let it be known that they were intervening to defend the baht, selling dollars for baht, along with the Bank of Thailand. Bank Negara Malaysia was also thought to have taken part in the intervention. The fact that other Asian central banks had intervened to support the baht was a shock to the market, taking the speculators off guard. The Bank of Thailand knew it would not have much time, for the speculators would soon work out that the MAS, HKMA, and possibly BNM had all intervened as agents of the Bank of Thailand and thus had not used their own reserves. On Thursday, the Bank of Thailand, which had been

cautioning Thai banks not to lend baht in order to stop speculators borrowing baht to then sell, came into the market to sell
dollars and at the same time ordered the domestic banks not to
lend at all to offshore parties, thus creating a two-tier market; the
two-tier system remains in place today.

The speculators suddenly had no way to fund their short baht
positions. As they watched their dealing screens in shock, the
overnight borrowing rate screamed through 100%, then 500%,
and then 1000%. At one point that day, it actually hit 3000%
before settling at around 1500% on an annualized basis. The
events of Thursday, May 15, 1997, are etched in the memory of
many traders, salespeople, and funds around the world. With
suddenly no liquidity to borrow offshore and the need to
instantly cover positions to avoid massive losses, many panicked.
Some screamed into their phones, into the broker boxes for anyone who would lend them baht in any form; some swore and
threw their chairs across the dealing room; others just looked
dazed at their screens. The only source of spot baht borrowing to
the offshore parties was the Bank of Thailand itself—at a rate of
1400%. The scramble became a panic; the panic, headlong flight.
Some proprietary desks were suddenly underwater by up to
USD50–60 million each. Hedge fund losses on a market-to-
market basis were estimated at up to USD450 million.

"They kicked our butts and they've taken a lot of profit we
might have had," said Stanley Druckenmiller, chief investment
officer for Soros Fund Management.[9] "They did a masterful job
of squeezing us out." The baht roared higher on the back of the
massive spike in baht borrowing costs.

Some funds and propietary desks managed to find initial
loopholes in the Bank of Thailand's strategy, buying Thai bills of
exchange denominated in baht. However, the Bank of Thailand
quickly moved to close the loopholes, saying financial institutions were only allowed to pay for unmatured bills of exchange,
promissory notes, or CDs in dollars. The Bank of Thailand also
forced the suspension of forwards, foreign exchange options,
and foreign exchange and interest rate swaps between the onshore and the offshore market. About that time, a large number

of hedge funds' short baht forward positions were coming due and the funds needed to find the baht with which to finance those positions. One hedge fund actually called up the Bank of Thailand desk and offered to stop attacking the baht if the Bank of Thailand would lend it baht at 25%. The Bank of Thailand quietly refused the offer. Many traders called it the "day of the blood baht." Several traders in European and U.S. banks in Hong Kong and Singapore were fired that day, such were the losses sustained. By Friday, the USD-THB had fallen back to around 25.6 in the offshore market. It would continue to fall, hitting at one point 23.80.

The Bank of Thailand had won a brilliant victory. The question now was, could the bank keep it up? Had it defeated the speculators or merely seriously wounded a few of them? The following week, Finance Minister Amnuay, in a strident address to reporters, said that fluctuations in the baht were normal, but that a deliberate attack on the currency was another story entirely and that Thailand would not allow "unethical people" to speculate against its currency. Amnuay added that it would be increasingly difficult for speculators to mount another attack given the resolve of the Bank of Thailand and the cooperation by other Asian central banks. In saying so, he missed the point—or rather avoided it—that the other Asian central banks would not intervene again to support the baht. Doing so once had been sensational and briefly effective, but they increasingly had their own worries to take care of, with the volatility in the baht spreading to Malaysia, the Philippines, Indonesia, and even Singapore. In addition, while the Bank of Thailand's tactics were effective in smashing the speculative attack that week, it also scooped up in the net many innocent parties, namely Thai corporates that suddenly were unable to fund or transact their usual commercial needs, and foreign funds that were trying to sell baht to get out of their asset positions. The pain of the former further hurt the economy, while that of the latter caused several fund managers, individuals who had invested for years in Thailand and had been welcomed in by the Thai authorities, never to come back. In a conversation with Standard & Poor's

MMS capital markets analyst Sheila Mullan, Amnuay reiterated, "The government is not considering a devaluation. We do not believe devaluation of the Thai currency will have any positive impact on the economy. Devaluation would do more harm than good."[10]

These were fighting words, but Amnuay himself had also been damaged in the battle. On the weekend, prior to that Monday, Prime Minister Chavalit had suddenly announced that he was taking command of the economy. The comment had been a straightforward answer to a question about who was running the economy—as in, I, as Prime Minister, am running the economy. However, it was interpreted as a signal that Amnuay was about to be fired. This was denied, but rumors lingered. There was known to be bad blood between Amnuay and Chavalit's coalition partner Chatichai, who did not favor the austere fiscal stance that Amnuay was attempting. The Bank of Thailand itself had also been damaged. Up until Thursday when it stopped intervening but pulled the liquidity out from the offshore market instead, the Bank of Thailand desk had spent up to USD10 billion (10 yards in market parlance) defending the baht, mostly in the forwards, in three-, six-, and twelve-month maturities. Bank of Thailand reserves, which had been about USD38.1 billion in March, had already fallen to USD37.3 billion by April. In May, they plunged to 33.3 billion—and that reserve figure was only counting spot sales of reserves by the Bank of Thailand, not the forward positions it had taken out. At the time, Standard & Poor's MMS estimated Bank of Thailand forward sales at a further USD10 billion, bringing total reserves down to USD23 billion, barely three months import cover.

Amid the confusion over who was in command of the economy, Thai officials blamed the media for the loss of market and economic confidence in Thailand. This was a trait that would reoccur throughout that year. The reality, however, was all too plain to see. The economy was in dire straits and getting worse by the day. Planned fiscal remedies had been stalled or delayed as the various cabinet and ministry elements sought to maintain their influence. The baht remained strong despite the fact that the overnight rate dipped back below 500%. But gradually spec-ulators looked for further ways of attacking it once more. The Bank of Thailand continued to plug loopholes as quickly as it discovered them, but it was like trying to plug a dike that was about to burst. Finance Minister Amnuay and Commerce Min-ister Narongchai, to their credit, continued to fight to the last to turn around the fundamental economic situation, focusing on the immediate need to cut spending and boost taxes in order to shore up the budget. If only they could visibly achieve this, and with Thai exports actually starting to improve again—May export data showed growth of almost 9% Y/Y—they might boost market support confidence long enough for speculators to lose patience and go away. The market restrictions could thus be gradually eased and normal market conditions restored, allowing them to get back to their other imminent task in hand of shoring up the salvable companies. All but the last were justi-fiable and indeed admirable aims. Shoring up all the finance companies was a recipe for disaster, and it was also wrong. If companies make mistakes, they should be allowed to fail if there is no viable alternative.

To this end, Amnuay and Narongchai proposed hiking an excise tax on motorcycles and batteries, a measure needed to close the budget shortfall. This was a seemingly modest and jus-tifiable measure, but it met with fierce opposition from within the cabinet. For Amnuay, it was too much. He had done every-thing he could to try to save the situation and now he was being actively blocked from within the government itself from doing so. In addition, his economic opponent, Chatichai, had just been made chairman of the cabinet's weekly economic strategy meet-ing. On June 20, he resigned. His resignation was quickly fol-lowed by that of Narongchai. It was the fatal blow from which Thailand, and the baht, would not recover.

In those last few days, the government scrambled to try to sup-port confidence, encouraging mergers within ninety-one finance companies. Bank of Thailand Governor Rerngchai made a some-what firmer gesture—if much too late—halting trading in sixteen finance companies to provide further encouragement. It was not the time for encouragement, however. More drastic measures were needed and even if taken might have been too late by then. Certainly, Thai investors and corporates had little apparent faith in such gestures, sending the SET and the onshore baht into free fall. The speculators started to come back, mostly in the offshore options, though also in spot through London and New York.

Thailand's last gasp came in the form of Chavalit declaring on Tuesday, July 1, that the baht would never be allowed to devalue. The very next day, at 8:30 a.m., on Wednesday, July 2, the time when the Bank of Thailand usually set the peg system rates, the desk said it would no longer defend the peg. For a split second, people stopped and stared at their screens in disbelief. It was a bombshell, so long in coming that some had begun to think, whatever their position, that Thailand might pull through. Then the silence was followed by dealers screaming their orders around the globe as they sought to sell the baht for all it was worth. On that day alone, the baht lost nearly 15% of its value against the dollar. From the Moody's downgrade in September of 1996, few would have guessed the terrifying speed of the subsequent economic and financial collapse that Thailand suffered. The banking system was teetering, and the reputations of the Finance Ministry and the Bank of Thailand itself—after that Pyrrhic victory—were lying in ruins.

In the Bank of Thailand's dealing room, no one spoke, the pain of defeat too great to bear. That pain would swiftly be felt by others. For many of Thailand's ASEAN partners, their worst fears had been confirmed. Thailand had devalued, proving that an Asian country could be defeated if attacked hard enough and for long enough. It would not be long before the speculators started to attack the other ASEAN currencies in earnest.

6

The Meltdown—One by One

MANY ANALYSTS AND TRADERS were stunned when it actually happened, shocked that the Bank of Thailand had just let the baht go rather than seeking a gradual depreciation of the currency. Of course, with the benefit of hindsight, one can safely say that such a gradualist option was no longer available to the Bank of Thailand. Only two weeks before, the baht had actually started to recover, but then the Thai Finance Minister Amnuay resigned, followed by the Bank of Thailand's announcement that its reserves had plunged USD4 billion in May to USD33.3 billion. Finally, the April Current Account was released, coming out at a massive THB38.0 billion deficit versus THB15.9 billion in March.

While some traders were disbelieving—albeit briefly—and others immediately sought to profit from the now free-floating baht, IMF Acting Managing Director Stanley Fischer welcomed the baht's flotation, together with the Bank of Thailand's parallel move to hike its discount rate by 2 percentage points to 12.5% from 10.5% as steps aimed at "addressing Thailand's economic difficulties and ensuring macroeconomic adjustment and financial stability."[1] Fischer added that the IMF would be available to provide technical assistance to Thailand during the subsequent transition period. As mentioned in the previous chapter, Soros Fund Management's Stanley Druckenmiller was gracious in his applause for the Bank of Thailand, calling the baht's devaluation "a great first step" and saying that it was positive for the Thai stock market.[2] Thai stock traders and brokers at the stock exchange agreed wholeheartedly, with the SET index registering its biggest gain of more than five years, some 7.76% to 568.21—seemingly ignoring the Bank of Thailand's rate hike on the view that since the baht no longer needed to be defended, rates would eventually come back down.

While the reaction from dealing desks and Western official circles ran the gamut from disbelief to relief and finally elation, that within Thailand's neighboring ASEAN countries was one of unequivocal horror. Their worst fears and nightmares had come true. After spending billions to defend the baht and then letting it go, the Bank of Thailand had shown the market that an Asian central bank could be defeated. Many had expected that, but here was proof. While the speculative sharks had gorged themselves on the carcass of an Asian currency, others, while not quite in such ailing condition, were still floundering in the turbulent financial and economic waters that prevailed. Some Asian government officials registered their private hope that the market would calm down. It had got what it wanted, and however onerous the cost and odious the speculators, the market would correct. Asian central bankers were more sanguine. Most knew all too well that the market had not yet sated its hunger. Sitting in their dealing rooms in Kuala Lumpur, Manila, Jakarta, and even Singapore and Hong Kong, Asian central bank dealing desks knew it was only a matter of time before the speculators turned their sights on them.

They did not have long to wait. Indeed, while the market reaction on July 2 was relatively calm in other Asian currencies, by the end of that week some were already starting to come under significant speculative pressure, particularly those of Thailand's ASEAN partners. Readers can find the Standard & Poor's MMS "Emerging Asia Chronological Developments" at the back of the book to help them with the day-by-day chronology of events that occurred subsequent to the Thai baht devaluation. I have, however, divided this chapter into the relative regions and then subdivided again into each country and currency because the crisis that spread from Thailand—subsequently to be termed a "contagion"—did so in specific stages, three to be exact. The first stage saw the other ASEAN currencies go one by one, while the Thai baht continued to slide. In the second stage, the North Asian currencies of South Korea and Taiwan came under attack. Finally the third stage occurred when Hong Kong was rocked by speculative pressure. While there are key similarities between these three stages, it is important to note this regional chronology, whereby tensions and full-scale speculative attacks transferred from one specific area to another—subsequently affecting the world's stock and bond markets. This typhoon elicited quite different reactions and policies from Asian governments and central banks as it passed through the region, some market-driven, others seeking control. If we are later on to look at their respective fundamentals and determine which one, subsequent to the crisis, has the most investment-friendly environment it is crucial to look at how each one dealt with the crisis in turn.

Stage 1 — The ASEAN

That very day, July 2, as the Thai baht plunged against the dollar, the first pressures in other ASEAN currencies started to be felt. In particular, the Philippine peso was the first of the ASEAN currencies to come under serious attack. Via the Philippine Dealing System (PDS) and in the offshore centers of Singapore, Hong Kong, Tokyo, and London, proprietary desks, short-term traders, and eventually the hedge funds began to take on the peso. Earlier in May, when the baht was under intense attack, the Philippine's central bank, Bangko Sentral ng Pilipinas (BSP), hiked the overnight borrowing rate some 175 basis points to 13.0% to try to avoid spillover from the baht to the peso. With the baht in free fall, the pressure on the peso began to rise again immediately. Initially, BSP responded to this unwelcome attack with vigor and determination. The Philippines was not Thailand. It did not have the debt problem that Thailand had, nor the excess capacity in property development and thus the banking system exposure to that excess. Indeed, banking supervision and standards, under the auspices of the BSP itself, were enviable relative to several of its ASEAN neighbors let alone Thailand. The Philippines had a current account deficit (4.2% of GDP in 1996) that was a valid concern, but here too what fundamental problems it had paled into insignificance compared with Thailand's massive current account deficit of 8%. On July 2, the day the baht was let go, BSP hiked the overnight borrowing rate from 15% to 24%, hurting the speculators by tightening market liquidity sharply. In addition, BSP's foreign exchange desk intervened in the market, selling USD543 million for peso.

Run by Governor Gabriel Singson, a veteran of the central bank with a keen sense of humor and a good man in a crisis who had helped steer the Philippines through financial difficulty during the 1980s and 1990s, the BSP had developed a reputation of being very market-savvy and market-oriented. Singson himself, who took up the position of BSP governor in 1993, was often quoted as saying that the market determined the exchange rate, not the central bank. Admittedly, such statements flew in the face somewhat of the reality that up until then the USD-PHP had effectively traded within a 1.5% band, which if broken would cause PDS dealing to stop. However, his more convivial relationship with the market—as was the case with his finance secretary Roberto de Ocampo—contrasted favorably with the approach taken by several neighbors of the Philippines. Unlike other central bank governors who remain relatively aloof from the market, Singson takes a very hands-on approach, watching his quote screens round the clock. "I watch the markets almost every hour," he told Standard & Poor's MMS in a discussion during a trip he took to Hong Kong.[3] Initially, Singson was relatively confident that the attack on the peso would die down and interest rates could be allowed to be lowered gradually. The attack did not die down, however, and going into that weekend it picked up in intensity.

Singson's job in defending the peso was not helped by an article in the Philippine *BusinessWorld* newspaper citing unnamed sources as saying that the peso "may be allowed to devalue" in the wake of Thailand's decision to float the baht.'In addition, a Singapore Sunday newspaper reported Finance Secretary de Ocampo as saying that the peso could weaken because of the Thai devaluation. On Monday morning, as soon as Asian dealers got to their desks, the peso came under wave after wave of speculative pressure. The BSP fought back with all it had, boosting its overnight borrowing rate to 30% through reverse repurchase agreements (RRPs) in the money market and intervening repeatedly in the foreign exchange market to sell dollars. In addition, de Ocampo denied that anyone in the Philippine government or central bank had said the peso would weaken or be devalued, emphasizing the country's strong fundamentals. Despite that, the peso continued to be sold aggressively, with daily volume on the PDS soaring from an average of USD200–250 million in the first half of the year to almost USD1.3 billion.

The pressure continued to build, forcing BSP to again raise its overnight rate a further 2 percentage points to 32%. On Wednesday and Thursday as the selling reached its climax, the BSP desk sold around USD1 billion in total to keep the dollar-peso (USD-PHP) rate below the 26.40 level. While its foreign exchange desk was frantically busy trying to stave off a devaluation of the peso, other BSP officials were trying to find out who was actually doing the selling. The first instinct was that it was mostly foreign selling, and the BSP asked local banks in Manila if this was the case. It got a variety of answers. There was indeed heavy foreign selling of peso through nondeliverable forwards (NDFs), which act like forwards but are settled in dollars on the basis of the difference between the initial buying/selling price and the selling/buying price on the day of maturity. No principal is exchanged, just the difference. BSP tried to get the Manila banks to close that particular loophole, though foreign speculators remained active sellers of PHP in the NDFs throughout that week. There can be little doubt, however, that Filipino banks and companies were also active sellers of PHP. Indeed, while some locals said they were selling PHP for offshore clients, they were in fact taking on proprietary positions based on the view that the PHP would eventually have to devalue. They weren't wrong. With only USD12 billion in foreign exchange reserves as of May, or three-months import cover, there was no way the BSP could hold the line for long. In addition, the high overnight borrowing rates would crush the economy if maintained. As interest rates soared, the stock market, which had strongly outperformed most world stock markets from 1993 to 1997, was getting smashed.

Singson and his team at the BSP are very realistic people. If daily volume continued at USD1 billion a day and they had to sell USD500 million or 1 billion a day just to support the peso, the BSP's entire reserves would have run out in a maximum twenty days. Between 1994 and 1996, the BSP had actually been a net buyer of dollars, to the tune of almost USD10 billion. The idea was simultaneously to boost its reserves and also to limit PHP strength, the latter being due to very strong foreign capital and FDI flows into the country. Now, here it was selling millions of dollars in a desperate attempt to save the PHP from being devalued. The writing was on the wall and Singson knew it. Not that such peso weakness was justified on fundamental grounds alone. However, with the Thai baht devaluation, market speculation against the baht was spilling over into general regional hysteria, or contagion, and that could not be resisted by the Philippines. Better to let the peso go and try to manage its depreciation rather than throw away the country's precious foreign exchange reserves. On Friday, July 11, only nine days after Thailand let its currency float free, the Philippines was forced also to let its currency devalue. The BSP announced that henceforth, the peso would be allowed to trade in a wider band. The BSP desk, and Singson at his terminal, watched silently as the peso promptly lost 11.55% of its value on that day alone. It was a defeat for the central banks, yes, but not nearly so bitter as that which the bank of Thailand had experienced. The BSP was realistic and gave up trying to defend the peso rather than waste reserves. In the subsequent turmoil, it would seek to manage the currency's fall, thus seeking in the process to try to achieve a soft landing for the economy itself—for in past peso devaluations, economic recession had always followed fast on the heels of the currency's plunge.

For that to occur again would have been a tragedy, an injustice, for the Philippines' fundamental problems were not nearly as severe as those in Thailand. Inflation, once a valid concern, had peaked in December 1996 at a Y/Y rate of 5.2%. With the peso having effectively been devalued itself, this would be a concern going forward, since about 40% of the Philippines annual output came from imports. But the BSP had shown prudent and even hawkish inflation management in the past, and there was no reason to expect any difference this time.

In the wake of the Thailand crisis, there were justifiable regionwide concerns about Asian property-sector oversupply and Asian bank exposure to that. However Philippine bank exposure to property was only around 18% of its loan book, compared with over 40% in Thailand. The Philippines had a current account deficit in 1996 of 4.2%, but this too was much lower than that of Thailand, almost half. Combined with a budget surplus of 0.3% of GDP in 1996, the overall economic picture was significantly more stable. Philippine GNP was 6.1% in the second quarter, above expectations and greater than 5.8% in the first quarter. Export growth in the second quarter averaged 27% Y/Y. All this should, in ideal market conditions, have saved the Philippines. However, conditions were far from ideal. In addition, the Philippines, like many ASEAN countries, suffered from overreliance on foreign capital, whether in the form of FDI, capital flows, or bonds or loans issued by domestic companies. In 1996, total outstanding external debt was USD38.3 billion—or 320% of foreign exchange reserves. Most of this was unhedged given the stability up to that point in the peso band system. With the peso under attack during the second week of July, domestic banks and corporates woke up to the threat that their balance sheets could be blown up by this unhedged risk. They started to buy dollars en masse.

For the BSP, subsequent to the peso devaluation, the main priority was to try to stabilize Philippine asset markets, then the peso, and finally the economy. With Philippine companies and banks continuing to hastily sell pesos for dollars to cover their new foreign exchange risk, both for receivables and to hedge dollar-denominated debt, stabilizing the peso was always going to be tough work. Trying to put a floor under the domestic asset market, particularly the stock market, was a more valid priority in order to avert total panic. From July 16 to July 31, the BSP cut its overnight rate back to 20% from 31%. This, together with persistent corporate selling of pesos into the market, boosted money market liquidity. As a result, BSP, while cutting rates to support the stock market and limit the economic impact of the failed attempt to defend the peso, hiked bank reserve requirements to mop up this excess liquidity, first from 2% to 4% on July 31, then to 5% on August 15, and again to 8% on August 28. Gradually, the peso began to stabilize. After having spiked to just shy of the 30 level on July 15, it ended the month at 28.98, still some 10% higher on the month, but off the highs.

For a time, indeed, Philippine market conditions appeared to calm down. While the BSP had clearly not won its battle, the situation had at least reached a stage of relative stability. The IMF and the U.S. government had been effusive with praise for the BSP's approach in letting the peso go, not wasting reserves, and focusing on sorting out the economy rather than trying to stage a vain, last stand against the might of the financial markets. And the IMF had put its money where its mouth was by offering the Philippines a USD1.1 billion loan facility to temporarily help replenish its reserves. The Philippines, however, was not isolated from developments in other ASEAN currencies and markets—no one was. In August and early September, the peso again came under pressure in the wake of precipitous declines in the Malaysian ringgit and Indonesian rupiah; this was further inducement for the BSP to hike bank reserve requirements. Domestically, there were also concerns that President Fidel Ramos, a former general who had done so much to improve the economic lot of his countrymen, might try to amend the constitution in order to run for office for a second term in the 1998 elections. After pondering the possibilities, and witnessing half a million Filipinos march peacefully through the streets of Manila against such a move, Ramos made a further pledge that he would step down when his term ended in 1998. Manila asset markets surged with relief. However, by the end of the day the stock market and peso had given back most of their early gains.

Even now, the peso was not out of the woods. Following the peso's devaluation on July 11, inflation started to pick up in August, hitting a 13-month high in September at 5.3%. The trade deficit was also worsening, to some USD1.029 billion in August and USD950 million in September, having averaged around 800 million a month in the first half of the year. With outright panic continuing in other currencies, the month of October started badly for the peso, with the USD-PHP soaring to as high as 35.61. Suddenly, the overnight rate soared to as high as 100% as the BSP drained reserves to meet IMF quarterly targets during a 10-day test period. The BSP was not done with its attempts to limit peso volatility and stabilize its markets. On October 7, the Philippine Bankers Association, in accordance with the BSP, implemented a new, three-tier volatility band designed to mute declines in the currency. Trading was to be temporarily suspended on the PDS if the 2% initial band (on either side of the previous afternoon's average) was breached, suspended a second time if the rate moved a further 1%, and finally closed for the day if the third band at a further 1% move was hit.

While this might have seemed a good idea at the time, at least in theory, practice was that this merely set targets for the market to hit. That day, Tuesday, October 7, the USD-PHP soared 3%, hitting two of the bands, and reaching a traded high of 35.98. The BSP then reopened its lending window (closed since August 20), though it set several conditions for borrowing. It only allowed banks to do so if they had a reserve deficiency, were not net lenders in the interbank market, and were not large buyers of dollars in the PDS. Overall, the BSP performed admirably during this period of significant volatility, in which the USD-PHP rose 36%. BSP policies were focused on smoothing out the market rather than directly opposing it, and more importantly on focusing on the economic fundamentals of the country, ensuring that the time in which market interest rates were hiked to defend the peso was as limited as possible (cutting the overnight back to

15% by mid-October) in order to try and achieve as soft an economic landing as possible in 1998. The one exception to this was the imposition of the volatility band, which I would suggest was a mistake. While understandable in light of the sharpness of the moves in early October, this did indeed give the market a further target to aim for—three in fact—and was not consistent with the trend in the Philippines to liberalize its financial markets, including foreign exchange. That said, that same month, Governor Singson was firm in parrying suggestions for the imposition of capital controls, saying he believed the extreme peso volatility of the summer and early autumn would soon come to an end—which indeed proved to be the case.

Such a sanguine and measured approach by the Philippine authorities contrasted markedly with that taken in Malaysia, at least by the Malaysian prime minister, Dr. Mahathir, who in the early months of the crisis continued to lambaste perceived external enemies of all sorts and in all quarters for bringing ruination upon his country. Malaysia, which had come to see 8%+ growth year after year, was not spared in the subsequent turmoil following the Thai baht devaluation. And this was not just because of the inflammatory comments made by Mahathir, though his comments unquestionably added to the decline in value of the Malaysian ringgit. Malaysia also had fundamental problems: excessive property supply, overreliance on external borrowing, and a large current account deficit. While these would be focused on subsequently, the initial wave of ringgit selling that followed the Thai baht devaluation and the initial attack on the Philippine peso was pure contagion. The crisis spilled over from one currency to another, rather than due to any new light focused on fundamentals.

Early in the second week of July, as the peso started to be attacked in earnest, Bank Negara Malaysia—which had developed a fearsome reputation for intervening in the foreign exchange market, both for and against the ringgit at various times—was forced to intervene repeatedly to sell dollars as the ringgit fell back across the board. On Tuesday, July 8, it was briefly successful, pushing the USD-MYR back down from

2.5240 to 2.5100, though such selling depleted its foreign exchange reserves and forced up the overnight rate (to 6.025% from 5.45%). It would go higher still, albeit briefly. Earlier in May, when the baht was being hammered and then subsequently recovered sharply as the Bank of Thailand won its Pyrrhic victory against the market, the ringgit had also come under significant pressure. At the time, BNM had also intervened heavily, selling around USD1.5 billion into the market for ringgit and orchestrating a liquidity squeeze in the swap market, effectively shutting the latter down. This caused liquidity problems for speculators who had gone short ringgit in the spot or forward markets and were trying to cover their positions by borrowing it in the swap market. Those tactics were highly successful, forcing a collapse in the USD-MYR from 2.53 to slightly above 2.47 in just over twenty-four hours. However, to achieve that, BNM had been forced to buy up MYR3.7 billion from the market, forcing money market interest rates to rise sharply. The one-week borrowing rate spiked from 7% to over 20%. This in turn caused several Malaysian banks to raise their prime lending rates by around 30 basis points to 9.6%.

That week, in July, BNM was faced with an even sterner test, with the baht having devalued and the peso already under attack. The trigger level, as far as the authorities were concerned, appeared to be 2.5250—and the market continued to gun for that level despite repeated BNM intervention and higher money market rates. Such was the intensity of the attack that in just over a week the central bank had spent over 10% defending the ringgit, with reserves falling some MYR8.5 billion to 61.9 billion. Of course, none of this went unnoticed by the Malaysian stock market, which reacted predictably to the spike in interest rates—by collapsing. Rates were tightened further: The benchmark three-month interbank rate was raised to 11.1% and then to 14.4%, prompting the Kuala Lumpur Stock Exchange index to plummet through the 1000 level for the first time since January 1996. As BNM Governor Ahmad Don said, there was always a cost involved in pursuing an objective, particularly when that objective was to defend a currency that was under attack, not in an isolated incident of market volatility but as part of a region-wide market crisis. Indeed, while many market commentators thought the ringgit safe given how determined BNM historically was and its war chest of reserves, some farsighted fund managers wondered how long even Malaysia could hang on in the midst of the currency market typhoon that was hitting the ASEAN.

Indeed, the initial knee-jerk wave of ringgit selling that had followed the baht's devaluation had changed and become more fundamentally focused. Like Thailand, Malaysia also had a large current account deficit (some 9.0% in 1995, falling to a "mere" 5.5% in 1996). Like banks in Thailand, Malaysian banks had focused on property lending, with over 30% of total bank loans made to property companies. High interest rates would mean a cash squeeze on these companies and thus hurt the banks exposed to them. This in turn would hurt growth prospects, not to mention Malaysian retail and institutional stock market investors who saw their share prices collapse. For the central bank and also for the government, the pain resulting from the defense of the ringgit, in terms of high interest rates and the plunge in the stock market, eventually became too much. On Monday, July 14, following the peso's devaluation the previous Friday, BNM gave up its expensive defense. With the domino effect of the ASEAN currency devaluations beginning in earnest—the peso having fallen 18% on Friday alone—and with the consequent impact on the trade competitiveness of those countries that did not devalue; Malaysian exports would be hurt in addition to the asset price pain (falling stock and property prices) and falling foreign exchange reserves that the economy would experience. Holding the line was just not worth the pain. BNM did not announce a new policy. However, with the USD-MYR already having blasted through the 2.5250 level and trading to within a whisker of 2.56, BNM stopped intervening.

It was effectively the green light for the market, and within a matter of hours USD-MYR had soared as high as 2.67 as money market rates fell and the stock market recovered. The ringgit was further buffeted by market reactions to frequent comments by Dr. Mahathir (which we will go into in greater detail in the next chapter) regarding the necessity (or rather the lack of necessity) for foreign exchange trading, the nature of markets and the like. BNM had not, however, finished with the market. On August 4 it imposed a limit on foreign customers for noncommercial-related ringgit swaps of USD2 million.

Up until then, the rating agencies had played a relatively small part in the story of the ringgit. That changed, however, on August 18 when Standard & Poor's Ratings cut its outlook on Malaysia from positive to stable. The long-term foreign currency and local currency ratings were affirmed, but by that stage the market was ignoring all positive news and simply reacting to bad news. While this was going on, the Malaysian stock market continued to slide. On Thursday, August 28, in an act of sheer lunacy, Malaysia imposed restrictions on short selling of KLSE index stocks. This action would cause one of the largest drops in the exchange's history, sufficient in fact to force the government to rescind that move the following day, Friday. Why lunacy? Because if you ban short selling, you first and foremost severely limit and damage overall liquidity—notably the other side of the liquidity needed to buy stocks. In addition, in the heat of the moment, who was to tell who was a short seller and who was just getting out of a position? Foreign investors, seeing this as the first of a number of likely restrictions on stock market trading, decided to get out at the first opportunity. In other words, it was like using a nuclear device to kill a wolf—thus in the process killing your own sheep as well and any friendly foreign sheep-dogs that had happened along. Dr. Mahathir talked about "good" and "bad" foreign investors. This hurt many investors he would have termed as "good," causing those who had managed to escape to leave and not come back.

Meanwhile, the USD-MYR continued to soar higher, breaching the 3.00 level on September 4. The Monday after Mahathir made his comments about George Soros at the IMF meeting in Hong Kong, and Soros had retaliated the following day, September 22, the ringgit was smashed as soon as Asian dealers were at their desks. Even Sydney, where ringgit trade was extremely thin, saw both commercial and speculative ringgit sell orders, as investors, corporates, and speculators alike dumped the currency onto the market—the speculators with almost disbelieving glee. That day, the USD-MYR hit 3.12, the highest level since 1971, while the KLSE fell a further 4%. Granted, the move was exacerbated by two major factors: liquidity and outright panic. However, those who looked further, beyond the rhetoric of nameless speculative "beasts" and "morons" attacking a defenseless and poor country—a ridiculous assertion in the first place—would have been rewarded with a notable discovery, one that had clear similarities with the case of Thailand and also to a certain extent with the Philippines and Malaysian companies that had plenty of foreign currency–denominated debt which remained unhedged. Total outstanding external debt in 1996 was some USD28.3 billion, most of which was in dollars and issued by corporates. Of that, most appeared to be unhedged. Indeed, the relatively young domestic derivatives markets in Kuala Lumpur limited the ability of Malaysian companies to hedge such foreign debts, particularly in longer-dated paper that was even more liquid. Besides that, hedging regulations actually required the company getting permission to do so.

More bad news was to come. On Thursday, September 25, as the IMF meeting wound down, Standard & Poor's Ratings cut Malaysia's rating outlook again, from stable to negative, citing the Malaysian authorities' reluctance to curb credit growth and the likelihood that bank asset quality would deteriorate in 1998. By the next Wednesday, the panic was in full control, with the USD-MYR screaming skyward, hitting 3.40 before stalling, amid general carnage in the regional currencies. Panic fed on itself, creating a snowball effect that pulled down everyone in the immediate vicinity.

"With no sign of BNM on the ringgit and every other Asian (ASEAN) currency getting smashed, everyone just jumped on the band wagon," said a dealer for a European bank in Singapore. "Who was selling it? I don't know anyone who wasn't!"[4] He added, "The lack of a clear policy on rates, the haze, and the barrage of comments about foreign exchange dealers. You put everything together and until there is some clarity on the economic outlook, you have to sell this thing."

Notably, the dealer in question and several others, in both Hong Kong and Singapore, said that by that stage there was little sign of the hedge funds. "They were in a lot earlier, selling the baht mostly. By October they were out and counting their profit." Indeed so. By October, most of the orders were commercially driven—corporates for the most part panicking in their effort to hedge (the unhedgeable). The ringgit, and the authorities, finally found some respite by the middle of October as the market, exhausted by its frenetic activity of the previous two months, sat and waited for the budget prepared by Deputy Prime Minister and Finance Minister Anwar Ibrahim. By then, Mahathir was beginning to tone down his rhetoric, and indeed Anwar himself, by being careful to support his prime minister, was taking a more conciliatory line with the market, seeking to woo back the "good" investors (if there were any left out there). In the end, it was something of a disappointment, though by that stage market expectations might have been overdone. Anwar sought to emphasize cutting the current account deficit, boosting savings, and deferring megaprojects—as expected. However, Standard & Poor's MMS and others were particularly disappointed by the lack of meaningful cuts on the government expenditure side.

Overall, the government sought to control the ringgit and failed and then sought to control the stock market and again failed. In stark contrast to the policies of the government of the Philippines and of the BSP, the Malaysian government sought to dominate market forces rather than channel and steer them into more constructive activity—or at least limit their destructive forces. By doing so, this only added to the woes of the Malaysian asset markets and the ringgit. Despite the strong headline growth numbers, there were valid fundamental concerns: a large current account deficit, a massively overinflated stock market (over 300% of GDP), property market oversupply and banking exposure to that, overinvestment relative to savings, and, like everyone else, falling export growth due to appreciation of the REER—none of which were dealt with in a timely or effective manner. As for BNM, it was not blameless either, though its policies were somewhat hampered by the government's fetish with headline growth.

By the end of October, the monetary base was still increasing at an annualized rate of 30%, yet the overnight borrowing rate was still 5.5–6.0%. In pure monetary terms, BNM was effectively printing money with the government's presumed aim at inflating its way out of a likely sharp slowdown in 1998. This was an exceptionally dangerous game. Seeking a high enough interest rate to ward off inflationary pressure and support the ringgit, while at the same time not braking the economy too hard, remains BNM's top priority. With the benefit of hindsight it is easy to say—though some did at the time—that a combination of tighter fiscal and monetary policy at an earlier stage would have undoubtedly caused a fall in Malaysian asset markets, but would have in the end avoided much of the subsequent collapse. The responsibility for that lies squarely at the door of the Malaysian authorities.

While Malaysia had fundamental problems but did little about them, at least initially, seeking to dominate and bully its way out of trouble, Indonesia had potentially worse problems but was at least trying to do something about them. In early July, with the baht floating freely—and heading downhill at terminal velocity—and both the peso and ringgit under attack, the rupiah also caught the market's attention. The reaction of Bank Indonesia (BI) was immediate and market-oriented. It widened the trading band of the dollar-rupiah (USD-IDR) rate from 8% to 12% on July 11, the same day the peso was devalued. It was designed as a preemptive move to dissipate speculative pressures before they had a chance to build up. In that regard, the timing of the peso devaluation and then the move to let the ringgit trade freely without intervention could not have been more unfortunate. On the Monday following the band widening, the rupiah started to fall, ending the session down 1.4% on the day. Prior to the band widening, investors had been attracted by interest rates in the

Indonesian money market of 15% or so. The band widening, in the context of the general regional currency hysteria of the time, actually increased rather than decreased the perceived currency risk in the rupiah. Bank Indonesia officials were quick to try to lessen any damage done. They pointed out that Indonesia had strong fundamentals and that the band widening was aimed at dissipating speculative pressures and allowing BI to get on with managing the economy via monetary policy. In a discussion with Standard & Poor's MMS, BI Monetary Management Director Dr. C. Harinowo explained: "The benefit [of widening the rupiah band] is providing us more autonomy to managing monetary policy. We do not need to be concerned with the exchange rate, which affects monetary aggregates. It gives us a bigger cushion if there are any speculative attacks [against the IDR]. It provides us with an experience of a floating-rate regime, but within a narrow confinement."[5] Those last few words were to prove ironic, for Indonesia was soon to experience a fully floating exchange rate regime whether it liked it or not. Hedge funds, having up until then concentrated on the baht, followed by the peso and ringgit, then focused on the rupiah. On Monday, July 21, IDR lost a stunning 7% of its value against the dollar, with USD-IDR rallying to as high as 2665, a whisker away from the top of the new band at 2682. This forced the Bank Indonesia foreign exchange desk to retaliate by selling dollars in the forward market. In addition, Bank Indonesia refrained from adding liquidity to the money market, allowing the overnight borrowing rate to spike. That week, Bank Indonesia spent around USD900 million, mostly through the forward market, to support its battered currency. While propping up the rupiah, Bank Indonesia moved to try to deal with perceived fundamental problems, notably property market over supply, issuing a ban on loans for new land acquisition.

Like the BSP, Bank Indonesia was concerned primarily with stabilizing the situation, one that had been at least partly forced on it by the devaluations of the baht, peso, and ringgit. Thus, it looked to ease interest rates as quickly as possible in order to limit the subsequent damage to the economy. In the week of

August 4, Bank Indonesia Governor Soedradjad Djiwandono invited foreign bankers in Jakarta to a meeting in which he urged them to remain calm and not to listen to rumors. Nevertheless, rumors persisted, notably that the band would be widened again.

Bank Indonesia lowered rates after the IDR calmed down briefly, only to have to hike them again when the regional turmoil spilled over once more onto the rupiah. Reports in local papers suggesting that the rupiah might weaken further or be devalued added to the rumors. And on Wednesday, August 13, the IDR fell a further 2%, briefly breaching the upper limit of the band to trade at 2684.50 despite repeated Bank Indonesia intervention. The overnight SBI rate was at 16% and yet still the wave of selling was all but irresistible. The next day, Thursday, August 14, Bank Indonesia let the rupiah go, with the bank's head of foreign exchange announcing that henceforth there would be no intervention band or conversion rate. The market had won yet another victory. On the day, the USD-IDR soared a further 5%, hitting 2800.

For the speculators who had hung in and bet on an IDR devaluation, just like the preceding devaluations of the baht, peso, and ringgit, it was yet more profit. For many Indonesian companies, however, it was a stunning blow, a shock of monumental proportions. Up until that point, they had been told or had persuaded themselves that Bank Indonesia would hold the band. When Bank Indonesia let it go, they could not believe it. On a more fundamental rather than emotional note, their fears were fully justified. Indonesia's external outstanding debt was about USD120 billion (1996), some 45% of which was corporate—and once again most of that totally unhedged against foreign exchange risk. The subsequent spike in the USD-IDR, cutting through the 3000 level like a knife through butter and then 3500, was totally driven by Indonesian corporates buying spot and forward dollars in a desperate bid to (belatedly) hedge this debt.

Bank Indonesia had had little choice in letting the rupiah go. Its reserves had already fallen around USD2.2 billion to

USD20.4 billion, and thus it had no wish to further deplete its valuable reserves in a futile exercise. This was little consolation to the Indonesian corporates, several of whom found that they were suddenly sitting on sizable foreign exchange–related losses. Bank Indonesia's reaction to this renewed wave of rupiah selling was to sharply tighten liquidity, so much so that the overnight rate soared to 42%. However, given that this dollar buying was hedge- rather than speculator-related, even this move did not immediately stop the IDR's slide in its tracks, though it did briefly attract investor interest back to the rupiah, given such high yields. Bank Indonesia also sought to introduce restrictions on the rupiah swap market, just as BNM had done, limiting transactions for foreign parties to USD5 million. This, however, was ineffective because most of the sudden increase in demand for dollars was local rather than foreign. Just the same, it was a brave try.

The Indonesian authorities were by no means giving up. Backed by a new economic crisis management team led by Finance Minister Mar'ie Muhammad and Bank Indonesia Governor Soedradjad, and including several leading and respected economists and financial officials, the Indonesian government unveiled an economic reform package on Thursday, September 4, including a ten-point plan of austerity measures, a two-step cut in the liquidity reserve requirement, and an easing of money market rates with a promise of more to come when market conditions allowed. Bank Indonesia cut the one- and three-month SBI intervention rates by 300 basis points and then on September 9 cut them by a further 200 basis points. Market reaction was initially positive and rightly so. This bold and speedy step at economic reform was just what was needed to at least put a floor under market confidence, contrasting notably with the rhetoric but lack of action by the Malaysian government on the economy (prior to the budget unveiled by Anwar, flawed as that was).

On September 15, just before the IMF and World Bank meeting in Hong Kong, Bank Indonesia again cut its one- and three-month SBI rates by a further 200 basis points to 23% and 21%, respectively. Mar'ie Muhammad said the government would reschedule up to IDR3.28 trillion in development and IDR39 trillion in infrastructure projects for fiscal year 1997–1998, in an effort to cut the current account deficit to 3% over the next two years.

At the IMF meeting, I had the chance to talk briefly with Bank Indonesia Governor Soedradjad. The head of the Indonesian central bank said that while the process of moving to a more free-floating exchange rate had been somewhat quicker than he might have wanted, it was nevertheless part of a process and a gradual trend that Bank Indonesia had been pursuing in any case:

> *We have implemented different kinds of systems. Since the end of the 70s, we have had a managed float. At the start, it was more managed than floating, and now it is more floating than managed. We have been opening up bit by bit. The widening of the band was a further step towards that, as was the move to abandon the band altogether. We do however retain the right to intervene in the market to smooth out market fluctuations and volatility and thus we would term it a managed float without band. Our long term goal is to stabilize the price towards the PPP level."*[6]

The governor said that while Bank Indonesia wanted to avoid excessive and precipitous falls in the value of the rupiah, it was the bank's policy to focus on interest rates rather than exchange rate targeting. He concluded by saying BI would continue to ease monetary policy as and when appropriate and would take appropriate and immediate measures to shore up the financial system, particularly with regard to the banking sector that was exposed, both to large amounts of unhedged dollar-denominated debt and to the property sector. "Healthy banks will be helped if they need it. Banks which face difficulties will be encouraged to merge. Those which do not merge will be liquidated."[7]

Once again, Bank Indonesia eased its monetary policy two days later when it cut the one- and three-month rates a further 200 basis points to 21% and 19% respectively. The rupiah again stabilized briefly, but then fell back as concerns continued to mount over Indonesian corporates and banks. The Malaysian rating outlook had been cut, so why not that of Indonesia? Particularly when it had considerably more debt. At the start of October, as the peso and ringgit went into meltdown, the rupiah plunged again. USD-IDR soared to as high as 3870 on October 6 amid persistent talk of rating downgrades and the potential for corporate losses, bond defaults, and banking system collapse—all such talk being exaggerated but fully understandable in the circumstances. Bank Indonesia again intervened, forcing the USD-IDR back down to 3700 on the day, but something had to be done. Two days later, Indonesia announced that it was seeking IMF assistance to bolster foreign exchange reserves and help stabilize the financial sector. While a theoretical relief, initial market reaction was muted, awaiting details. While desks waited for those details, Standard & Poor's ratings decided to cut Indonesia's foreign currency and local currency ratings, causing the rupiah to lose all it had gained on Indonesia's IMF announcement.

Subsequently, there were fears that the Indonesian government might not reach an agreement over an IMF loan package and the necessary terms and conditions, causing the IDR to fall further. Bank Indonesia then again cut the one- and three-month rates by 100 basis points and cut the overnight rate to 14% (down from the high of 42%). Finally, on October 31, an IMF-led assistance package for Indonesia was announced, totaling USD23 billion in loans (USD15 billion from the IMF, USD4.5 billion from the World Bank, and USD3.5 billion from the ADB), with a further USD10 billion pledged from individual nations, notably Singapore and Japan. In return, Indonesia pledged major financial-sector reforms, announcing the closure of sixteen banks and deregulatory moves including lifting the monopoly of the state commodities regulator, BULOG. The following Monday, to ram the point home, the Monetary Authority of Singapore (MAS) and the Bank of Japan stunned the foreign exchange market by intervening with Bank Indonesia to sell dollars for rupiah. This caused the rupiah to rally 12% and the USD-IDR exchange rate to fall back to as low as 3271. Singapore Finance Minister Richard Hu and Japanese Finance Minister Hiroshi Mitsuzuka said in statements that day that rupiah stabilization was a key part of achieving the success of the assistance package and that the Monetary Authority of Singapore and Bank of Japan stood ready to act again in the market if necessary in order to achieve stability. The U.S. added its weight to the proceedings by saying that it would send officials from the Federal Reserve and Federal Deposit Insurance Corporation to help the country restructure its financial system. That same week, on Thursday (November 6), the MAS again intervened to sell USD-IDR, confirming the action publicly.

From July 1 to mid-November, the rupiah had lost almost 20% of its value against the dollar, and at one point was down 28%. Yet this seemed exceptionally rough treatment of the authorities by the market since conventional wisdom suggested the authorities had done almost everything right, subsequent to the Thai baht's devaluation—letting the rupiah band widen and then abandoning the band to avoid losing valuable foreign exchange reserves, tightening policy to try and stabilize the currency and then gradually easing policy back, cutting the budget and promising to delay projects and government spending, and pledging more deregulation. Yet, in the end, Indonesia was forced to go to the IMF to achieve some sort of stabilization. Why? The key—yet again, a point that was made with Thailand, the Philippines, Malaysia, and finally Indonesia—was domestic corporate and bank exposure to unhedged foreign currency-denominated (usually dollar-denominated) debt. Indonesian companies by that stage had upward of USD55 billion of dollar debt, much of which was unhedged given the previous gradual band widening system where foreign exchange risk was more or less totally disregarded—the risk was predictable so there was no risk. Surprised by Bank Indonesia letting the rupiah go, they all tried to hedge, by buying dollars, at the same time. If even 50% of that debt exposure was unhedged, to hedge that portion would have required buying USD27.5 billion for rupiah.

Indonesia was not without its own economic problems as well, as noted earlier. While it had achieved 8.0% GDP growth in 1996 (who hadn't?), it had a current account deficit of 3.9% of

GDP, not yet in the danger zone (some economists look for 5% as a danger level). Fiscal policy while relatively tight had still allowed a fractional budget deficit in 1995. Meanwhile, credit growth was expanding at a rate that suggested the potential for overheating, with M2 growth of 26.0% in 1996. Lastly, export growth fell in 1996, an ASEAN-wide phenomenon admittedly, though notably Indonesian non-oil export growth fell by a third in 1996 relative to 1995. In sum, Indonesia had similar symptoms of the disease that was continuing to rage in Thailand, and that had also appeared in smaller doses in the Philippines and Malaysia. After the Thai baht devaluation, the Indonesian authorities did everything they could to stabilize the situation. But the momentum of the market by that stage, the belated realization of massive Indonesian corporate exposure to unhedged foreign currency debt, and the fragility of the banking system defeated their best efforts and forced them to seek IMF assistance. Many lessons have no doubt been learned by the Indonesian authorities during this crisis, but at least they appear ready and willing to learn.

Such was the ferocity of the attack on the ASEAN currencies that even the mighty Singapore dollar was not left unscathed, reversing a ten-year bull phase that had paralleled the rise of the yen against the dollar. Particularly in October, when the frenzy of regionwide currency selling was at its height, dollar-Sing (USD-SGD) blasted through the 1.50 level and then 1.55. Singapore's reaction was a lesson in acting *with* rather than *against* the market. Summing up the situation, Singapore Prime Minister Goh Chok Tong noted that "you cannot fight the market" and that if the market has decided that for competitive reasons the USD-SGD should trade higher, then the Singapore government was happy to accept that. Such prudent realism contrasted notably with others in the region, particularly Malaysia.

Growth in the first half of the year had slowed markedly from the heady levels of past years—to 5.8% in the fourth quarter of 1996 and 3.8% in the first quarter of 1997. Since exports of electronics and electronic components make up a substantial portion of Singapore's non-oil exports, and the latter had seen sharply lower growth in the wake of the 1996 collapse in world semiconductor prices, such realism was necessary to allow for a more competitive exchange rate for the Sing dollar. Dealers in Singapore had from as early as the end of August interpreted a new approach to the Sing dollar by the MAS, given the actual declines in Singapore non-oil exports that were experienced on a year-on-year basis in January, February, March, and May. "They did not say anything overtly, but the little they did say seemed to suggest that they were allowing the Sing dollar to weaken in order to restore trade competitiveness. A lot of people made a lot of money riding that trend [betting that the Sing dollar would subsequently fall]," said a European bank treasurer based in Singapore.[8] An excessively sharp fall in the Sing dollar would presumably be unwelcome. However, the focus is clearly on restoring a more suitable exchange rate for Singaporean manufacturers, without threatening any spike in inflationary pressures. With a current account surplus of about 13% of GDP, Singapore's economic fundamentals are the strongest in the region, although there are still structural problems that should be addressed for the continuation of long-term prosperity. The fundamentals, the changes that are occurring and the necessary steps to be taken by governments, by both Singapore and the other governments of the region, will be covered in Chapter 9.

Meanwhile, as the peso, ringgit, and rupiah were dropping, the Thai baht itself started to slide again after a temporary lull. Initially, following the baht's devaluation, Thai officials expressed the view that Thailand would not seek IMF help because this would make its situation seem like that of Mexico. The reality was that Thailand was already like Mexico. Indeed, potentially it was in worse shape and notably burdened by an overbearing false pride and sense of "face" that had already had major (negative) economic consequences. To replace Amnuay as finance minister, Prime Minister Chavalit had chosen Thanong Bidaya, the president of the Thai Military Bank, after asking four people if they wanted the job and being rejected four times. A Japanese-trained professional manager, Thanong was hectically busy from the very start. Bank of Thailand Governor Rerngchai

Marakanond was replaced by his deputy, Chaiyawat Wibul-swasdi. Then three finance companies were shut down. Pressure mounted for Thailand to accept IMF help, but the Thai government resisted to the last. Going cap in hand to the IMF would be an unacceptable loss of face, in theory. In practice, there was no option if Thailand wanted to avoid a systemwide collapse and major social tensions, including the potential for a military coup to restore order. Not that the army wanted to take to the streets, because many senior Thai military officials viewed the Thai financial situation with justifiable horror and wanted no part of it whatsoever. However, if the situation reached a stage where it looked as if the government could no longer control the country and the financial system appeared on the verge of collapse, the army may have taken over on the simple basis that if it didn't, the country might completely fall apart.

As for the IMF, it was getting increasingly irate with the Thai government. For over a year, the IMF had been urging Thailand to sort out its fundamental problems, notably its current account deficit. Now, here was Thailand on the verge of collapse, because it had not taken IMF advice, and it was dithering about whether to ask for IMF help or not. Toward the end of July, Thanong tried one last face-saving measure. He flew to Tokyo to speak with the Japanese Ministry of Finance and the Bank of Japan. The message from Tokyo was polite but firm: Don't ask us to bail you out and we will not refuse. Japan would help Thailand but only as part of an IMF package of assistance. Thanong and the Ministry of Finance described the meeting as positive, but in reality Thanong went home empty-handed. He had no choice but to accept IMF help, however bitter that realization. The immediate baht reaction was positive, though such gains were quickly wiped out on fears that the Thai government would bicker with the IMF over terms—as indeed it did subsequently for several months.

Despite that, on August 5, the IMF unveiled the rough outlines of the Thailand bailout package and on August 11 announced a package totaling about USD17.2 billion from the IMF and Asian-contributing countries. This included USD4 billion from the IMF itself, USD4 billion from Japan's EXIM (Export-Import) Bank, USD1 billion each from Singapore, Australia, Malaysia, China, and Hong Kong, USD500 million each from Indonesia, Korea, and Brunei, USD1.5 billion from the World Bank, USD1.2 billion from the ADB, and USD1.1 billion from the Bank of International Settlements. Included with the loans were IMF-set macroeconomic targets for Thailand and agreed (grudgingly) measures to deal with the various fundamental problems. Among the macro targets, the IMF set out that the Bank of Thailand's foreign exchange reserves must be a minimum of 3.5 months of imports, or around USD25 billion for 1997. In addition, the current account deficit must be cut from 8% of GDP in 1996 to 5% in 1997 and 3% in 1998. GDP growth was to be maintained at 3–4% for the 1997–1998 period (this will be impossible to maintain) and inflation limited to 8–9% (also unlikely). Finally, fiscal and monetary disciplines were to be maintained by rebalancing the state budget, and achieving a budget surplus of GDP of 1%. As for the measures needed, Thailand would have to raise VAT to 10% from 7% on August 16, cut the THB980 billion budget by THB59 billion (the IMF originally asked for THB100 billion), scrap subsidies for utility tariffs and state enterprises, maintain wage restraint, boost privatization, further rationalize the banking and finance company sectors, and deregulate further by allowing foreign investors increased ownership of local Thai banks.

This was tough medicine, but much needed given the mess the Thai authorities had allowed the economy and the financial sector to get into. One question remained: While the USD17.2 billion in loans was extremely positive in shoring up Thailand, what exactly was the total size of Thai bad loans within the financial sector and what was the size of the Bank of Thailand's reserves if one included the forward contracts the bank sold to defend the baht before the devaluation? The Bank of Thailand itself provided an answer to the second part of that question when it stunned the market by announcing that it had some USD23.4 billion in outstanding forward sales of dollars on its book, maturing within the next year, thereby absorbing much of its USD30.4 billion reserves as of the end of July. In other words, the Bank of Thailand desk had potentially expended over two-thirds of its reserves in its desperate attempt to stop the devaluation of the baht.

"In effect, the Bank of Thailand was the Nick Leeson of central banks. Bank officials threw good money after bad, trying to take on the market and it didn't work. It must have been pretty clear to them that they were not going to succeed before the 20 billion mark yet they did it anyway," described one senior dealer for a European bank in Hong Kong.[9]

More Thai official money might have to be found, but from where and from whom? Meanwhile, the Thai political system continued to quarrel over the IMF terms and conditions demanded in return for the loans—so, like Nero, Thailand fiddled even as it burned. While Thai politicians continued to attempt to stall the much needed budget cuts, anxious about the social reaction to such austerity, there was also talk that the Bank of Thailand was on the warpath. Dealers were saying that they had heard the bank had a "blacklist" of foreign banks that had attacked the baht and would subsequently impose sanctions against those it deemed as being responsible for the baht's demise. The Bank of Thailand denied the existence of such a blacklist, though two foreign investment banks were subsequently searched by Thai authorities. While the search for a scapegoat was more obvious in Malaysia, it was also prevalent in Thailand.

In addition, a new constitution was proposed for Thailand. Initially, the ruling government led by Chavalit strongly opposed this. However, realizing such opposition would likely bring down the government itself, it gave its grudging support. Meanwhile, Thai markets were once again rocked by the rating agencies. Moody's said it was again placing Thailand's long-term foreign currency debt rating under review for possible downgrade, while Standard & Poor's Ratings cut Thailand's long-term foreign currency rating and also cut its outlook to negative. The Thai parliament passed the constitution, a positive if somewhat belated move, for the political system. However, in early

October, the local Thai press reported that Finance Minister Thanong had submitted his resignation, frustrated beyond measure at internal government opposition to budget spending cuts. Officials denied the reports, but suspicions persisted, and rightly so, for on October 20 Thanong finally gave up. When Chavalit had reversed his proposed oil tax hike, which had been approved the week before, Thanong had had enough. The baht was hurt not only by Thanong's individual resignation but also by the confirmation that the Thai government remained reluctant to implement the full series of measures stipulated by the IMF. The USD-THB soared to a new high of 38.10. Two days later, thousands of Thai citizens marched in the streets of Bangkok to protest against government infighting and indecision amid the economic crisis that the country faced. To follow Thanong's resignation, all forty-eight cabinet ministers also resigned, causing the USD-THB to soar to 39.95.

The new finance minister, the third to be appointed in Chavalit's ten-month term as prime minister, was Kosit Panpiemrat, the executive director of the Bangkok Bank and former agricultural minister. At fifty-four, he was a respectable technocrat without any known affiliation to political parties. Holding a master's of economics from the University of Maryland in the U.S., he insisted that he would not tolerate political interference. Again, this was fine in theory, but the political system itself might disagree. Still, there was good news to come. On November 4, Chavalit announced that he would resign as prime minister, amid declining public and market confidence in his government. Subsequently, Chuan Leepkai, head of the Democrat opposition party, was to take over as prime minister. While being responsible for the BIBF which resulted in Thailand's overdependence on dollar-denominated debt, his government from 1992 to 1995 had at least pushed for reform. Thus there was the consequent hope that, aided by yet another cabinet reshuffle, his new government would be equally forthcoming with significant measures, aimed at turning around both the economy and the financial system.

To review the situation from July 2 to early November, Thailand let the baht float and then did its level best to ignore reality, much as it had done up until the flotation. How was this possible? Thailand's technocracy had long been renowned for its professionalism and impartiality. However, the political system, which focused on a dynamic equilibrium between power in the office of the prime minister and that of the separate ministries, resulted in factionalism within the technocrats. This in turn diverted the technocracy from its basic task of steering the economy. By early 1997, Thailand was a very sick patient indeed, a lame animal all too vulnerable to attack. The IMF surveillance system that the Washington-based institution had set up had worked in part. The IMF notified Thailand several times of the need to boost economic fundamentals. Yet, despite that, Thailand ignored the advice. Thai government officials who seek scapegoats have in reality no one but themselves to blame. They allowed the mess to develop in the first place.

Stage 2—North Asia

While the financial market typhoon raged and seethed in the currencies of the ASEAN, in Southeast Asia, those of North Asia also felt its blast, notably in South Korea. While Korea was not burdened with the real estate worries that so plagued Thailand and to a certain extent Malaysia and Indonesia, it was most assuredly weighed by debt concerns. Devastated by the Korean War of 1950–1953, it had risen from the ashes to become a major world exporter of manufactured goods, competing directly with such mature economies as Japan's. Yet, in order to achieve that, it had kept monetary policy artificially low and directed lending, rather than let market forces of supply and demand direct credit growth. The result was an impressive exporter base but a balance sheet disaster, with companies and the economy as a whole weighed down by massive gearing levels. Low rates generally encourage borrowing as opposed to saving, and indeed this was the case with Korea, though to be sure

Korea equally took governmental measures to sharply boost the savings rate. Nevertheless, dependency on borrowing, and particularly foreign currency–denominated borrowing, was to prove an Achilles' heel for the economy. Korea had been acquiring other bad habits as well, notably in its current account, where the deficit reached some 4.8% of GDP in 1996. As noted previously, current account deficits are not of themselves sell signals; however, they are usually driven by sentiment—and thus equally vulnerable to a sharp reversal in sentiment.

Korean exporters had been ecstatic when the USD-JPY fell during 1993–1995, as this gave them a huge competitive advantage over Japan, their closest competitor. However, when the USD-JPY started to rebound in April 1995 and then continued higher in 1996 and early 1997, they felt their margins get hit hard. The result was widening trade and current account deficits, the only remedy for which was a fall in the Korean won to compensate for the decline in the yen, in order to reassert Korean trade competitiveness. In late 1996 and through May 1997, this did indeed occur, with the won gradually weakening against the dollar, if not against the yen. When, in May 1997, the USD-JPY collapsed from a high of 127.47 to a low of 110.55, it was a godsend—the won thus collapsing against the yen. As a result, Korean exports started to pick up again after seeing growth of only 4.1% in 1996, as opposed to 31.5% in 1995. In May itself, Korean export growth was 3.6% Y/Y, followed by 12.8% in June, 16.4% in July, and 17.8% in August. During May and June, the Bank of Korea intervened several times to prevent actual appreciation of the won against the dollar. Yet, persistently high debt levels remained the scourge of an otherwise prosperous economy. On July 13, following the earlier bankruptcy of the Hanbo Steel Group, creditor banks announced they would grant emergency support to help the Kia Group, Korea's eighth largest chaebol and parent of Kia Motors, avoid bankruptcy itself. Given the bank sector's exposure to Kia and other debt-ridden conglomerates, Standard & Poor's Ratings and Moody's placed several Korean bank ratings on negative outlook ten days later.

The result was increased credit risk within the Korean financial system as a whole and thus rising market rates and bond yields to compensate. Kia defaulted on some KRW280 billion of debts in mid-July and was subsequently seeking bankruptcy protection before the Korean government announced that it would seek full court receivership for the group (October 22). Thus effectively it nationalized the financially troubled automaker, with the state-run Korean Development Bank converting its loans into the largest equity stake. Kia's gearing ratio of around 520% was extraordinary by Western corporate standards but not by those prevailing in Korea. Much of this debt burden was in short-term paper and thus susceptible to a rise in short-term rates given the combination of tighter liquidity and investment aversion to increased risk as well as closer maturity dates. That September, Jinro, Korea's largest liquor group and nineteenth largest chaebol became the third largest Korean firm to go bankrupt. In addition, the Bank of Korea said it would lend KRW1 trillion to Korea First Bank and the government would boost its capital with a purchase of KRW600 billion in Korea First stock. Looking at the economy as a whole, bad loans hurt the merchant banks, which then called in short-term loans, creating a vicious circle of liquidity (illiquidity).

In addition to the debt problems, Korea continued to record current account deficits month after month. While these were gradually falling in nominal terms, by July the market was focusing on any current account deficit in Asia. With July seeing a deficit of USD978 million, followed by USD714 million in August, compared with only USD242 million in June, this was a further concern—one that was felt even in the overregulated Korean foreign exchange market, with the won reversing its previous strength. The decline gradually became a slide as the combination of debt and current account concerns began to build, to the extent that the USD-KRW managed to breach the 900 level. Into October, amid general Asian bond market woes, Korean corporate bond spreads relative to the U.S. Treasury continued to widen. Then on October 24, Standard & Poor's Ratings downgraded both Korea's long-term foreign currency rating, from AA– to A+, and also its short-term rating, reflecting the escalating cost of supporting ailing businesses. This rating move affected the credit ratings of such state-affiliated companies as Korea Development Bank, KEXIM Bank, Kepco, and Korea Telecom. Moody's followed suit four days later, also cutting Korea's credit ratings. The USD-KRW continued to soar higher, breaching 920, then 950, despite repeated interventions by the Bank of Korea to sell dollars. By that stage, a further negative in regard to the won was that the yen had begun to weaken again, thus hitting Korean exporters once more in relative competitiveness terms. With the exporters having no incentive to immediately convert dollar receivables to won, while importers had every incentive to buy dollars just in case they had to buy dollars at a more expensive rate in subsequent sessions, commercial activity alone would have driven the USD-KRW higher. The Bank of Korea itself had said that some USD67 billion of USD115 billion in outstanding external debt was to mature in a year or less, a reminder of corporate Korea's propensity to borrow short term. With banks trimming credit lines across the board because of the generally more adverse liquidity conditions, this hurt Korea Inc.'s ability pay back such debt—and reduced the willingness of the banks to roll over or refinance the credits.

Such was the buildup in market concern over Korea that various rumors circulated in early November that Korea might have to turn to the IMF for assistance—which both Korea and the IMF denied the need for—and that the Bank of Korea was running out of reserves and was preparing to devalue the KRW. At the time, the bank had reserves of around USD30.5 billion, though it also had an unknown amount of forward contract commitments. Dealers speculated that this could equate to around USD10 billion, leaving only USD20 billion reserves left. With no Korean won forward market available, offshore parties, including proprietary desks and hedge funds, started to attack the won via the nondeliverable forward market. This was the same market that the BSP of the Philippines had tried to close out from foreign speculators. The USD-KRW spot hit a high of 990.90 on November 10, but the one-year NDF USD-KRW hit an equivalent value of 1500 at one point. Subsequently, the Korean Ministry of Finance and the Bank of Korea sought to explain to the market and to media sources that Korea could fully meet its debt obligations, that the current account deficit was shrinking and would likely fall to around 3% of GDP in 1997, and finally that its approach to liberalization of markets was gradual, thus restraining speculative forces from attacking the economy. While the Korean economy is a marvel relative to its restart in 1953, and all due credit should be paid to this, its debt burden remains a major concern despite these assurances, as does Korean exporter price sensitivity. It is not enough merely to seek a cheaper currency to export your way out of trouble as Korea has sought to do for the past decade or more. Korean companies have to go further up the line in terms of added value, as their Japanese counterparts have assuredly done.

With the ASEAN currencies having been swept away and the Korean won also dragged down, it was not long before the Taiwan dollar also felt the full force of the prevailing market turmoil. The pace of the decline in the Korean won and the consequent slide in the Korean stock market spilled over into the Taiwan asset markets. This in turn hit the Taiwan dollar (TWD) and caused money market rates to spike. For 2½ months, the response of the Central Bank of China (the Taiwanese central bank) to this was unequivocal. The USD-TWD rate would be capped, first to around the 28.55–60 area and then to 28.727. However, with the ASEAN currencies devaluing some 25% on average against the dollar and the Korean won falling over 10% from July 1, Taiwan's trade competitiveness was getting measurably hit. Not that exports were not doing well. In September, they were recorded at about USD10.864 billion, up 3.6% Y/Y, the seventh straight month that they had been over USD10 billion. However, import growth was by that time sharply outstripping exports. Exporters were consequently in no hurry to convert dollars to Taiwan dollars, while importers were anxious to buy U.S. dollars immediately.

Meanwhile, the Taiwan stock market continued to tank, reflective of the high interest rate environment needed to protect the currency. For 2½ months, the Central Bank of China (CBC) held the line. Eventually, however, the costs of holding that line became too much, even for the CBC, which in May had some USD90.01 billion in foreign exchange reserves, the third largest in reserves. Having spent about USD5 billion of that by the end of September, the CBC decided that enough was enough. The Taiwan benchmark stock index had plummeted about 25% in just two months. In a two-pronged strategy, it cut the reserve requirement in mid-October by 1.5 percentage points, in order to ease liquidity constriction. Then on Saturday, October 18 (when Taiwan markets are still open), it announced it was no longer defending the USD-TWD rate. The USD-TWD immediately soared higher. The Taiwan dollar lost 3.3% on the day, trading as high as 29.76, and then hit 30.45 on the following Monday. The stock market initially panicked on the news, but later stabilized as the Taiwan authorities eased margin buying ratios from 50% to 40% and urged investors to be patient, saying there was no fundamental reason for capital flight.

Stage 3 — Hong Kong

Yet it was the move to let the Taiwan dollar float freely, completely reversing a strongly held and bitterly defended policy, that drew the attention of speculators to Hong Kong, rather than the activity in the Taiwan stock market. At the time, few market players had believed that the CBC would give in to market forces. When it finally did, this was almost as cataclysmic an event as the initial Thai baht flotation on July 2. For if the CBC, with its USD90 billion in reserves, could be defeated, then so too could Hong Kong—at least in theory. Speculators throughout the U.S. and in Europe began to pay very close attention to the Hong Kong dollar and the Hong Kong asset markets. On August 7, the benchmark stock index in Hong Kong, the Hang Seng, had reached a peak of 16,673, shrugging off the massive declines in the stock markets of the ASEAN, Korea, and subsequently Taiwan. Confidence was sky high. The "handover" from Great Britain to the People's Republic of China had been achieved with the maximum of world publicity—celebrated long into the night by parties all across Hong Kong—but with the minimum of fundamental change or concern. Hong Kong fundamentals were strong, and several U.S. banks were forecasting 20,000 for the Hang Seng by or even before year-end. Sadly, it was not to be. For while Hong Kong growth was sturdy (at 4.6% in 1996) and the newly proclaimed Special Administrative Region had a fractional current account deficit of 0.1% of GDP, combined with a budget surplus, it too had an Achilles' heel—property.

Like Thailand, Hong Kong had experienced a property boom, with some luxury residential houses actually doubling in price in the first six months of 1997. Real incomes, as a result of wages, together with increased asset portfolios due to rising stock and property prices, were rising sharply, leading to ever-increasing demand. Yet, unlike Thailand, Hong Kong strictly limited the supply of property sold to the market—a property developers' dream in many ways. By the summer of 1997, however, there was anecdotal evidence that, with both commercial and residential prices, some areas of Hong Kong had actually become more expensive than Tokyo. Further anecdotes suggested that following the handover, tourism to Hong Kong had fallen sharply, particularly from Japan. In the late 1980s, and early 1990s, many Japanese tourists had seen Hong Kong retail prices as extremely cheap relative to their own in terms of the yen, and thus had regularly taken weekend trips to the territory. By 1997, Hong Kong, boosted by the rise in pre-handover consumer demand, was no longer so cheap. Economists also fretted that Hong Kong exports would be hit in relative competitiveness terms by the devaluations of the ASEAN currencies, and then the currencies of South Korea and Taiwan. In sum, asset prices had to come down or the Hong Kong dollar also had to devalue, which meant the Hong Kong dollar peg had to go.

In technical terms, the Hong Kong dollar is not linked to the U.S. dollar with a typical peg so much as a currency board. It has been this way since October 1983 when the peg—for want of a better word—was fixed at HKD7.8 to the USD. The link is designed to allow Hong Kong interest rates to automatically adjust to currency pressures via changes in domestic money supply, whereby selling of Hong Kong dollars automatically results in a decrease in the Hong Kong dollar money supply. This in turn pushes up interest rates, which causes investors to buy back into the Hong Kong dollar once they reach a sufficient risk premium. Hong Kong's manager of the currency board—erroneously though understandably called Hong Kong's central bank—is the Hong Kong Monetary Authority. Known as the HKMA, it guarantees to exchange HKD7.8 for each U.S. dollar (and vice versa), allowing interest rates (and thus asset prices) to bear the brunt of any shock to or volatility in the Hong Kong financial system.

Pressures had started to mount as soon as mid-August, amid the general regional turbulence, when it was announced that the HKMA had earlier sold USD1 billion into the market the previous month in order to counter speculative pressure. Such pressures rose considerably after the Taiwan dollar was let go on October 17 and then the following Monday, on October 20. That day, as the Taiwan dollar continued to fall, unsupported by the Taiwan authorities, and the Taiwan stock market also fell, the Hang Seng came under a major wave of selling, losing some 630 points on the day. On Tuesday, it lost 568 points and then on Wednesday 765 points, as money market rates started to edge higher in reaction to the selling in the stock market and weakness in the Hong Kong dollar itself against the U.S. dollar. That Tuesday evening, I was in the office late (writing this book, in fact) and was phoned by a senior trader at a prestigious U.S. investment bank in New York, who wanted a rundown on the Hong Kong economy and the Hong Kong dollar's fundamentals. "Basically, tell me why Hong Kong is not Thailand," he demanded.[10] Such was the growing interest, worldwide, in the affairs of the Hong Kong dollar and particularly in the strength— or lack thereof—in its currency. The activity of speculators was already being seen in the Hong Kong dollar forward market, where the forward points were starting to twitch, shifting out "to the right" (one adds the forward points to the spot to get the agreed rate for an agreed future date of settlement). With the DJIA in the U.S. and the Japanese Nikkei 225 also starting to tremble, Thursday's session for the Hong Kong stock market was a scary ride. For stock market investors, it was a white-knuckle, screaming nightmare. Within just a few hours of the opening, the Hang Seng had fallen a stunning 14.6%, or 1699.3 points. In September, the Hong Kong assets had pulled back as global fund managers sought to take a profit on their holdings in the liquid Hong Kong markets, frequently unable to do so in some of the less liquid ASEAN markets. That day, however, there was real fear in the air as volume, both in "cash" stocks and in Hang Seng futures, soared. Hedge funds were attacking in force, going short both against the Hang Seng and against the Hong Kong dollar via the forwards. Seeing their returns disappear before their eyes, retail and institutional investors ran for cover by dumping their stocks on the market.

More than anywhere else in the world, with the possible exception of China's Shenzhen and Shanghai exchanges, where people have died in the crush to get stock certificates, the Hong Kong stock market is a punters' market, a casino where retail investors—you and me—take their chances. Granted, there are solid fundamentals to be concerned with, and many retail investors watch those closely. But such are the participation levels of ordinary working men and women in Hong Kong in the stock market that overshooting, in either direction, is bound to happen, whatever the activity of the mutual or pension funds. As I said in my introduction, the average taxi driver will have a position in the stock market; so will the window cleaner, bartender, truck driver, and secretary. Indeed, a person I know, not satisfied with the risk in the stock market, was taking leveraged speculative positions in the foreign exchange market in the dollar-mark involving several million dollars. If there is a spirit of no risk, no reward in places such as New York, then such a spirit is epitomized here. If you do not take part, you are the exception.

That Thursday, people from all walks of life stared up in horror at the stock monitors of bank branches, or looked in shock at their pocket price trackers, all across Hong Kong, as billions were wiped off the value of their shares. Talk of ruin was in the air, some individual investors suffering paper losses of several hundred million Hong Kong dollars that day. By the end of the session, the Hang Seng had come back off a low of 9,938.50 to close at 10.426.30; yet this was still the largest one-day fall in unit terms in the exchange's history, some 1,211.47 points. What had caused this? The speculators, using leverage of up to 30 to 1, had launched a massive attack against the Hong Kong dollar peg, selling Hong Kong dollar forwards and also selling thousands of Hang Seng futures contracts. This prompted the HKMA to react immediately by refusing to add liquidity to the money market and instead draining liquidity to the extent that the overnight borrowing rate screamed to as high as 300%. In addition, the HKMA foreign exchange desk sold dollars to the market for Hong Kong dollars. There was even talk of the desk spending some USD10 billion, out of its total reserves of USD88.1 billion that week alone, although such a figure seems vastly inflated (and most likely put out by speculators themselves). The combination of soaring interest rates and foreign exchange intervention was a double blow for speculators, many of whom lost heavily in the subsequent panic to buy back the Hong Kong dollars they had sold. The USD-HKD collapsed from its usual rate of around 7.7450/90, falling as low as 7.5000 on the day before stabilizing. Speculators had been smashed—for the time being. The HKMA desk had tasted blood. The next day, that Friday, it allowed the overnight rate to fall back, initially to 100% and then to 16% by the close. There was no one left to take advantage of this. They had all been hammered the previous day.

Speculators had tested the resolve of the HKMA, and the HKMA had responded unequivocally. The peg would be held, whatever the cost. If asset prices had to fall, then they would fall. Such a correction was probably warranted in any case, given the extended gains during the first half of the year. Hong Kong Financial Secretary Donald Tsang (wearing his trademark bow tie) was adamant that day and subsequently that the peg would be held and speculators would be burned if they attacked it. "Let me repeat, we have no intention of changing our exchange rate system or our dollar link," he said.[11]

Yet, despite this victory, there was a very real cost to bear, as well the HKMA knew. Hong Kong banks raised their prime lending rates by 75 basis points to 9.50%. As a result, even when the domestic markets had subsided somewhat the following week (after the Hang Seng had to live through a 554-point plunge in the DJIA), the premium in the Hong Kong curve to the U.S. was still around 600 basis points. This was excellent news for people looking to put their money in Hong Kong dollar time deposits—as many did—but bad news for the domestic economy as it of necessity meant a slowdown in 1998. The HKMA was resigned to that. It was a price that had to be paid. The peg had provided the base for stability and strong growth for more than a decade. To let it go would be a financial disaster, worse than Thailand, given the parity between USD and HKD assets in the system. The banking system itself would explode, interest rates would rise (skyrocket) rather than fall, and the stock market would go into meltdown. There were absolutely no benefits to the HKMA letting the peg go, and every reason to keep it for the long-term health of the economy. The peg would stay, whatever the short-term cost to the economy or to the population. And it is the population itself, as HKMA Chief Executive Joseph Yam has said on many occasions, that is the fundamental strength of the peg. On Thursday, October 23, when the Hong Kong dollar came under such violent attack and the Hang Seng was smashed, the reaction of the population was not to change their savings into U.S. dollars, but rather to stay in Hong Kong dollars and seek the higher savings rate through time deposits. Local confidence is a key factor in maintaining the peg and that day it held rock solid. The market tested Hong Kong as a whole, and no doubt will do so again, but Hong Kong is a different story to the ASEAN, with different fundamentals. Besides, the Hong Kong economy is being increasingly integrated into that of mainland China, providing its parent with the necessary international financial center to service that country's massive financing needs.

In sum, the ASEAN currencies fell like dominos after the baht's devaluation, the cost of supporting them too high, each falling prey to the competitive devaluations of the others. Each currency and country had their own unique fundamental problems, but the key common theme of Thailand, Indonesia, the Philippines, and Malaysia was overreliance on external finance relative to their institutional infrastructures and huge levels of unhedged corporate debt. Singapore let its dollar float to reestablish trade competitiveness in the midst of devaluations against it; while Korea was additionally loaded down with massive total debts, in addition to its current account deficit; and Taiwan was burdened by falling domestic asset prices and strong demand from Taiwan importers for dollars. Hong Kong stood alone, undefeated, yet also bearing a cost of battle. All will have to restructure in this new, and significantly more uncertain, environment. As we shall see in the next chapter, it is all too evident that some are willing to do so while others are decidedly not.

7

The Aftermath — Recrimination

HAVING SEEN BILLIONS wiped off the value of their stock markets, having also lost billions in foreign exchange reserves trying in vain to defend the currencies, and seeing prospects for their most ambitious projects in tatters and growth forecasts for their countries scaled back by banks, Asian authorities could have been forgiven—briefly—for being a touch angry. Those who had been on the front line, the central bankers, for the most part kept their mouths shut. For others, the pain and the humiliation were too much to bear, resulting in vitriolic comments from government officials in Indonesia, Malaysia, the Philippines, and Thailand itself.

Recrimination flowed, albeit sparingly, considering the results and cost of the devaluations on their countries. The embodiment of that recrimination, of blaming others, was Dr. Mahathir Mohammed himself. His remarks at the IMF meeting, mentioned in the Introduction to this book, were perhaps the most notable, given the venue and the occasion, but they were most certainly neither the first nor the last such remarks he would make—nor even the most notorious. Well before the conference in Hong Kong, the Malaysian prime minister had made public his thoughts regarding the evils of speculation, mentioning U.S. fund manager George Soros repeatedly by name and blaming him for the ringgit's fall. Indeed, for a brief time, it had seemed possible that Mahathir and Soros might meet in Hong Kong to discuss these "conflicting views." However Mahathir quickly scotched this idea, saying that he had no desire to meet Soros.

On September 8, well before the IMF meeting took place, Mahathir called for the outlawing of currency manipulation. This was said in relatively general terms, thus no doubt causing alarm but not outright investor panic. At the IMF and subsequently, Dr. Mahathir would become much more specific. Following his remarks on Saturday, September 20, he gave an interview with the *South China Morning Post,* a Hong Kong newspaper, which appeared on Sunday. In it, he said that foreign exchange trade for purposes other than for financing trade was not only immoral but unnecessary and that consequently it should be banned in Malaysia. He stated that "we have decided that continued speculation cannot go on because there is no benefit to us. Why should we allow something which is damaging to us? Currency trading, so far as we are concerned, will be limited to financing trade."[1]

Deputy Prime Minister and Finance Minister Anwar Ibrahim tried to soothe the market's understandable nerves, saying that there were no plans for Malaysia to change its existing regulations on foreign exchange trading and that the country was committed to open markets and financial liberalization. On the Monday after the initial comments from Mahathir and the fierce rejoinder from Soros, branding Mahathir a "menace to his country," Anwar attempted to bring an end to what had become a public mud-slinging match, saying "I think the exchange is now equal. What we have to do now is deal with the problem. Dr. Mahathir has his supporters and Mr. Soros also has his own sympathizers." He emphasized that there was no point in extending the debate and that his job was to stabilize the Malaysian economy.[2] Initially, however, dealers and investors alike were not in the least comforted, seemingly selling everything they had. And Mahathir had by no means finished yet. The Malaysian prime minister subsequently went on a visit to Latin America. It is not known whether he learned useful lessons from Mexico in particular and other LATAM countries in general on how they dealt with the Mexican currency crisis, but what became clear was that he was intent on continuing to hammer away at his message that evil "speculators"—foreign ones, naturally—were responsible for the market turbulence and consequent economic instability that Malaysia was experiencing.

Malaysia, so the message went, was a poor, developing nation, being punished by interests in the developed West for having the temerity to try to better itself. There were rich, scavenging parties within the West who wanted to see developing nations like Malaysia kept low and enslaved to the West and they would do anything to ensure this. Furthermore, while there were still "good" Western investors who bought into Malaysia for the long term—thus aiding in the prosperity of the country—all Western investors had not been there to help in the defense of the Malaysian ringgit and asset markets when they had been needed. There was thus a sense that Malaysia had been "betrayed" by these said investors. This ignored the converse argument, naturally, that the Malaysian government might have equally betrayed the interests of long-term Western investors. In addition, it revealed a startling naïveté: Portfolio investment can benefit nations by infusing much-needed capital, but that is not its prime purpose, which is, after all, to make money. Pure and simple. Amazingly, Mahathir would go even further, almost predicting ringgit weakness. On Monday, September 28, he said that the following day in a speech in Santiago, Chile, he would "say nasty things" about the ringgit, adding, "We are being punished for speaking freely. We are not supposed to speak freely."[3] The result was entirely predictable, although the extent of the ringgit's subsequent collapse must have surprised even the most gloomy of forecasters, with the USD-MYR breaching 3.20 and hitting the highest level since the initial flotation of the ringgit in 1973. To the cynical, it seemed Mahathir was deliberately trying to debase his own currency. Indeed, given the fact Mahathir, whatever his faults, has a fierce intellect and has been directly responsible for much of the economic good that has occurred in Malaysia, there seems no realistic alternative to this view. To suggest otherwise is to say he had no idea what he was doing or did not care.

Whatever his realization or motives, the Malaysian prime minister continued to lash out in ever-more strident tones, accusing the "great powers" of deliberately pressing "poor" Asian countries to open up and deregulate only to then plunder them by forcing their currencies to devalue in order to eliminate them as competitive threats. Western speculators had been responsible for wiping out billions of dollars' (and an increasing amount of ringgit) worth of wealth within the Malaysian economy solely for the purpose of enriching themselves. By mid-October, the comments had become even more inflammatory. The enemy was no longer an amorphous West, nor more specifically the hedge funds, but the Jews. The suggestion was made that the devaluation of the ASEAN currencies was possibly the result of a Jewish plot to destabilize Muslim nations including Malaysia and Indonesia. Predictably, the U.S. reacted angrily, describing the suggestion as outrageous and deeply damaging to Mahathir's country. Finally, at a meeting of fifteen developing nations in Kuala Lumpur, Mahathir used the opportunity to warn against such countries lowering trade barriers to the West and thus making themselves unnecessarily vulnerable to speculation, discrimination, manipulation, and all such evils. Mahathir was still planning dire retribution for speculators in mid-November, though he refused to give details. Eventually, however, the markets wearied of such rhetoric, no longer reacting—or at least not so much—to the vitriol of the defeated, but instead looking forward to the economic consequences of the devaluations.

While the stream of remarks by Dr. Mahathir Mohammed were perhaps the most inflammatory in their execution, he was by no means alone in either feeling or voicing the sentiment that external parties were solely to blame for the woes that had befallen ASEAN. In Indonesia, Thailand, and even the Philippines, there were those who sought revenge—though they did not have the moral courage to call it that. In Thailand, there was talk, as mentioned previously, that the Bank of Thailand was keeping a list of suspected foreign banks that had speculated against the Thai baht, and that would subsequently be banned from taking part in forthcoming Thai privatizations or underwriting Thai corporate or sovereign bonds. The Bank of Thailand denied the existence of such a list; however, the foreign banking community in Bangkok remains relatively unreassured, awaiting developments warily. Certainly, the investigation by financial and police authorities of ABN-Amro and Capital Nomura in Bangkok on the premise that these two institutions were spreading rumors that the Bank of Thailand was going to shut down several small Thai banks—the allegations having been found to be totally baseless—did nothing to improve confidence.

In Indonesia, matters took on a somewhat more final note, following the forced floatation of the rupiah, when the Indonesian justice minister mused that currency speculators could face subversion charges if their activities were found to be destabilizing or damaging to the economy and that the ultimate penalty for subversion, whether political or economic, was death. While alarming, and not representative in general of the approach taken by the Indonesian authorities toward dealing with the crisis, it was not an isolated incident either. At around the same time, the Muslim-oriented newspaper *Republika* published a public service announcement featuring a Westerner (presumably a dastardly Western currency speculator) wearing a terrorist mask and headdress made of 100 dollar U.S. bills—the headdress resembling a kaffiyeh, making this somewhat ironic—questioning, "Are you a terrorist of this country?" and exhorting Indonesians everywhere to "Defend the Rupiah, defend the nation." Even in the Philippines, where the authorities, led by BSP Governor Singson and Finance Secretary de Ocampo, had been eminently realistic in their dealings with the markets despite the unpleasant, forced devaluation of the peso, President Fidel Ramos was heard to utter that foreign speculators were clearly responsible. In Taiwan also, there were efforts to find scapegoats, with the authorities investigating whether foreign brokerages and banks had been speculating against the Taiwan dollar and/or asset markets.

The effort to seek external reasons for the calamities that befell the region from July to October reflected not only the understandable political desire to find convenient scapegoats but also the deep sense of injustice felt by many Asian governments, seeing much of their effort over the past years going up in smoke. While Mahathir talked of speculators wiping out a third of Malaysia's wealth overnight, and however exaggerated this might be, someone clearly had to be blamed. The logic, even to sincere believers, was eminently attractive. Overall, it was better to blame offshore parties immediately than to allow the thought to take hold among the domestic populace that mistakes by the government had in fact been responsible. The example of Thailand, where social tensions were already growing as a result of the economic hardship that the country was facing and the thousands of people who had taken to the streets in protest at perceived vacillation by the government, reflected the crystal clear message of the political dangers inherent in the economic and market crisis in the region.

To be fair, Western commentators who single out Asia in general or the ASEAN more specifically for seeking financial scapegoats and talking about retribution have either short or convenient memories themselves. After all, it was not that long ago that so-called developed nations were doing exactly the same thing and in a language that was not too dissimilar.

Following the sterling's ejection from the ERM in September 1992, the United Kingdom government's first public reaction was to blame the German central bank for either not coming to the aid of the United Kingdom in defending the ERM parity or in fact deliberately seeking its ejection. There was talk that the Bank of England was drawing up a list of banks that had played a part in speculating against the sterling—a ridiculous measure given that the whole market had been selling sterling and the Bank of England had effectively been the only buyer. Equally, after the forced widening of the ERM bands to 15% on August 1, 1993, the hysterical reaction by officials within the French and German governments, lambasting the implied devaluation of the ERM currencies as the result of nefarious activities by heinous Anglo-Saxon speculators—presumably the German officials, simultaneously forgetting their own ethnic origins—would have made some of the comments by Dr. Mahathir seem shy and retiring by comparison. Europe's best and brightest didn't only talk either. Some of them, like the Danish National Bank, the Bank of France, and others, sought to punish those who had dared go against their precious plans for currency union by keeping interest rates at punitive levels subsequent to the band widening—in the process, hurting the "innocent" along with the "guilty." Unlike in the U.S., where the Federal Reserve's independent status is explicitly aimed at being the guardian of financial stability as well as being the creator of sound macroeconomic management in tandem with the Department of Treasury, many European central banks, while publicly independent for the purpose of achieving the Maastricht criteria, in practice act as conduits for deliberate, interventionist policies, whether their own, of the government, or for the purpose of furthering the drive for EMU. These objectives run counter to the usual objective of a central bank of assuring a sound platform for healthy, long-term growth.

In the specific case of Asia, Thailand created a two-tier foreign exchange and interest rate system, while Malaysia, the Philippines, and Indonesia all slapped on limits to swap market trading. While the dividing line is somewhat thin, these measures were not so much aimed at punishing speculators after the fact than they were efforts at self-defense during the climax of the speculation and panic. Indeed, given the relative lack of political development in the region as opposed to economic development—though, no doubt Asian leaders would disagree with this clause—the overall reaction of the political and financial authorities was remarkably restrained, with one obvious exception. The comments by Dr. Mahathir Mohammed were no doubt aimed at his home audience rather than the West, and indeed they went down very well at home. Many Malaysians remained strongly in favor of both his policies and his rhetoric, and not just the bumiputras. On Monday, October 27, around 2000 members of the Indian community burned an effigy of George Soros, pledging allegiance to Mahathir. Chinese business leaders were also supportive of the Malaysian leader. Indeed, the fact that Mahathir mentioned all sorts of external enemies, including Western speculators and Jews, but not the Chinese, was notable in itself—and no accident. The essence of Asia's official protest at its rough handling was twofold: first, a natural reaction to such treatment whatever the reasons, and second, an issue of control. The authorities had lost control, or at least a high degree of it, and the market had gained it. Of necessity, control is a subject close to the heart of any government or central bank.

This was the case in Europe after the two ERM crises, and it was also the case with the Asian currency crisis. Control was relevant not only for economic reasons but also because the go-go years of growth had masked or postponed underlying political and social problems. Control was particularly relevant in Asia because there had been a de facto (if not de jure) social pact between populations and governments that rapidly growing economies and consequent rises in personal incomes (income disparities notwithstanding) replaced the need for increased political representation. The devaluations of the ASEAN currencies and the consequent economic impact were thus not only an economic but a political threat, as this boosted the chances of the social pact unraveling—and people taking to the streets or worse to voice their dissatisfaction. Such a possibility was not to be underestimated. In Indonesia—where the price of such basics as rice, vegetables, and cooking oil had soared, small business had been hit hard, the country had experienced its worst drought in decades, and subsidies on fuel and food had been cut or eliminated due to IMF loan stipulations—the threat was very real indeed. To some, the very loss of complete control itself, whether political or economic, was totally unacceptable. Most took a somewhat more sanguine view. There were economic problems to be faced and they had to be dealt with, however unpleasant the relative loss of control.

The people who took that view were largely those responsible for economic policy in the first place. They were people who had practical, front-line experience of the prevailing economic and financial imperatives rather than the more theoretical politicians. This was not particularly surprising, at least to those who have been following Asia for some time, as Asian financial authorities have a history of being practical and realistic in the face of adversity—despite the excesses that subsequently develop. Asia had dug itself out of more than a few scrapes and often with astounding results. An excellent example is the crisis in Thailand in 1983–1984. Thailand was forced to devalue the baht and then repeg it to the dollar after its current account deficit exploded in the wake of a spike in import costs arising from the rise in the price of oil coupled with falling prices in other commodities. In 1985–1986, several ASEAN nations faced recession, with Malaysia notably reacting by making deep spending cuts. In 1991, India was faced with a severe fiscal crisis, forcing a much-needed turnaround in economic policy which entailed market liberalization, cuts in import tariffs, and increased openness to foreign investment through deregulation. Asia's traditional answer to economic problems had usually been managed liberalization: opening up the domestic markets and economies to increased penetration, while at the same time keeping a core element of control. The dynamic balance in Asia (as elsewhere) between elements seeking greater openness and those looking for greater control, even pushing for a reversal of liberalization, continues to push inexorably in favor of the former rather than the latter.

Asian authorities are as hard-nosed as anybody when it comes to economic realism, despite the rhetoric of some, knowing all too well that there is no choice but to go forward toward greater economic integration and globalization. To go back, through capital or exchange controls, is to face a far greater risk of economic and political strife. The realization has dawned—at least within the economic and financial elites—that increased global economic integration requires ever-closer financial integration; the one cannot go without the other. In a global economy, both the domestic economy and the financial markets are increasingly judged by international rather than regional, much less national, standards. To go backward and actually increase financial and economic regulation, to the detriment of open markets and trade, rather than just talk about it, simply results in global capital going elsewhere. As capital markets, and more importantly capital flows, liberalize around the world, economic and financial policy management becomes increasingly complex and difficult. In particular, the ability of capital to move at light-speed around the world, of necessity, narrows the policy deviations between national financial authorities, whether they like it or not. Asia was for a time the only game in town in terms of investing in emerging markets, but that is no longer the case—and quite frankly has not been for some time. In the past, the market bought the Asian story as a whole. Going forward, it will increasingly look to relative value investment. This is an exercise that will go some way to forcing economic prudence upon the more recalcitrant and boosting the efforts of those who are already seeking to open their economies.

One of the most prudent and realistic financial operators, Mar'ie Muhammad, the Indonesian finance minister, reacted (predictably) to the crisis facing his country by calling for greater economic and financial deregulation, rather than reverting to previous restrictions. As early as the second week of October, following a meeting with twenty Western fund managers to discuss market developments and projections, Mar'ie acknowledged there had been a sea change in market sentiment, toward a more negative view of Indonesia, and that the only way to reverse this was to open up the economy further. His comments were backed by those from Bank Indonesia Governor Soedradjad Djiwandono, who stressed that the Indonesian authorities had been moving in favor of ever-greater liberalization in any case and that the abandonment of the intervention band was just a further stage in that process.[4] He added that the recent turbulence was irresistible: "We cannot shield ourselves from this kind of development. We go along with it." He said further that the authorities remained committed to financial and economic liberalization. Both Anwar and Thailand's Thanong Bidaya have echoed similar sentiments, while de Ocampo of the Philippines said that attempts at renewed protectionism, whether in the fields of trade or finance, would do considerably more harm than good and that the best protection for a country's currency and asset markets was prudent economic policy.

In sum, Asian authorities as a whole went through several stages of reaction—to varying degrees, depending on the individuals concerned—starting with shock, followed by anger, denial, and finally (partial) acceptance. Of these, denial is by the far the most dangerous in terms of handicapping the country's ability to subsequently recover; that is, to deny the existence of a problem is to exacerbate it. Such denial was predictable in light of the amount of hype emerging markets had received (see Chapter 2), particularly in Asia. Some Asian leaders had begun to believe their own press, always a dangerous activity. In addition, such denial was extended because the effects of the currency crisis took longer to feed through into the real economies than was the case, for example, in Mexico. Until the data stared them in the face, some refused to believe that the Asian economic miracle had been derailed—albeit temporarily—and a near-term future of painful restructuring, austerity, and much slower growth loomed large. The economic reform and budget packages by Thailand, Malaysia, and particularly Indonesia showed that despite the occasional rhetoric at least some of the necessary lessons were sinking in. This coincided with the first signs, whether in the streets or in the regular economic data releases, that economic hardship (in relative terms) was potentially at hand and immediate measures had to be taken to stabilize the situation. Korea remained in denial the longest, with Finance Ministry officials claiming the economy as healthy—ignoring the massive burden of debt (particularly the USD100 billion of debt that fell due within one year) that weighed down on it. Indeed, Korea attempted all forms of denial. Saying it would defend the 900 level to the last on the USD-KRW, then 950, and finally 1000, inevitably it was forced to let the currency go. Clinging to the belief that all debt obligations, whether national or corporate, could be met without help, eventually, it was forced to admit the truth: It needed financial aid. Even when this realization came, Korea sought to retain at least some semblance of face, requesting financial aid from both the U.S. and Japan, before eventually facing the bitter necessity of accepting help from the IMF.

Despite the anger of Mahathir and the attempts at denial by Thailand and Korea, acceptance—albeit grudging—finally dawned. Going forward, there seems every likelihood that

Asian countries and their governments will seek to restructure according to the prevailing necessities of the global economy rather than to the whims of rhetoric or wishful thinking. As we have seen, Asia has a history of being practical when it counts, despite the stream of invective that has also periodically been noted. Many challenges lie ahead, and to steer a safe course through the treacherous economic waters that have resulted from the currency market crisis will require such pragmatism in abundance.

The fiscal austerity so necessary to offset the shock of devaluations and to cut into current account deficits will mean severe economic pain in the short term, in terms of sharp rises in unemployment. This, coupled with the inflationary impact of the currency declines, has the potential for creating political instability. If this seems melodramatic, consider the existing social tensions, particularly with regard to ethnic groups, that were papered over during the boom period when everyone prospered. The risk is that the inevitable economic turndown in 1998 could exacerbate these tensions. Aware of this, the Malaysian authorities have left alone the issue of the bumiputra-Chinese ethnic divide. In Thailand and Indonesia, the tensions are not so much focused on ethnicity as they are on wealth disparities between the privileged few and the many whose prosperity is more modest, or indeed the outright poor. Government fear that an economic downturn could lead to an explosion of popular anger was a key reason—though not the only one—why such a high priority was placed on growth (at any price). The violent events of the summer of 1996 in Jakarta were ample warning to the authorities, not just in Indonesia but throughout Asia, of the dangers of any perceived breach in the growth-rights contract. Now that the downturn is here, the way forward must be to open up further not only the economy, but the political systems also.

To do otherwise is to risk not just popular opposition to, but outright rejection of, the status quo, a much more dangerous situation. In addition to dealing with wealth gaps, real and imagined, Asian governments must also seek to address relationship distortions—"cronyism," for want of a better word—that have been prevalent in Thailand and Indonesia. Although this cannot be uprooted (whether it should be or not is another question), the emphasis on it must be gradually phased out. Domestic players, whether the people on the streets or investors who have up to now not been favored by the government, will demand a more level playing field. In the past, Asian governments could ignore such calls. To turn a deaf ear now would be to risk a social backlash, the extent of which might not be controllable. The crisis also comes at a particularly difficult time for several Asian countries, notably Indonesia and the Philippines, which have crucial presidential elections this year. Thailand got over this particular hurdle with the (re)appointment of Chuan Leepkai as prime minister, replacing Chavalit; however, the political system as a whole remains shaky, and the government is caught in a bind between the need to implement fully the IMF strictures and thus cause the economy (and the populace) untold economic pain and the threat of a public backlash (as happened in October of last year) if it is seen to hesitate. Even in Malaysia, there remains the question of succession to Mahathir. His number two man, Anwar, is of course the favorite; yet the styles of the two show marked differences, not least with the press and foreign parties.

To be sure, the network of cozy relationships between government, business, and the banking industry will not be fully dismantled, but the process by which contracts are won (and lost) will no longer depend solely on contacts and will become more competitive. Note that this takes the optimistic view, as I do. To be a pessimist is to say that Asian governments will hold on to the system of relationships without allowing for great political equality, thus ensuring a reversion to third-world status. Asian governments have in the past, whatever their overt political views, had a remarkably flexible approach. This has been largely adopted with regard to the economy. The challenge going forward will be to loosen the political reins, in terms of both allowing the burgeoning middle classes a greater voice and at the same time relieving some of the pressure from below by allowing those who perceive themselves as not having a voice at all some degree of speech. A crucial lesson of political just as much as economic history is that it is better to give the carrot so as to avoid the need for a (bigger) stick later on.

Foreign investors also will demand a more equitable system and greater return on capital. Asian stock markets soared in 1993 but since then have as a whole produced miserable returns. The economic recoveries in Mexico and Argentina in 1996 and the subsequent outperformance in LATAM asset markets—the stellar performance by the U.S. markets notwithstanding—will require that Asian companies match international standards not only for supply, but also for returns. This will in turn require that Asian companies restructure, not so much to serve national interests, but to satisfy the requirements of international investors. Chapter 9 will look at this in much closer detail and the resultant opportunities that are and will be apparent within Asian asset markets. Suffice it for now to say that there will be a key shift in how corporate Asia—and also Asian governments—both see themselves and act within the global economy. To act independently may be theoretically desirable, as some politicians would have it, but is it feasible anymore? I would argue that the answer is unequivocally no. The global economy increasingly requires uniform standards. Ideologically, emerging market countries may resent having to obey the standards of the West, but if they are to receive the West's capital they have little choice. To reject Western standards totally would be hugely detrimental—both for the West and for Asia. On the ideological front, the West has reached an understanding—certain diehards in the Republican Congress notwithstanding—with regard to the gradual approach taken by China toward political liberalization (and wisely so, given the inherent difficulties of even the gradual and prudent approach, let alone a Russian-style "great leap forward" to full capitalism with the political and social chaos that would inevitably entail). The only reason why this has not been extrapolated to the ASEAN members is the somewhat more combative stance taken by one or two ASEAN members, Malaysia in particular.

Cynics might argue that Western politicians would sell their own mothers (at a discount) for a chance to get at the Chinese domestic markets and that therefore this parallel does not apply given the smaller domestic markets available within the ASEAN. However, I would disagree. For one thing, Westerners now view prospects within China with a much more cynical eye than they first did. China—rightly—is insistent on not being recolonized (the briefcases and cell phones of Western manufacturers replace the cannons of old, but most assuredly not the memories of old, passed down by generations), while Western companies on their part are looking at participating or retiring from the field of corporate battle rather than plunder. For another thing, with regard to the ASEAN, Indonesia is the fourth largest country in the world by populace—yes, one-fifth or less of that of China—but still of tremendous economic value to the West.

On the market front, fund managers are even more practical. They have to be, given the necessity to balance available risk and reward on a global basis. The gradual opening of capital market borders is, of course, reversible; and those within the ASEAN who threaten to limit, restrict, or tax financial market trading might have theoretically important viewpoints. However, to attempt to put those into practice would be an entirely different matter and one entirely injurious to the ASEAN itself, let alone "speculators," whose activities such limitations would seek to curb. Capital would simply flow to those regions where there were no or fewer restrictions. It is easy for regional leaders to pontificate that offshore capital is not necessary, but just try getting by without it—particularly in the face of others prospering with it.

Despite the penalties of attempting to push back the tide, there are of course, historical precedents—the trade wars in the 1920s that preceded the Great Depression being perhaps the most notable and prescient example. To attempt to do so again would be to threaten a rerun of that time, in effect a meltdown of the trading system and thus of global asset markets, and world depression followed by war. If it happens, it will have started in Asia. There, too, there were emerging trading blocks and a

Europe hell-bent on crucifying itself on a single monetary standard; there too political transmission mechanisms were in place which led to instability and conflict within what would now be deemed the emerging markets. The exceptions to this rule are Germany and Japan, for long now fully democratic states. Yet the continued subjugation of Iraq following the Gulf War is a parallel in at least one sense—force a rat (regime) into a corner and it will eventually bite you, for it has nothing to lose. Conflict, whether political or economic, does not have to start from the source to develop within. Needless to say, such musings are pessimistic, let us trust overly so. Yet it pays to consider the dangers of words, for words sometimes lead to actions, in many cases not deliberately, and in such cases actions that are not desirable to any party concerned.

Looking at both words and actions, two nations within Asia should be singled out for praise: Hong Kong (albeit a Special Administrative Region), and by inference China, and Singapore. Both have demonstrated admirable pragmatism. The former has developed the most free and liberalized capital markets in Asia. And the latter has adopted a fully market-oriented policy toward its currency and asset markets—at the same time seeking to limit the rapid internationalization of its currency. In these two countries, contact-based capitalism faced checks and balances—individuals might argue about the rigidity of such, but they could not deny their existence. The benefit of both countries' strong domestic financial institutions to act as they did was essential in limiting and containing the contagion that flowed from other parts. Indeed, those kinds of institutions, with their fierce reputation and independence, were notable by their practical, as opposed to theoretical, absence in the likes of Thailand and Indonesia. Granted, the Bank of Thailand had a fiercesome reputation, but when push came to shove it did not do its job. One can argue that it was not allowed to do so as a result of pressure by the political establishment, but this is merely to confirm that contact-based capitalism, having become exceptionally venal in the case of Thailand, triumphed over the requirements of a modern financial system and its institutions. If one denies this, then the Bank of Thailand simply did not do its job—in which case, Thailand has to achieve the requisite standards for these institutions. The case of Indonesia is somewhat more complex since Indonesia had not suffered from the same degree of current account imbalance as had Thailand. Yet the Indonesian authorities had let develop a sizable external debt burden for whatever reason.

The hollowing out that is to come, within economies as a whole and more specifically within Asian financial sectors, will eliminate or reduce inefficient capital—if Asian leaders allow the process to proceed. One nation in particular has more than a passing interest in this process—Japan. Japan, more than any other country, has funded Asia's expansion through government and commercial loans, FDI, and portfolio flows. Just as has occurred in Japan at the start of this decade, Asia's asset bubble has burst. While the lessons of the need to provide more acceptable returns and more transparent financial, economic, and political systems remain from this crisis, Asian leaders would do well to look to Japan to learn what mistakes to avoid.

As for Japan itself, the Asian currency crisis represents a further sickening blow to a persistently belabored economy—burdened by more inefficient capital than the ASEAN countries have dreamed of. The likely results will be that Japanese banks will have to set further loan losses and security companies stock losses against their books (at least in theory). How this crisis will affect the Japanese banking system, industry, and the economy as a whole and where Japan goes from here are examined in detail in the next chapter.

8

The Banker — Japan's Exposure

IT IS AN EXAGGERATION—but not much of one—to say that Japanese capital and Japanese technology were the building blocks for the rise of Asia. More than any other country, even than the U.S., Japan was exposed to Asia, in terms of both commercial bank lending and foreign direct investment. For Japanese bankers and businesses, the Asian currency crisis is a nightmare that could not have possibly come at a worse time. Japan's economy, having to endure the domestic hike in the consumption tax from 3% to 5% from April 1, 1997, had peaked in the first quarter and subsequently fallen back sharply—GDP falling 11.2% on an annualized basis in the second quarter. Consumption had fallen sharply and inventories built up as corporate estimates of domestic demand all across the range of products had proved overly optimistic.

Then Thailand let the baht go, and the ASEAN currencies fell like dominoes, one after another, followed by the Korean won and the Taiwan dollar. Corporate Japan woke up to the sickening prospect of its cherished profit rebound, driven largely by Asian-based manufacturing plants, being threatened. Japanese banks, which had spent the previous seven years trying to gradually write off massive bad loans, the result of credit profligacy during the go-go 1980s, were suddenly faced with a new and significant threat to the health of their loan books. For seven years, Japanese authorities, principally but not solely the Ministry of Finance, had delayed, fudged, and dissembled, hoping that somehow they and the financial system could emerge without having to admit that a crisis situation existed. Huge public works' programs were tried—to be accurate, not solely or even principally aimed at the financial system—followed by "moral suasion" to boost the stock market and thus alleviate losing bank and life insurer stock portfolio positions. Finally, with the prospect of EMU looming in Europe, following the successful implementation of NAFTA and the benefits that brought, Japan's new strongman, Prime Minister Ryutaro Hashimoto, announced that Japan's financial markets would have their own "big bang" liberalization by 2001.

All of this was merely tinkering with the problem of bad debts, putting a Band-Aid on a weeping sore rather than excising it with a scalpel. That was fine for a while. Indeed, up until June 1997 it was thought in some circles, both foreign and domestic, that the Japanese financial system had turned the corner and banks and financial institutions were on the mend, the result of further bad debt write-offs and reductions. Overtly, the sore had healed. Internally, however, the sepsis had spread, infecting the financial system, becoming a gangrene within the economy as a whole. Asia's currency, banking, and economic crises brought that reality sharply into focus. As investors—and governments and central bankers, somewhat belatedly—concentrated increasingly on such weighty issues as asset quality and foreign exchange risk within loan exposure, the failing health of Japan's financial system was brought to light. Such illumination forced a stark rethink by the Ministry of Finance and the Bank of Japan.

"There is no doubt that the catalyst for the new reality we are seeing in Japan was the Asian crisis," says Simon Ogus, SBC Warburg's executive director of Asian Economics.[1] Indeed, so. In the past, Japan has changed its ways only as a result of being forced to do so. The hope is that this time will be no different, for change it must. Estimates vary as to the full extent of the Japanese banking industry's loan exposure to Asia, and the parties themselves are somewhat reticent to divulge the information.

However, an approximate figure is around USD150 billion, roughly three times the U.S. banking industry's loan exposure to Asia. Much of this has been to Asian subsidiaries of Japanese firms rather than Asian companies, and thus the threat is largely—though not completely—of the need to roll over or refinance loans rather than one of default. However, coming on top of the existing bad loans in the system (Japan's top twenty banks have around Y18 trillion in bad loans), this is a further blow, in terms of both financial institution profitability and the ability to operate—news of such bad loans resulting in a so-called Japan premium whereby Japanese financial institutions have to pay above the market in order to get funding in the money market. Added to the bank loan exposure to Asia, one should also include bank deposits and the purchase of Asian stocks and bonds by banks and other Japanese institutional investors. Japanese investors are major investors in Asian corporate and sovereign bonds, second only to the Koreans.

As we saw in Chapter 1, Japanese manufacturing companies had also become heavily exposed to Asia, initially as a low-cost labor center for production facilities and later as a strategic area for production and sales, representing an increasingly important part within the global production wheel. Japanese corporate FDI in Asia has long surpassed that of the U.S. in the region (European FDI in Asia is not even worth considering) and continued to represent a growing share of total Japanese FDI worldwide. After Japanese multinationals set up in the region, suppliers, either within their own keiretsu or outside, sold them needed parts from Japan—a traditional pattern in Japanese offshore investment. The results were impressive, at least from a Japanese point of view. Between 1985 and 1993, Asia's trade deficit with Japan exploded, rising to almost USD55 billion from just over 9 billion in 1985. Granted, this was not just Japanese companies selling and buying parts and finished products among themselves. Such activity played a crucial role, however. Japan also increasingly exported technology to Asia, both because it wanted to boost the technology of its own plants and because such technology no longer had a comparative price/value advantage and thus could afford to be used by others rather than kept in Japan. Between 1986 and 1993, total Japanese technology exports to Asia rose from 38% to 47%.[2] Some 40% of Japanese corporate offshore profits, as opposed to just sales, were generated in Asia in the fiscal year to March 1997. The combination of Asia's low-cost base and Japanese high-volume production technique was irresistible, resulting in higher margins and higher profits. The yen also played an important role. By weakening sharply from April 1995 to May 1997, not only against the dollar but also more importantly against the Asian currencies, it reduced import costs for Japanese companies based in Asia. Asia took on increasing importance for corporate Japan, with 45% of Japanese total exports going to Asia.

Japanese banks were keen to lend in Asia, principally because their own customers—Japanese manufacturing companies— were already there. Domestic demand in these countries was very strong, and for Japanese banks as well as the manufacturers, Asia offered the chance of higher margins. While focusing on their Japanese customer base, Japanese banks were not shy about making loans to the Asian corporate sector either. Of Thailand's total external private debt of around USD96 billion in the third quarter of 1997, around 35% of that was to Japanese banks. Japanese bank lending made up around 25% of Indonesia's troublesome external debt of USD120 billion. For the past decade, Japanese banks and companies had been shifting "human capital" to Asia, and away from Europe and North America—in relative rather than nominal terms. Their involvement concerned long-term fundamentals, just as much as short-term profit potential. In addition to using Asia as a cheaper export base, they were attracted by the demographics of the region—large youthful populations whose increasing consumption and yet high savings rates represented strong potential, in terms of both markets to be tapped and labor.

Within Japan itself, the only area of the economy which was actually doing well in the second quarter of 1997 was exports. Domestic consumption, as measured by retail sales, collapsed after the tax hike. Corporate bankruptcies rose sharply, land prices continued to fall, and total "domestic aggregate demand," as economists term the real economic activity of the population, plunged. With banks offering near-zero deposit rates, the population preferred to keep more money in cash—but not spend it. The monetary base slowed, as shown by MI data following April. In the first quarter, there was a rise in domestic demand, but it was in fact due to "front loading" whereby manufacturers and consumers sharply increased production and consumption, respectively, ahead of the consumption tax hike. Taking an optimistic view that the solid performance of the first quarter would continue, manufacturers had built up inventories only to realize that such a view was overly optimistic and an inventory adjustment process would have to be faced. As for the banks, life insurers, and securities houses, the resulting fall in the Nikkei 225, due to the more bearish economic outlook, hurt their stock portfolio holdings. This is particularly important in Japan because banks and other financial houses count paper profit on these stock positions toward their capital base—and thus their capital adequacy ratios. The Nikkei 225 continued to decline and with it the paper profits on their books—and thus their capital base.

Exports were the only light at the end of the tunnel. Thanks to the fall in the yen and the significant productivity improvements that Japanese companies had been forced to achieve during the period of *endaka,* along with strong demand in Asia and North America, Japanese exports in the first half of calendar 1997 boomed. Month after month, the overall Japanese trade surplus showed Y/Y gains of well over 100%. And then came the Asian currency crisis. It took some time for the market to digest the likely effect of this on exporters. The bottom line, however, was that if some 45% of Japanese exports went to Asia and ASEAN currencies had devalued against the yen by an average of 40%, Japanese trade competitiveness would be hit hard. When this realization dawned, the Nikkei 225 fell even further. The light at the end of the tunnel now suddenly appeared to be an oncoming train.

The banks, life insurers, and brokers were faced with the triple whammy of tightened global liquidity, falling stock prices that hurt their balance sheets, and the prospect of yet more bad loans as a result of the situation in Asia. In sum, the Asian currency crisis caused instability within the Japanese financial system given further bad loans incurred by the banks, reduced stock portfolio profits on bank balance sheets, valuation losses to Japanese exporters in Asia, and a worsened outlook for Japan trade. It did have some positive impact, however, although it most certainly was not seen that way initially. The Ministry of Finance had long held the view that Japan's twenty largest banks were too large—and would not be allowed—to fail. However, the Asian currency crisis and the resultant instability within the Japanese banking system forced it to take a different view. It did not take immediately to this different view. When the Hokkaido Takushoku Bank (commonly known as "Takugin") found itself facing financial difficulty—as in immediate financial difficulty in terms of an inability to raise cash, for it had been in trouble for years—the expectation still was that the Ministry of Finance would bail it out or save it by merging it with another bank. The Ministry of Finance tried, but plans to merge it with Hokkaido Bank failed as did attempts to get life insurers to boost the bank's capital base. Eventually, on November 17, Takugin, reluctantly on the part of the Ministry of Finance, was allowed to fail.

Initially, the Nikkei 225 rallied—by over 1000 points on the news—on the view that the authorities were finally getting serious about sorting out the mess that the financial system was in and might even use public money as part of the promised third economic stimulus package. The reality eventually dawned, however. The Ministry of Finance had not simply stepped aside and allowed Takugin to go under. It had fought that prospect until the last and had only allowed the collapse because there was no other option. Even worse was to come, and the market began to anticipate that. Japan's financial system was in trouble and the authorities did not appear to know what to do about it. The following week, the financial markets received the stunning news that Yamaichi Securities, one of Japan's Big Four brokerage houses, had also failed. Japan's oldest brokerage, it left behind some Y3.2 trillion in debt. Announcing the news, Yamaichi President Shohei Nozawa broke down in tears, saying he was to blame, not his employees, and disclosing that Yamaichi had hidden losses and debts of Y265 billion. Japan's financial authorities were also to blame. They knew for years, perhaps not about the Y265 billion, but about repeated annual losses at Yamaichi and they did nothing. The cost of years of sweeping unpleasant problems under the carpet and hoping they would go away, or that growth would reverse them, was coming to the fore with a vengeance. More important than the nominal profitability reduction, increased bad debts, and stock portfolio losses of Japanese banks, brokers, and life insurers which followed on from the Asian currency crisis was the overall threat to financial system confidence. It has not been strong for some time anyway, but in 1997 it received a body blow. Japanese banks faced the prospect of a rising cost of funding—the "Japan premium" in the money markets, falling asset markets, rising bad loans, and depositors standing in line to get their savings out. The financial system itself faced the threat of meltdown. Because of Japanese bank loan exposure to Asia, this in turn fed back into falling stock prices in Asia, the two feeding off each other.

Up to now, we tried to answer the question of where Japan has gone before and why. Now we turn our attention to the question of where it is going in the future. The rest of this chapter seeks to address this crucial question. Japan's period of economic and financial pain is not yet over. Despite the promise of public money and the authorities providing ample liquidity for money market needs, the failures of Sanyo Securities, Takugin, Yamaichi Securities, and Tokuyo City Bank will most certainly not be the last. Through falling stock prices, credit lines being cut, and the rising cost of funding via the Japan premium, the market is doing the Ministry of Finance's job, albeit in extremely brutal fashion. Given the extent of bad loans still in the system and stock portfolio losses on books, there will be further failures of financial institutions, including second-tier securities houses and banks. The smaller life insurers are also threatened. Given Japan's market structure of cross-share holdings, lifers are among the largest holders of bank-sector shares. They are also heavily exposed to banks and brokerages through subordinated loans, which incidentally are not covered by Ministry of Finance guarantee. In addition, while the largest of the lifers are on a relatively sound balance sheet footing, the smaller ones are faced with low interest rates, rising cancellation of insurance policies, and stock losses. If a lifer fails, it will not be the first to do so. That dubious honor went to Nissan Mutual Life last year. Given deregulation to date, which has resulted in higher premium and dividend obligations for the lifers, together with the low returns available at home, many have no choice but to invest in the offshore markets, notably, of course, in the U.S. Treasury market, given its liquidity, size, and high real and nominal yields. Fears that Japanese financial institutions could repatriate large amounts of offshore investment thus seem overdone. To do so would be to take away their highest-yielding assets, thus essentially committing corporate suicide. There could, however, be some repatriation if the authorities require the financial institutions to mark-to-market low returns or actual losses on their books. These would have to be offset by profit from higher-yielding assets. Needless to say, for this very reason, the authorities are unlikely to do so.

In late November, following the collapse of Takugin and Yamaichi, the Bank of Japan intervened heavily in the money market to offset a real credit crunch—the result of market unwillingness to lend to any financial institution with even a hint of problems—adding massive amounts of reserves to the system, or failing to drain reserves in order to stabilize the unsecured call loan rate around its target level at 0.50%, and provide the requisite liquidity to the system in order to prevent further failure, both specific and systemic. Still, a concrete plan to stabilize the financial system remains to be found. Many of the ideas suggested in December by the Ministry of Finance were positive, but the authorities as a whole appear remarkably relaxed about the entire matter given the severity and urgency of the problems that are faced.

Several things are needed. First and foremost, the Ministry of Finance and the Bank of Japan need to clearly say that the financial system as a whole will be protected. They have indicated this by their actions in the market; however, it needs to be made clear verbally as well. Not all of this concerns poor fundamentals—not all the lifers, banks, and brokers being hit by the vicious combination of stock market losses, higher cost of funding, and bank and insurance policy withdrawals are financially weak.

The second point is that the Ministry of Finance must make it crystal clear that those financial institutions that do not face up immediately to their situation, by either merging with others or writing off huge loan/stock losses, will be closed down. This sounds potentially dangerous, but not to do so is much more dangerous. At present, almost all financial institutions are being tarred with the same brush. The threat is thus that relatively healthy institutions could be dragged down, even to the point of failure, given the general crisis in confidence. Going back to the patient analogy, if one or more limbs have to be amputated, so be it. The operation is not only necessary, it is critical. Otherwise, make no mistake about it, the patient could die. And if Japan fails, then so does the entire world financial system.

Third, the Ministry of Finance also has to make crystal clear—rather than its usual dissembling and prevarication—that deposits are safe and will be guaranteed. The interests of stockholders are not guaranteed and should not be. The price of investment has to be the possibility of losing everything you put in. That is part of the game. Second-tier banks have faced deposit runs because depositors had little faith about the guarantee or were uncertain. Such faith has to be shored up, for confidence, although not everything, is certainly a lot. Many a patient has given up hope and has died as a direct result of that loss of hope.

In addition, rather than the Bank of Japan just injecting countless trillions of yen into the financial system, the fledgling Deposit Insurance Corporation (DIC) should be given real powers, in both financial and regulatory terms. On the financial side, the DIC's own reserves are paltry and completely inadequate to deal with the task in hand. These need to be significantly boosted, most probably by bonds guaranteed by the government which would be bought by the Ministry of Finance's own trust fund bureau. The funds from these would be used by the DIC to buy failed financial institution bad debts in order to protect depositors and at the appropriate time (not for a long time) sell these on. In addition, the DIC should be given regulatory "teeth": It should be allowed to investigate the entire financial system and if necessary shut down errant banks, rather than just wait for them to fail before guaranteeing their deposits through bad debt purchases. Also, public funds have to be used. There is nothing wrong with this despite the understandable anger and opposition it has caused. Public funds were used in the U.S. banking crisis, and they should be used again in the Japanese banking crisis, first to shore up confidence and then the system itself. Some Y685 billion was needed to deal with the failed jusen—mortgage finance companies. Significantly more will be needed this time, possibly up to half the bad loans, or some Y9–10 trillion. Politicians, despite pledges to do so, are understandably reluctant to use public funds given the public and political opposition to this, not an insignificant concern given the parliamentary elections later this year. The need for public funds has to be addressed and explained, however. Again, the alternative is decidedly less palatable. Finally, the Bank of Japan needs to keep interest rates where they are for the rest of this year at the least, to allow banks and other financial institutions to rebuild their battered balance sheets. This is what Greenspan did with the U.S. banking crisis at the start of the decade. The bank's tactics of adding massive liquidity, reopening the discount lending window—which allows banks to borrow uncollateralized funds at the 0.50% discount rate—and making "special (uncollateralized) loans" to troubled financial institutions worked well and stopped the financial system as a whole from meltdown.

Further measures of a more structural nature—such as the ones suggested above—are needed in order to avoid the possibility of a reoccurrence of the credit crunch and panic that happened in late November and early December. Like Asian current account deficits, potential systemic problems arise not from bank bad debts per se, but from a crisis of confidence—and thus doubt over the ability to fund those debts. Since the bubble burst, Japan has spent at least Y60 trillion in economic stimulus packages to try and shore up the economy and financial systems. Despite this, growth was anemic from 1992 up until FY1996. Radical change is needed, and not just within the financial system.

Japan's financial crisis of last year, which followed from the Asian currency and financial crisis, has accelerated the process of deregulation within Japanese finance, which had begun in earnest ahead of the prospect of big bang. Deregulation is needed in the corporate sector as well. Many authors and market commentators have noted how Japan's form of "cooperative capitalism" directly or indirectly creates excessive labor cost bases—the reluctance to fire people weighing on the bottom line and at the same time limiting liquidity within the labor market as a whole. Not that I am suggesting U.S.-style capitalism for Japan. Japan is different—as indeed is the U.S.—and is perfectly entitled to have its own form of capitalism, as long as its form is fair and equitable for all concerned (competitors and the Japanese domestic population) and allows efficient transmission of capitalist mechanisms.

On all three counts, Japan fails in this. First, Japan still has restrictive tariff and nontariff trade practices (again, as does the U.S.). It should move further to reducing these. Indeed, to do so would be entirely in its own interests, let alone anyone else's. Second, while Japan has an extremely high living standard, the burdens on the Japanese people in terms of living costs are also extremely high—unnecessarily so, representing a key inefficiency. The system, either deliberately or indirectly, creates incentives for saving rather than consumption. This need not be radically altered, but consumption should be boosted in relative terms, and the way to do this is by deregulation and increased competition. Third, the system is inefficient, allowing pockets of inefficient capital—such as in the banking system—to develop and grow. The cross-shareholding system should be ripped out root and branch. Either the authorities do that, or the market will do it for them by hitting every stock price linked with troubled firms or banks. Further Nikkei 225 losses will also cause dumping of stocks on the market by disillusioned institutional investors, an eminently healthy process.

Back to the corporate sector, Japanese companies are among the finest in the world in terms of the products they make. However, this should not allow for complacency, particularly given the Asian crisis and the resultant impact that will have on Japanese exports to Asia, coupled with weak domestic demand in Japan. The result will be profit and margin pressure—a key reason why manufacturing stocks have been hit in Japan as well as financial counters. Slower growth in Asia and rising prices due to currency devaluation will hit Japanese exports of capital goods to Asia particularly hard—which just happen to represent some 65% of total Japanese exports to Asia. Rising import costs will also hit Japanese production plants in Asia in the short term. Given that Japanese Asian subsidiary corporate debt was in either dollars or yen, both of which have risen sharply against the local currencies, the cost of funding those loans has just increased markedly. Either the subsidiary will have to pay these higher costs, or the parent will have to help the subsidiary out. Either way, it is not good news for earnings.

Looking at specific country examples, Japanese exports to Thailand make up 4.4% of total exports. Japanese exports to Indonesia are 2.2% of the total, to Malaysia 3.7%, to the Philippines 2.0%, and to Singapore 5.1%. Taken together, these five currencies lost an average 20% against the yen in 1997. J-curve theory suggests an immediate rise in the Japanese trade surplus with these Asian countries given the higher yen value; followed by a steep drop in volume terms, given higher yen-based prices; and then a sharp drop in revenue terms. The speed of the slowdown in Asian countries will dictate how quickly this process takes place. My bet is that despite the efforts of some Asian governments to delay the inevitable, the slowdown will take place in short order. Indeed, we are already seeing signs of that. Thus, Japanese exports will be hit by the combination of slowing domestic demand and rising costs. This year, Japanese exports to Asia are likely to fall very sharply indeed, possibly by 25 to 30%. The one saving grace for Japan's net trade balance with Asia, however, is that with Japanese domestic demand also remaining extremely weak, imports from the ASEAN, which make up around 15% of total Japan imports, will remain relatively soft despite their newly found competitiveness.

All is not doom and gloom, however, for the Japanese corporate base in Asia. For one thing, the devaluation of the ASEAN currencies, together with the rise in the USD-JPY, will eventually make Japanese exporters to Europe and North America even more competitive. In regard to the structure of Japanese corporate capitalism, Japanese manufacturers focused on the twin virtues of continually increasing technology and added-value product content and at the same time investing in and boosting the skill base of their labor force. By doing this they have created what has been termed the "cost structure revolution" which, supported by technological comparative advantage, has resulted in the "global natural monopolies," as I noted earlier in Chapter 3.[3]

The technological advantage is crucial because it allows greater pricing power and flexibility—Japanese exports of very high added-value product ranges that are not subject to cyclical disturbance will continue to Asian countries despite lower prices in those countries because there are not (as yet) available domestic substitutes. Japanese manufacturers have applied an extremely strategic approach to investing and producing in Asia. Rather than just using it as a low-cost center, they have sought to maximize output efficiencies by placing production facilities in each Asian country that has a specific production comparative advantage. By making the domestic economy dependent on their capital and production, they frustrate domestic attempts at competition. This is by no means an accident. It is a deliberate policy. Equally, while lower-value technologies are exported from Japan to take advantage of cost advantage, high-value technologies are most assuredly kept at home in Japan—to the chagrin of many Asian leaders who have complained in vain for years at this practice. In order to maintain its overall trade competitiveness, corporate Japan is thus exporting its production facilities and technology of low comparative advantage while maintaining its high-comparative-advantage potential at home.

The inability to develop similar domestic bases—which requires extensive government and business cooperation—within Asian countries keeps them dependent on Japan, from both within and without. This is borne out by just looking at the auto industry in Asia. Japanese manufacturers produce 94% of all auto production in Thailand, 90% in Indonesia, and 80% in the Philippines.[4] You can see this in action any time you visit these places. On a short trip to Bali, every single car I saw was Japanese. That's the domestic production, let alone what is exported, the technology and economies of scale which only the Japanese companies have. Japan is thus exporting the way it does business to Asia, creating a complex, interlinking, and integrated production network. When the inflationary and growth impacts of the Asian currency crisis eventually subside, this, together with the currency devaluations against the dollar, will give Japanese manufacturers a huge advantage when exporting to the West, particularly to the U.S. It will have important consequences for the global economy and for world financial markets. Later this year, look for the U.S. trade and current account deficits to explode, with predictable impact for the dollar. This in turn will impact the deutsche mark (the USD-DEM will fall sharply) and thus the ERM.

What about the Japanese economy itself? Standard & Poor's MMS's economists in Tokyo—who nine months ahead of time called the peak in the economy in the second quarter of 1997—remain extremely bearish on near-term prospects. In addition to sustained sluggishness in nonmanufacturing, weak domestic demand for manufacturing output will put the brakes on any potential rebound in the domestic business cycle. The continued process of inventory adjustment has led the business cycle into a severe downward slide, and S&P MMS does not expect this to bottom out until the middle of this year at the earliest.[5] Despite this, industrial production data should pick up ahead of this, as Japanese exporters look to increase output to the U.S. and Europe. This eventually will lead to a renewal of trade tensions with the U.S., and possibly voluntary export limitations. The former will happen first, however. As for the dollar-yen outlook, the dollar should remain well supported initially given the prospect of a fall in the overall Japan trade surplus (though not the bilateral one) together with extremely accommodative Bank of Japan monetary policy. In addition, the first major stage in the big bang liberalization process takes place on April 1, 1998, when the foreign exchange law, limiting Japanese retail investment abroad, is revised. With Japanese asset market returns likely to remain extremely weak into the second quarter, Japanese institutional investors will also continue to invest offshore for yield, a factor that will at the least limit any pullbacks in the USD-JPY and more likely lead to further gains. Finally, the combination of the lost trade competitiveness with Asia and persistent weakness in Asian currencies given their own fundamental problems will result in a sharp fall in Japan's trade surplus with Asia during the first half of the year. Note that the Nikkei 225 usually anticipates a turnaround in the economy by at least six months. A major reversal in the Japanese stock market, rather than the various false rallies we saw last year, will in turn feed into a reversal in the yen.

What is needed most for Japan as a whole is deregulation. Yet the authorities in each economic sector remain reluctant to carry this through on a "you first" process. The crisis in Japanese finance, and the resultant need for immediate restructuring and deregulation, has led to this taking place. In the longer term, two key incentives for reforming the finance sector are the big bang, which will lead to much greater competition and for which the healthy Japanese financial institutions are furiously preparing, and the demographic question. Japan's budget deficit remains a critical structural problem. This may sound strange—particularly against the backdrop of previous Japanese fiscal prudence—but set against the prospect of the "graying of Japan," which is likely to accelerate in earnest from around 2010, it no longer appears melodramatic. In order to finance the ensuing need for rising social welfare payouts and a falling tax base, the Ministry of Finance faces the task of cutting deep into the budget deficit, in fact making it into a surplus. Deregulation will be a crucial platform for this, because spending cuts and tax hikes alone will not produce the desired results, given weak consumption and domestic demand. Further, deregulation is crucial in freeing up the Japanese financial sector to produce better and higher returns—to offset the higher obligations they will face in the years to come. Deregulation is the key, whether in finance, real estate, or manufacturing. Yet there remains the threat that other economic sectors will only deregulate when they, like the finance sector, face a crisis. Certainly, despite the merits of doing so, they will not give up without a fight if history is anything to go by.

One final aspect with regard to Japan is its role going forward in Asia, not just as the principal manufacturer in the region—neo-imperialism as some might see it—but as a participant in the political, financial, and defense spheres. Japan's willingness to help in the financial bailout packages for Thailand, Indonesia, and Korea was not only because it served its own interests—though this of necessity was the principal reason—but because it sees itself taking up a greater role in interregional and intra-regional affairs. The U.S. has long moaned that Japan does not pull the equivalent of its economic weight on the political stage. As ever, the counterargument to that might be: Be careful about asking for something, because you might just get it.

With two powerful trade blocks emerging in the world—NAFTA and EMU—an Asian trade block has to be developed, led by Japan, so the logic goes. This need not and should not be overt from the political side, since to be so conspicuous could risk unsettling Asian sensibilities—and memories of what Japan did to Asia in World II. Such memories remain slow to fade and will remain an important geopolitical factor in the region. That said, Japanese manufacturers, in alliance with their natural cooperative partners in the Japanese government and labor, are achieving this de facto. Despite an overall political shyness, the examples of Japanese officials planting a flag on the Daeiyu Islands and the increasingly militant call for U.S. troops to leave Okinawa or at least be significantly reduced represent a significant shift in Japan's political thinking. In addition, the tensions between China and Taiwan when the PLA (Peoples' Liberation Army) decided to hold military exercises close to Taiwan to remind the latter that independence was NOT an option served also to remind the U.S. and Japan of the importance of their mutual security interests and needs.

Not surprisingly, beneath an otherwise serene surface, a vigorous debate is taking place in Japan about its role in the new world (dis)order. Inevitably, that role will become a more assertive one politically, in whatever form, if only because the prevailing situation is one of lack of political assertion (though this is gradually changing). The very idea of setting up an Asian bailout fund, a suggestion put forward by Japan at the recent IMF meeting in Hong Kong (and viewed as heresy in the West because it could potentially reduce IMF dominance, for good or ill), would have been inconceivable a decade ago. Japanese politicians have to face the question of why Japanese companies lead the world, and more importantly Asia, and yet Japan's government political "sun" has failed to rise. Indeed, the Ministry of Finance's Sakakibara-san said explicitly that Japan was now prepared to play a greater role in the region, though it was not willing to act as a "big brother," the way the U.S. operated in Latin America. (Such an analogy while fully accurate up until the mid-1980s no longer seems accurate given the greater degree of economic progress and independence exhibited by these countries.) Deregulation of the economy and structural changes, notably shifting consumer patterns and thought processes, will force such questions into the open.

On the financial side, the Ministry of Finance has fought the internationalization of the yen for decades, concerned that greater usage of Japan's currency could threaten its control over the economy—which it undoubtedly would, and no bad thing either given the Ministry of Finance's appalling economic record over the past five years. Yet, going forward, it seems unlikely that the Ministry of Finance will be able to fully halt this process. The very breaching of the dollar peg systems by Asian currencies will likely entail some greater degree of reserve diversification on the part of Asian central banks. Asian central banks, including the Bank of Japan, manage around 75% of the world's foreign exchange reserves. Thus this is of more than passing relevance to the global economy and world financial system as a whole. To facilitate this, Japan needs to develop liquid and efficient financial instruments in which these reserves can be invested. In short, it needs to develop a Treasury bill or financing bill market similar to that which exists in the U.S. These securities are of short-term maturities, are extremely liquid, and possess good yields—and are thus ideal for central banks to park reserves until they are needed for intervention purposes. Despite the fact that the Bank of Japan has been calling for liberalization of the financing bill market, the Ministry of Finance continues to oppose this idea, mainly because the Ministry of Finance itself uses the financing bill market to sell FBs to the Bank of Japan, which are then used for intervention.

Again, the issue is one of control. If the Ministry of Finance continues its opposition, however, reserves will simply go elsewhere. With the approach of EMU, this could mean increases in diversification into European currencies before the creation of the Euro. Or it could mean increased reliance on the dollar as the main reserve currency by those who are uncertain about what will happen in Europe in regard to the soundness of the EMU project and the Euro as a currency. The Ministry of Finance and the Bank of Japan are thus deadlocked. However, eventually it seems likely that the Bank of Japan will win. If Japan's politicians and bureaucrats see it as inevitable that Japan is to gradually play a greater role in world and regional political and economic affairs, then it is equally inevitable that the yen will also take up a greater role in the world financial system. This in turn means that a partially or fully financing bill market must be developed. Central banks from around the world, but notably in Asia, will demand no less.

The Bank of Japan is furthering its efforts to internationalize the yen by seeking to achieve yen-denominated (rather than dollar-denominated) repo agreements with other Asian central banks. This makes sense to the central banks given the high degree of Japanese-related (and thus yen-related) trade going on in Asia, along with the rising percentage, against a historical context, of yen-based loans to Asian governments and companies and central bank reserves. Such a realistic view by the Bank of Japan is again prompted by external threats—the rise of NAFTA and the approach of the Euro, both of which take away some degree of Japanese economic control in any case. There are still some diehards in the Ministry of Finance who do not see it this way, but they are in the minority. The big bang liberalization itself is aimed at increasing the importance of Tokyo as a world and regional financial center and thus is indirectly aimed at increasing the international importance of the yen. To compete in the global economy, increased deregulation is needed, and the Bank of Japan and Ministry of Finance officials such as Sakakibara-san realize this. The currency markets with specific regard to the yen and the yen money markets will be no different.

On the trade side, around one-third of Japan's global trade is done in yen, leaving two-thirds to be translated back, notably from the U.S. dollar. This leaves Japanese exporters and importers facing heavy foreign exchange risk. Some of this can be reduced or eliminated by moving production facilities, but this by itself is not sufficient. The yen has to take up a greater share of Japan's trade. U.S. companies will likely be reluctant to acquiesce to this. However, Asia could be more willing given the increased interdependence of Asian economies as a result of rising interregional trade.

In addition, the loss of the dollar-based peg systems could by itself serve as an incentive for diversification. Japanese authorities who agree with the view regarding the need for further internationalization, instead of the politically splendid isolation practiced since the war, are also looking for greater use of the yen with regard to investment. This is hard to achieve at present because of the miserable returns in yen asset markets. While a reversal in the Nikkei 225 could help, higher returns are also needed in the yen yield curve in order to attract investment. Yet to achieve this would entail higher market and official interest rates, which would be detrimental to the aim of getting higher levels of foreign investment into yen fixed-income assets in order to help finance the budget deficit—a tough dilemma. It seems logical that the deregulation and liberalization of the financing bill market will have to occur first. This will be followed—or preceded—in any case by a rising yield curve as the Japanese economy starts to recover in earnest in the second half of this year. This will in turn attract higher foreign investment, thus helping to at least limit the rise in market rates and therefore the budget deficit. The yen still has a very long way to go in terms of catching up with the dollar's share of world foreign exchange reserves—around 8% compared with 55%. Still, logic suggests that it can only increase over time.

Lastly, in the area of defense, Japan has also become (quietly) more assertive, with defense spending gradually increasing as a percentage of national GDP. Despite Japan's deeply pacifist stance over the last fifty years, nature abhors a vacuum, particularly when it is given a prod—in the form of Japan's supremacy in electronics, which can in turn be used for defense-related purposes. In this regard, Japan has developed highly sophisticated radar and antiballistic missile capability, the latter being of direct use given that North Korea has the capability to hit Japan with its Rodong 1 intermediate range ballistic missile. Increasing technological supremacy—U.S. Air Force capability is heavily dependent on Japanese-manufactured electronics—will gradually lead to a more assertive role in defense-related issues. It is already happening. The peacekeeping missions by Japanese troops in Cambodia and Rwanda would have also been inconceivable a decade ago. This is not to say that the Japanese government or people have a desire to see any renewed overt military role for Japan's defense forces—quite the contrary. Japanese would not stand for any such move given the horrendous memory of Hiroshima and Nagasaki. Rather, the long-standing political and defense relationship between the U.S. and Japan is changing, and the essence of that change is increased Japanese independence from the control of the U.S. This process will no doubt be temporarily halted given the Asian and Japanese financial crises. However, this emerging trend of independence from the U.S. and interdependence within both a global and an Asian context appears clear.

Despite Japan's significant financial contribution toward the Gulf War, it was seen as insufficient or grudging by many Western nations, because Japan did not contribute any direct military presence. This did not go unnoticed back in Japan. While as yet not wanting to increase Japan's military role, either regionally or globally, there are growing elements in the Japanese government and population who would like to see Japan's increased political presence and role be extended to defense-related spheres, particularly in light of Japan's technological importance. Equally, Japan could easily, if it so chose to, develop nuclear strike missile and deployment capability. There is clearly no chance this will happen any time soon given the Japanese repugnance of nuclear weapons (having experienced them firsthand). However, Japan's development of conventional delivery systems, which theoretically could be used for nuclear weapons, together with space exploration technology through satellites (both built entirely with Japanese technology), continues unabated. Historically, there seems only one possible way that Japan's greater defense role could be used in more overt military fashion—if its access to natural resources were cut off (again).

In sum, despite the Japanese financial crisis, Japan is likely to play an increasing role across all spheres of economic and political activity within Asia. Of course, much depends on what happens in Asia as to how this plays out. The next chapter examines in detail my projections for Asian fundamentals going forward, including country breakdowns.

9

The Fundamentals — Problems, Challenges, and Opportunities

THE TWO CHINESE CHARACTERS for the word "crisis"—*weiji*—literally mean "danger" and "opportunity." In the context of the events that have beset Asia, no word (crisis) and no two characters (danger and opportunity) are more appropriate. Asia faces a period of exceptional volatility—and danger—in economic, political, and social terms, but there is also unparalleled opportunity to be had. The doomsayers out there will say this region has passed its prime, that the "Asian miracle" is over. Don't believe them. A detailed look at the long-term fundamentals strongly suggests otherwise. That said, Asia must also face up to a number of serious fundamental concerns. Hence this chapter seeks both to examine the prevailing fundamentals—what I have termed "short-term problems" and "medium-term challenges"—and also to suggest some broad ideas for investment potential. Before looking at the "opportunity," an examination of the "danger" is not only instructive but vital.

To be sure, the immediate fundamental picture for much of Asia looks pretty grim. While 1997 was the year that marked the collapse of Asian financial markets, 1998 will be characterized by the sharp downturn in Asian real economies. The outlook for Thailand looks especially grim—it is staring economic recession in the face. There will be no escape. Bank of Thailand has revised down its growth forecasts several times (the last one to 0.6% for 1997), but in truth Thailand faces the prospect of negative growth, possibly for both 1997 and 1998. Of the other Asian countries, Indonesia and South Korea are also likely to see negative growth in 1998. Together with Malaysia, they all suffer to varying degrees from the same sort of economic problems that currently ail Thailand—overleverage, whether in domestic or foreign currency terms, which will now be replaced by a credit crunch. Some Asian politicians have tried to put a brave face on things, but a general slowdown is foreseen. This actually is no bad thing given the extraordinary growth rates that both the ASEAN and North Asia have seen throughout the past decade. The spike in market and official interest rates following the start of the crisis, along with the sharp rise in currency volatility and consequent downsizing of private and official projects, will hit investment. Consumption will be hit by heightened pessimism along with the wealth effect from plunging stock markets. On the trade side, exports should boom, first in currency and then in volume terms on the back of the devaluations, while imports will be hit by the combination of the currency effect and a collapse in domestic demand. This will partly but not fully compensate for the domestic slowdown in terms of net growth (or the lack of). The rapid deterioration in Thai systemic asset quality in Thailand is well known, but it has not been the only case. While not to the same extent, Indonesia, Malaysia, and the Philippines have similarly, though to varying degrees, faced the effects of overleverage to cyclical-type demand such as the property and stock markets (in that order).

Interestingly, an examination of nonperforming loan (NPL) data prior to the events of the summer of last year would have given no clue about the impending asset bubble in Thailand (or elsewhere) which would finally burst. This is because NPLs are of necessity a lagging indicator and have little if any predictive ability. You cannot include an NPL in the data until it has actually occurred; but by the time it has actually occurred, it is too late. A better tool for prediction is to look at net foreign total liabilities—external debt plus the current account deficit. This would have shown, and did show, Thailand to be a sell before it actually was. By the time of this writing (the end of December) Thailand was still a sell on all counts. By the time you read this (April onward), it will be a buy. This will not necessarily be on fundamental terms, but asset markets are bought first on liquidity terms, then correct, and then fundamentals return to focus and act as the driving force for the second wave. The current account deficit was around 8% in both 1995 and 1996 for Thailand. This is likely to narrow sharply given the fiscal austerity measures put in place. However, the Achilles' heel remains external liabilities—and not just for Thailand.

The collapse in the financial and property sectors in the countries of the ASEAN, not including Singapore, will be the most protracted, as previous outperformance in expectations and thus asset price reality reverts to sustained underperformance and rerating of asset values. Much of this has already occurred in the initial fallout to the Asian currency crisis. Bank Negara took—or tried to take—prudent steps to slow the property market, and thus banking-sector exposure to this. However, Malaysia still faces the risk of a sharper slowdown than the Philippines because of property market oversupply concerns. By contrast, Indonesia, which was swift to address medium-trend concerns via its economic package and easing in monetary policy, faces a much greater problem than Malaysia regarding its own net foreign liabilities.

That said, market concern of a slowdown in Asian growth should be put clearly in context. GDP growth should remain comfortably positive overall and indeed remain favorable to that existing in the developed world. Although the Standard & Poor's MMS revised forecasts for the Philippines, Indonesia, Singapore, and Malaysia are significantly off the pace of recent years, they remain strongly favorable. Asia is unlikely to be the fastest-growing region in the world in 1998 because of the crisis, but it will still be a respectable second to Latin America. Looking at the NIEs (Hong Kong, Singapore, Korea, and Taiwan), China, the ASEAN, India, and Vietnam, the average GDP growth is likely to be at least 6.0% in 1997 and 4.4% in 1998. Where the ASEAN and Korea stumble, South Asia and China will pick up the slack. What anticipated moderation there is reflects some cutback in government and private investment spending in the face of a reduction in the heavy inflow of foreign capital that had helped fund sizable deficits in nations other than Singapore. Current account deficits should shrink as a percentage of GDP in 1998 as the currency depreciation enhances export competitiveness. The downside of the weaker currencies will be a notable pickup in average annual inflation, though the monthly CPI Y/Y figures should peak in early 1998 and moderate by year-end. A similar picture applies to South Korea, where along with several ASEAN nations, the 1998 outlook remains clouded by the lingering threat of a banking crisis.

Lower growth will be the initial and immediate result of the crisis, with the consequent impact for corporate earnings. In addition, however, the currency devaluations will result for a time in imported inflation on goods. This will be brief since domestic demand will fall sharply. However, given the increased risk premium that investors will place on Asian asset markets following the crisis, Asian central banks—even if they are allowed to do so—will be in no mood to take chances. They will hold official interest rates for higher and for longer just in case. This will have further bearish implications not only for growth, but for the asset markets themselves. Eventually, however, given this expectation that the demand side will slow markedly, the inflation threat should fade. On a microeconomic level, personal incomes will be hit, by both the hike in rates—which will hit mortgages and house rentals and ownership valuations—and the fall in the stock market. Retail investor exposure to leverage was particularly notable in the stock markets of Malaysia and Thailand, and consequently the fallout from the asset bubble bursting will be that much worse. For the S&P MMS macro-outlook on the Asian economies, see Table 7.

Table 7
Emerging Asian Economies

	1998 GDP	CPI	C/A as a % of GDP
China	8.8% E	5.0% E	+0.2% E
Hong Kong	4.2%	7.0%	−5.2%
Indonesia	−3.0%	25.0%	+2.0%
South Korea	−1.0%	9.0%	+3.0%
Malaysia	4.5%	5.3%	−5.8%
Philippines	3.0%	8.5%	−3.0%
Singapore	4.8%	2.5%	+13.5%
Taiwan	6.4%	3.0%	+2.8%
Thailand	−2.0%	8.5%	+3.5%

Source: Standard & Poor's MMS, *Asian Markets Outlook.*

Following the initial stages of the crisis in the summer of 1997, the newspapers were full of stories of wealthy Thais selling their sports cars and even jet aircraft to raise cash—the prices of which were plummeting as they attempted to unload these luxury items. Unfortunately, the real economic impact will be felt not only at the top end of the income scale—as painful as this itself has been—but throughout the economy. Government austerity, in the form of less spending, less investment, and perhaps even higher taxes, will have to be matched by similar austerity in retail economic patterns. In other words, ordinary people will have also have to tighten their fiscal belts, in some cases severely, forced to do so by higher costs and, initially at least, higher prices. So much for the individual. For the banks, the key for the authorities will be to clean up, voluntarily or by force, overexposed balance sheets—ironically, in many cases the direct result of government-directed targeted credit policies. In Asia as a whole, the go-go years of the late 1980s and the early 1990s are gone. Demand and supply habits will have to change across almost all sectors—depending to varying degrees on the specific countries concerned. Going forward, Asia has a number of short-term problems that it must face, most notably its external overreliance, together with an equal number of medium-term challenges, such as pollution, poverty reduction, and further integration into the global economy. Both consist of microeconomic and macroeconomic issues, the difference being the time span they focus on.

(Short-Term) Problems

As noted above, a key problem for Asia, both in the past and going forward, has been its overreliance on the outside world. In a world of free trade—or as close to it as the world has ever got—it is, of course, impossible to be free of external factors. However, Asia has been overdependent on the outside world in a number of key ways, which have both shaped its initial growth phase—reliance on exports for industrial expansion—and played a key role in the continuing crisis that unfolds before it in the markets and the real economies. First, on the manufacturing side, Asia's dependence on the electronics industry—and thus vulnerability to downturns in this area—has been graphically demonstrated by the events of the past two years. Given criticisms by some that Asia has not gone up the added-value chain sufficiently, this may seem an odd statement to make, and yet the statement and the criticisms are not at all incompatible. While several Asian countries, notably Thailand and Korea, have achieved major successes in elevating their added-value potential, involving greater use of technology-oriented industries such as electronics and computing, their manufacturing potential has largely been focused on low-tech, high-volume production. In other words, they have been focusing largely on price relative to added-value content. In 1995 and 1996, electronics, including most notably semiconductor chips, made up an increasingly large proportion of Asian exports—an average of 34%, taking Singapore, Malaysia, Korea, the Philippines, Thailand, Taiwan, and Hong Kong as a group. As the Asian Development Bank noted, manufacturers in Singapore prior to the crisis made up 40% of the world's disk drives, while one-third of PC microprocessors were packaged in Malaysia. Some eight out of every ten circuit boards in the world were made in Taiwan as well as half the world's keyboards.

Encouraged by strong demand levels and good margins, Asian manufacturers who were not already in semiconductors rushed to set up production facilities. Those who were already there counterattacked by boosting production. By the beginning of 1996, Asia accounted for over 50% of world memory chip sales. Needless to say, this increased supply had a predictable effect on semiconductor prices, which began to slip back. New and innovative chips, along with consequent heavy discounting on older and less technologically advanced models, added to this situation. At the same time, demand for PCs themselves was starting to shrink. This was a fatal combination. PC sales had grown a stellar 25% in 1995. In 1996, this cooled to a "mere" 16% Y/Y growth; yet even this slowdown was enough to trigger a chain reaction that was to have a major effect on Asia's economies. The initial reaction from the disk drive and semiconductor makers was to increase production further on the view that PC sales would pick up. The pullback in semiconductor prices hit the bottom line, and this had to be made up in volume terms. Anticipating a rebound in both, Asian manufacturers ramped up production—and in the process, added to an ever-expanded glut of excess capacity. What had been a modest pullback in semiconductor prices became a collapse. Semiconductor prices fell some 90% on average in 1996. Given Asia's exposure to the world electronics industry, this bit hard into exports. Indeed it was a crucial factor in the overall falloff in Asian exports. Even so, the overappreciation of real effective exchange rates was of more importance. The correction in semiconductor prices was indeed cyclical—and thus is likely to be reversed given that PC demand, albeit demand for ever more sophisticated PCs, will remain strong into the next century. As a result, there should be a rebound in Asian exports of semiconductors and other electronics industry products and components—aided by the devaluation of the Asian currencies, which along with the fall in chip prices has now made them significantly more competitive.

But how should Asia deal with this problem in the future? Over the long term, Asian manufacturers clearly have to go further up the added-value chain, producing more technologically advanced chips. In addition, they need to be the manufacturers of those chips rather than just an export base of Japanese or U.S. companies. In the short term—in order to build a base to achieve those worthy aims—the industry has to be rationalized. I will go into the general issue of corporate rationalization and restructuring in greater detail, but suffice it to say that Asia, at whatever product price, has too much capacity. This is most notable in Korea, where there is extreme overcapacity in virtually every manufacturing industry. Lower asset valuations, for both products and share prices, will act as a boost to this rationalization. Second, Asian nations need to develop a critical mass of production and funding potential that can then be guided, along with incentives from the governments, to developing higher technological capacity in order to move up the value-added production chain. The focus must always be on added value—as in any business. Low-added-value products inevitably—after periods of cyclical upturn—result in low-price, low-margin businesses. High-added-value businesses have the opposite effect, boosting long-term margins—until competitors catch up. Neither the U.S. nor Japan, especially not Japan, is going to hand this technology over to Asia on a plate. Asia has to develop this technological capacity itself. Note that I am talking about Asian industry developing it, with a (modest) helping hand from government. I am most certainly not talking about government-directed national technology drives—which can be variously called "white elephants" or perhaps more accurately "black holes," sucking in finances and producing little if any returns. The drive, to be able to achieve the desired results, must be industry- and market-led. At present, the country that appears to have the best chance of achieving this is Taiwan.

Asian external overreliance has taken many forms. On the finance side, the most obvious example is exposure to foreign currency–denominated debt. In 1996, before the Asian currencies devalued against the dollar, thus greatly exacerbating the exposure to dollar debt, total combined external debt outstanding of Indonesia, Malaysia, the Philippines, and Thailand was about USD265 billion, according to the ADB. By the end of

1997, this is likely to have risen to over USD310 billion. Most of this was corporate, most in dollars, and most completely unhedged.

How had this come about? Asian domestic bond markets were relatively small—but they will get considerably larger as we shall see later. Outstandings were only around 25 to 30% of GDP in East Asia compared with over 100% in the United States. Withholding tax rates in many nations were prohibitive. Even then, the Asian institutional investor also remained lamentably small—hence the failure of the dragon bond market. For an Asian bond market to develop and succeed requires most importantly a strong domestic institutional base. U.S. corporate bonds are primarily bought by U.S. investors, though significant tranches are allotted for foreign investors. The aim should be for Asia to be no different. Asian bonds should be primarily issued by Asian entities, in Asian currencies, and bought by Asian entities—and preferably not just Korean banks.

Funding in other currencies and offshore investor bases is perfectly fine, but the aim is to reduce offshore financial dependence. As it is, most of that external outstanding debt is short term, resulting in high rollover costs and exposure; the exposure is similar to Mexico's *tesobono* exposure, though this was government as opposed to corporate or banking debt. Yet Asian corporates have had little alternative if they wanted to issue debt but to do so in short-term, foreign currency–denominated paper. Initially, the corporates took this route. And the banks themselves were not far behind. Some demanded ridiculously tight spreads over Treasuries or dollar LIBOR for dollar-denominated paper in return for the promise of more mandates. Soon the whole system was leveraged to offshore funding—that is, except the Asian governments that had no need to issue debt because most of them ran budget surpluses. Then the currencies went down and suddenly everyone woke up to gaping holes in their balance sheets. The structure has to be created to wean banks and corporates off short-term, foreign currency–denominated debt and onto domestic yield curves—though, of course, those yield curves have to be created first. As for existing debts, hedging now is bolting the stable door after the horse has fled, though it could reduce the risk of more losses. Foreign exchange–related losses that have already occurred will simply have to be taken as extraordinary losses on corporate and bank balance sheets.

Taken as a whole, overreliance on external manufacturing demand and funding is a liability that can be ill afforded. Such exposure has to be reduced if Asia is to prosper. Why? Because taken together with high domestic demand and thus imports of capital goods—which widens the trade deficit—it weighs on the current account balance, resulting in increasing deficits and thus eventually hurting the currency. The current account deficits of Asian countries such as Indonesia, Thailand, Malaysia, and the Philippines were their most visible Achilles' heel. The causes lie in manufacturing and financial external overreliance. In the immediate term, Asian current account deficits will shrink substantially due to the combination of falling domestic demand and the foreign exchange effect on imports, causing them to lose trade competitiveness. Over the longer term, however, finding ways of staying at home will pay great dividends—as long as it is market- rather than government-based.

Asian corporate and bank overreliance on external debt ties in closely with the general weakness of the Asian banking system. To be sure, there are exceptions. In particular, Hong Kong and Singapore, as seen by their capital adequacy ratios, are the most strongly capitalized and the most stringently and prudently regulated. It is no coincidence whatsoever that their external exposure is significantly less. A significant percentage of Asian banks, particularly in the ASEAN region, have developed from a single family base. This core structure has led to two things: overcapacity (too many Asian banks) and a strong reluctance to do anything about that overcapacity—like merging. In addition, the model of Asian growth from 1960 to 1995 required targeted credit policies. Governments, businesses, and banks worked hand in glove. For the purpose of providing the requisite funding for rapid industrialization this worked superbly well. However, with no major alternatives of funding available, via, say, a domestic bond market, the decisions on credit policies were made solely at the discretion of family-run banks. And occasionally the decisions were helped along by a political word in the ear. All of this resulted in distortions of credit flow.

Simply put, too much credit went to the wrong people at the wrong price, in turn encouraging irresponsible manufacturing behavior. Thailand's banking and finance company system is often touted as an example of such credit lunacy. However, Korea was also well on the way to the asylum before the crisis hit. With interest rates kept artificially low, the government targeted bank credit at industries that were seen to be in the national interest and for the national future. The results were great in terms of allowing Korean companies to expand but horrific in terms of balance sheet stability. But then, in 1995 and 1996, who cared about that? Average corporate gearing levels (debt/equity ratio) ranged from the "conservative" 150% to the positively exhibitionist 500%+. Some of the largest Korean chaebol had gearing levels of over 400%. I do not cite this example to pick on Korea. Rather, it is an attempt at demonstrating that any "national policy," whether it be in manufacturing or finance, will inevitably lead to distortion. It is a recipe for disaster in almost all cases.

The only ones to get around this have been the Japanese. Japanese manufacturing—a model for the world in terms of product quality and technology—has been built along targeted rather than purely market-driven lines. The various ministries have played a large part in this achievement. Yet an ever-larger part has been played by the idea of consensus, rather than simply dictated and *diktat* handed down by the ministry from on high. The consensus is among the banks, government, business, and even competing businesses. The key is to build a critical mass and to avoid what the Japanese call *kato kyoso*—excessive (and in their eyes, wasteful) competition. At least on the manufacturing side, it has been a remarkable success. The story in Japanese banking and finance is somewhat less rosy. Overall, however, the rule does appear to hold true: Markets are far better at determining price than governments or bureaucrats. Price in turn determines future activity, whether in manufacturing or finance, which in turn determines future price, and so on.

Targeted credit policies and the resultant (over)accommodative monetary policies produced massive credit overcapacity, and thus they were a key cause of manufacturing overcapacity. For the next two years, such irresponsible and profligate lending practices will be replaced with a credit crunch—from boom to bust, in both the manufacturing and finance senses. It need not have been so, but that is the way it will be near term. The overcapacity in the banking system in Asia will be significantly rationalized. In two years' time, half the banks in Asia (including Japan) will have gone one way or another, either merged or liquidated. There is nothing wrong with this, though it will certainly be a painful adjustment process. For instance, to have 239 banks in Indonesia is sheer lunacy. High numbers of banks inevitably lead to declining margins in normal, responsible banking activities and thus tempt bankers away to higher-margin, but more risky, businesses. It is so in the developed world. There is no reason why Asia should be any different, and indeed it is not. Whether in manufacturing or finance, it all comes down to two simple elements: demand and supply. At the moment, there is way too much supply. One way or another, that is going to get substantially reduced.

Such a view is not likely to sit well with certain elements within Asian governments that work closely with—or rather in—the industries that could be rationalized, but this comes to the heart of the problem. "Crony capitalism" cannot go on. It has had its day. To allow it to continue is to risk a reversal of economic progress, to see such countries being bypassed by direct and portfolio investment. This would occur not necessarily (though justifiably) for any moral reason, but because crony capitalism inevitably produces a collapse in returns. It is what Marx and Lenin talked about when they predicted the demise of capitalism. Though they completely underestimated the ability of the market itself to develop and change to suit changing conditions, they saw that certain types of capitalism were inherently inefficient. Crony capitalism left unchecked will inevitably produce ever-decreasing rates of return. Why? Because it distorts the pricing mechanism. The market is not allowed to price goods and services correctly, and this leads to incorrect pricing, which has serious—and potentially fatal—consequences for business. Critics of this view may argue that Asian business has traditionally been more focused on networks, family or ethnic, and that as a result such networks will inevitably come into contact with government. Undoubtedly so. There is nothing wrong whatsoever with networks nor with such contact. The problem arises when the network, contact, and business activity all merge. Then the reason for the network and the business is no longer price and value determination of the goods and services that the business produces, but the contact itself. For efficient economic development, there has to be an intermediary between the two. Otherwise, it is like ivy growing on a tree. Eventually, the tree is choked of its resources and finally of its life. Looking at examples, the transparency, lack of crony capitalism, and strong institutions to ensure that crony capitalism does not develop within Hong Kong and Singapore are major fundamental positives and will act as safeguards for future economic progress and development. The greatest challenge in terms of the need to change the structure is in Indonesia, though to be sure it also exists in Malaysia and Korea. Change must come for the good of the government itself, not just the people. Asian governments of whatever hue essentially share a deeply pragmatic perspective. They have changed before and many will change again, allowing greater transparency and a greater division between state and business. To fail to do so is to threaten their own survival.

Back to the economy. Debate continues to rage about the real threat to Asian economies. That is, is the threat one of inflation or rather one of deflation? There is no general answer to this. For a start, it depends largely on how Asian governments respond to the crisis. In addition, the crisis is taking different forms and is developing to different degrees in each country. The one generalization that can be made, as indeed Federal Reserve Chairman Alan Greenspan himself has noted, is that periods of deflation almost always occur after periods of inflation, in that order. Looking at three cases in the 1990s—Germany, Switzerland, and Japan—this has undoubtedly been the case. Excessive price rises were met by zealous tightening of overall monetary conditions, first in terms of nominal rates, then in terms of currency appreciation. This subsequently led to actual declines in asset prices, in terms of both the CPI indicator of goods and the stock and bond markets, rather than just lower price growth. In all three cases, the subsequent period of deflation lasted for several years, a minimum of three years in fact. The duration of both inflation and deflation has much to do with the flexibility of the economy to change and adjust to different economic conditions. In the three cases mentioned, the most notable feature is extremely rigid labor markets, a factor that must surely play a part in delaying the transmission mechanism—and therefore the recovery from deflation—of price changes.

Looking at the Asian countries, given that money supply growth in many countries affected by the crisis remains excessive, the appropriate policy response by the central bank must be tightening of nominal interest rates. Here again, many have indeed tightened rates. On the other hand, Malaysia is the most glaring example of a country where monetary policy is unquestionably lax relative to money supply growth. There the authorities are in effect printing money in order to try and inflate their way out of the crisis.

The two countries where there is the greatest threat of inflation—and thus of deflation, if the rule holds true—are Indonesia and the Philippines. In Indonesia, the Y/Y CPI rate in November was 9.96%, the highest rate since February 1996, this despite an overnight borrowing rate of 15/16%. Part of this relates not to the Asian currency and economic crises, but to the effects of the El Niño–related drought on food prices. This is the same drought that allowed the fires to develop and prosper so rapidly, choking the region with haze. Indeed, November food prices saw growth of 17.3%. In the Philippines, the key fundamental weakness is that old chestnut, external overreliance, in this case on oil. A rising dollar increases the price of importing oil. In addition, the Philippines was also badly affected by weather, which in turn caused food prices to spike in the last quarter of 1997 (to around

15% Y/Y). The one saving grace is that domestic growth was not nearly as strong in the Philippines to begin with and thus there is less demand falloff for these higher-priced goods—food, notwithstanding. This suggests the process should be relatively swift. The Achilles' heel, however, remains the oil dependency. The Philippines relies for 95% of its total energy needs on imported oil. Every 1-peso decline in the USD-PHP exchange rate is thought to translate into a 1.5–2.0% rise in domestic petroleum prices. Traditionally, high fuel prices have led to accelerated overall inflation. As of October CPI, this was "only" 5.7% Y/Y, remarkably tame. That said, the central bank, led by Governor Singson, will remain vigilant. He has not come this far to throw it away now.

Given the domestic credit crunch that will occur, the greatest threat of deflation would appear to lie in Thailand, Indonesia, and Malaysia. The case of Malaysia is different because domestic credit is inflating the economy and thus the immediate threat is, of course, inflation. Malaysia's problem, unlike that of the Philippines and Indonesia, was not overreliance on external funding or resources but on excessive domestic credit leverage to the stock and property markets. Here, it shares much in common with the case of Thailand. Indeed, the risk is that by not facing up to the fundamental problems now, Malaysia faces the risk of a Thai-style meltdown. Excessively low interest rates and high money supply growth will not only fuel inflation but also cause further widening of the current account deficit. This is bad news for the ringgit. Eventually, Malaysia will have to deal with this through tighter monetary policy—tighter than might otherwise have been necessary. This coupled with the developing credit crunch could bring about deflation. It is not beyond the bounds of possibility that Malaysia might have to go to the IMF for aid.

In sum, it is actually extremely difficult to predict which countries will experience inflation and/or deflation given the varying fundamental problems that each one is experiencing and the remaining uncertainty over how each rises (or falls) to the challenge. There remain too many variables. The one safe prediction (always a dangerous statement) is that we will see neither inflation nor persistent deflation in Singapore and Hong Kong. Indonesia, Malaysia, Thailand, Korea, and the Philippines all remain at risk to one or both of these scenarios. If I were a betting man, I would say the greatest long-term risk lies in Korea and Malaysia. In both cases, there seems to be the greatest institutional unwillingness to deal with the problems. Looking back to the example of Japan, which was mired in a combination of recession and deflation for four years in the 1990s, this is one (of many) lesson that Asia should have learned ahead of time. The risk is that at least one and possibly two Asian countries will refuse to learn it.

In the past decade, intra-Asian merchandise trade has steadily grown. It is the result of both trade liberalization and a focus on export industries within an Asian context given the rise of Asian consumption and an Asian middle class. This is the start of what could be the most important economic development since the similar rise of the U.S. middle class. In 1995, some 39.1% of all Asian DMC (developing member country) exports went to fellow DMCs.[1] If you include Japan, the figure is around 50%. In the next two years (from January 1998), given the currency and economic crises that have befallen the region, and the consequent belt tightening mentioned earlier, intraregional trade is likely to be a liability just as much as an asset. Just as in banking and finance, there is far too much capacity out there, in this case manufacturing capacity, for the available demand. Furthermore, the level of demand is likely to shrink substantially. The alternative to a reduction in that capacity is to attempt to alter its final destination. This will occur to some extent, particularly since the Asian currencies have been devalued. Southeast and North Asia have now become competitive once more (the exceptions being Hong Kong and China). There is, however, a limit to the amount of this kind of transfer of destination. For one thing, demand levels and types are different in the U.S. and Europe, and thus substitution may not be easily achievable. For another, an explosion in Asian trade surpluses with either Europe or the U.S. may cause renewed trade and political frictions that would be undesirable for both sides. The only alternative to this is rationalization of the excess manufacturing capacity within Asia itself, given the falloff in Asian consumption and therefore demand.

"In 1998, there will be fire sales all over Asia," predicts Simon Ogus, executive director of Asian Economics at SBC Warburg, in Hong Kong.[2] Ogus predicts the fall in asset prices will be extensive but eventually will be met by acquisition interest from both within and outside Asia. The process will be painful but extremely necessary. In the past, Asian countries focused on industrialization per se, with a smattering of specialization and comparative advantage thrown in. However, once asset prices have hit bottom—and that will take some time—the focus will be on demerging, unbundling, and specializing, as well as on strengthening core businesses. Government need not play any part in it. Indeed to do so risks extending the process. Market forces will do it better and more quickly. In finance, for the next two years, M&A (mergers and acquisitions) is going to be a great business to be in. In autos, semiconductors, chemicals, and commodity-based businesses, massive overcapacity exists. This is particularly true of those businesses linked to the construction and property sectors, though base commodities will be hit as well.

It is high time these businesses were cut down and made leaner and fitter, better able to compete in the new global economy. Many of the old Asian companies were conglomerates, unwieldy, autocratic, centralized—family-run—and uncompetitive in global terms. New Asian companies, start-up companies together with the old ones that have seen the future and restructured ahead of time, will have only a few key competencies, or even just one. There will be a much greater focus on profit and shareholder return than there was before, and also on professional managers and added value—high technology and management and product innovation. It is about time. The rates of return in Asia have been declining sharply across the region in terms of asset prices and FDI. In comparison, those in the U.S. continue to strongly outperform. The U.S. performance is the result of the painful restructuring process the country went through in the early 1990s, first during a period of recession and then via "reengineering." Asia's future economic performance will depend to a large degree on the ability of its companies to restructure themselves to achieve greater focus on comparative advantage and thus on profitability. Lessened access to easy credit will necessitate this. And in the long run, this is not a bad thing, though it will mean painful rationalization. A lot of people are going to lose their jobs before this is all over. Asia will thus be faced with the need to achieve ways of retraining these people.

A final problem, identified most clearly in the case of the Thai economy, is low skill-sets. While many Asian economies have done exceptionally well at developing primary and secondary education institutions, progress has been less broad-based with regard to university-level education and beyond (such as technological- and managerial-oriented institutes and colleges). In the case of Thailand, the country has indeed attempted to set up a high-end education system. However, relative to the needs of the country as a whole, this remains inadequate. Again, this was a factor that propagated external overreliance. Wealthy sons and daughters went abroad to study in the U.S. or Europe rather than stay at home. This has had real economic consequences because in many cases they did not come back! Such a system of educational growth and transfer is incredibly random and inefficient, forcing companies to again seek external expertise. This in turn limits the total skill-set within the domestic workforce, condemning it to remain a relatively low-skilled labor market that relies only or chiefly on price to be "exploited" by (again) external manufacturers. It is stating the obvious to say that education is the basis of long-term economic development and prosperity. Without it, in every case, development will surely flounder.

It is a relatively recent phenomenon (excluding Japan) for Asian university students to be able to get their degrees within Asia. Nevertheless, it is a major step in the right direction. Asia can no longer afford to depend on price, particularly when much of it has overpriced itself relative to other global competitors. It must rely to an increasing extent on raising skill-sets, on producing more added value—in other words, *in getting more bang for your buck (or baht, or ringgit, etc.)*. To rely on price is to risk business going elsewhere. Just look at how manufacturing moved from Hong Kong to Guangdong, and from Thailand to Burma, Vietnam, India, and Bangladesh. If Africa ever gets its act together, Asian businesses that rely on price alone will be in a lot of trouble. Many will go out of business altogether if they do not change their focus quickly.

To sum up this section, which has looked at short-term problems facing Asia, we have considerable overcapacity in finance and manufacturing, external overreliance, weak banking systems, crony capitalism, the threat of inflation/deflation, and low skill-sets. What can be done about all this and indeed about the immediate economic difficulties that Asia faces throughout this year and the next? SBC Warburg's Simon Ogus suggests the following macroeconomic remedies: (1) Governments have to lead by example with regard to fiscal belt tightening "pour encourager les autres" ("in order to encourage the others"—the people). Governments cannot be seen to be hesitant in fiscal tightening; they *have* to lead. Unfortunately, Malaysia appears to be dragging its feet in this with the October budget not having shown the needed spending cuts. On the other hand, Thailand seems to be finally getting the message, albeit after having been dragged kicking and screaming to that point by the IMF. (2) Monetary policy should be depoliticized. Governments should allow central banks to get on with their job. Central banks should be independent and be seen to be independent. Thus, they should be allowed the authority to close down financial institutions without political interference or influence. (3) New bankruptcy codes need to be set up. (Thailand has recently restructured its bankruptcy code, and none too soon given that the old one was extremely tortuous, an indirect incentive for irresponsible activity given the difficulties of investors or lenders recapturing assets. (4) Who is refunded (to whatever degree) and who is not must be clearly and unequivocally stated. Those who lent or bought stocks should lose; that is the price of investment. Depositors, on the other hand, must be protected. Finally, with regard to this, the powers of the regulators must be improved. This is crucial. The political will has to be there to do these things.

"Mexico took all the requisite measures, rationalized and restructured its economy because it had to, because it was told to," Ogus says. "The trouble here in Asia is that there is no one in that position to enforce needed change." In other words, such change may or may not occur—Asia's future hangs in the balance. "Asia does not realize that it is actually not that important in relative terms, yet despite that Asia is arrogant. That combination does not make progress easy."[3] Indeed not. Several Asian countries may resist needed restructuring and change to the last. This may be overoptimistic, but I believe that market forces will eventually have their day. Asian governments and regimes have faced economic crises in the past. In the recent past, they have usually taken the pragmatic approach. If they fail to do so this time, the costs, both political and economic, will be very high.

(Medium-Term) Challenges

In addition to the short-term problems that have to be faced, Asia is also confronted with a series of medium-term challenges with varying priorities and time spans. First among these is to integrate further into the global economy. Over the past decade, Asia has achieved its phenomenal successes largely by opening itself up to trade, by lowering trade barriers, and by increasing investment incentives, whether for FDI or portfolio investment. The ongoing financial market and economic crises could cause Asian authorities to hesitate from opening up further their economies (that is, the economies that are not now influenced by the IMF via the loan packages and accompanying terms) given the damage done by the swift reversal of capital flow and currency devaluations. The lesson, however, is not that capital flow is bad—in the global economy it is vital. Rather, the lesson is that it has to be better managed and channeled to achieve the best returns for both sides. To achieve this, financial regulatory and market institutions need to be strengthened. The temptation (for some) will be to clamp down, to reverse the process of openness to trade and investment. This will be a critical mistake if it is ever made. The likelihood, as I continue to believe, is that pragmatism will prevail. It is in Asia's own interests to open its economies and markets further to the world. In the long run, it can only benefit from doing this.

First and foremost, capital and exchange controls must go. This includes the swap market restrictions in Malaysia, Indonesia, and the Philippines and the two-tier system in Thailand. Central banks imposed these restrictions in order to try to limit speculative activity, but this is akin to King Canute trying to stop the sea coming in. Eventually, if the fundamentals are misaligned and dealers and speculators sense a profitable opportunity to attack a currency or asset market, the market will always find a way. The process of globalization has already to a great extent taken financial control out of the hands of Asian political and financial authorities. The trick is not to fight that process— thereby denying yourself the necessary capital for growth—but to ride the trend, at the same time seeking to secure long-term national health and prosperity through the requisite long-term macroeconomic and microeconomic policies. With regard to this, supporters of free trade and open markets, including myself, received some welcome news in the form of the APEC (Asia-Pacific Economic Cooperation) communiqué of Wednesday, November 26, last year:

> *We, APEC's economic leaders, met today in Vancouver, Canada, to reaffirm our commitment to work together to meet the challenge of sustaining regional prosperity and stability. Certain of the dynamism and resilience of the region, we underline our resolve to achieve sustainable growth and equitable development and to unlock the full potential of the people who live there. We agree that the prospects for economic growth in the region are strong, that Asia-Pacific will continue to play a leading role in the global economy. The goals we have set, including the achievement of free and open trade and investment in the region . . . are ambitious and unequivocal. . . . We remain convinced that open markets bring significant benefits and we will continue to pursue trade and investment liberalization that fosters further growth. Prudent*

*and transparent policies, particularly sound macroeconomic
and structural policies, human resource development strategies and effective financial sector regulation are key to restoring financial stability and realizing this growth potential.*[4]

The ASEAN also confirmed its commitment to liberalized
trade. The prospect of an AFTA (Asian Free Trade Area) by 2003
remains, at least in theory, in place. Even those few who, in their
understandable time of grief and despair at the financial market
and economic turbulence that had been unleashed, railed against
foreign influence have not (yet) done anything to carry out their
threats of closing, rather than opening, their economies. Watch
what they do, not what they say. Emotional rhetoric, however
understandable (but damaging), has given way to good sense and
pragmatism. Participation in the Uruguay Round of the GATT
previously compelled Asian countries—for the better—to liberalize, deregulate, and open up their trade regimes more to the outside world. If the Asian currency crisis plays a part in accelerating
this process, it will have played a major part in securing the long-
economic viability of the region. And this is not for the purpose
of enslaving Asia to external parties as some might suggest, but
instead securing Asia's own role in being able to influence global
economic decisions for the good of its peoples and that of the
global economy.

Under negotiations subsequent to the completion of the
Uruguay Round in 1994 (in Marrakesh), Asian countries committed to full market access being made available at varying
times (1998–2006) depending on the country concerned. Fulfilling these commitments is vital for the prosperity of Asia itself.
The new global economy poses increasingly complex and rapid
challenges to national governments and businesses. In order to
be able to meet those challenges—indeed, just to be in the game,
let alone win it—governments everywhere must give domestic
businesses the help they need by eliminating subsidies (no
incentive is a greater boost to success than survival), lowering
tariff and nontariff trade barriers, creating and maintaining corporate (and government) transparency, and upholding intellec-

tual property rights. As seen by the speed and extent of the Asian currency and economic crises, this process of globalization magnifies and accelerates the costs of poor economic policy. The analogy of not providing the appropriate supports for a building despite the threat of an impending typhoon is not inaccurate. That is exactly what happens to weak financial institutions. The market exacts a terrible price for mistakes. Yet this process actually helps the long-term health of the economy—again, the analogy of the gangrenous limb. It is better to amputate the limb and save the body than wait and hope—and risk death.

While continuing to welcome foreign investment, the specific challenge for Asia is to match the unquestioned success of NAFTA (and to a certain extent Mercosur) by continuing to emphasize intra-Asian trade. This mutually ensures the demand side of the equation as well as supply. Intra-Asian trade is set to take on an ever-increasing preeminent position within the region given the expectation that, after a brief (in historical terms) lull of one to two years, the rise of the new Asian middle class will resume. Asian authorities, both financial and political, must seek to support domestic financial and manufacturing business—through market-driven policies—in order to ensure this rise will not simply renew Asian external dependency but lead to broad-based domestic prosperity. In light of their successes to date, the events of the crisis notwithstanding, they appear well capable of achieving these goals.

Apart from the trade side, a crucial lesson for Asian governments must be that foreign capital has to be used more efficiently. Thailand could have used the waves of foreign capital to build infrastructure, which in turn would have led not only to better road and rail systems (itself a major plus for anyone who has waited for hours in a Bangkok traffic jam) but also to profitable ancillary investments—accompanying property and service centers. Instead, the Thai government allowed a massive property bubble to develop, a sea of unwanted, unused buildings. Eventually, this caused misery for home owners who saw the equity of their own properties plummet in line with the general market fallout after the bubble burst. Integration in the global economy and the global financial markets magnifies and accelerates both the benefits and the weaknesses within domestic economies, requiring faster and more effective government responses than would otherwise have been required. In the end, we all benefit from this.

The process of globalization makes what has become known as the Asian model of growth—or "command capitalism"—less appropriate or relevant to the current economic and market conditions. This might appear a contentious statement to make. However, just take a look around at financial markets, or retail sales, or manufacturing. What are the key common denominators? Speed, flexibility, and technology. The prevailing model was built on the cornerstones of industrial capacity, market share, and revenue growth (rather than actual profit); it does not have the flexibility needed for the increasing global focus on relative returns and is not capable of the requisite speed to alter or upgrade product lines to meet the rapidly changing needs of both domestic and global demand. Equally, it does not possess the level of technology required to continue to rise up the added-value chain. In the global economy, as in business everywhere, either you rise or you fall. If you think you are standing still, you are actually falling. The Asian countries that are able to prosper from the current adversity will be the ones that have fully comprehended the depth of structural reform needed to achieve a globally competitive position—one not based just on price but on quality, on added value.

This is of course (a lot) easier said than done. Here, Asian countries can take at least one lesson each from the U.S. and Japan.

Lesson 1: The U.S. is the most competitive (and by no coincidence at all also the wealthiest) economy in the world. The focus must be on allowing the market to determine both supply and demand. The age of the great Asian credit cycle is gone. The next cycle of growth, following the period of restructuring that will occur over the next two years, will be founded on (relative) returns, on the bottom line, on earnings per share. The next cycle will see the rise of the Asian shareholder, and and none too soon! Up to now, stock markets have been vehicles for domestic speculation by retail investors. In relative terms, there has been little (or any) focus on corporate fundamentals. That will change. The challenge is to ensure that that changes. For Asian companies to compete in the global economy this is essential. This is not to say that Asia need slavishly follow the U.S. (or Western) model of capitalism. Asia has its own cultural dynamics that make such a change difficult to achieve in a relatively short period of time, if at all. The challenge therefore will be for governments to mold the new needs of the global economy to the demands of Asian culture—neocapitalism with Asian characteristics, as it were. That said, the market economy must be (once and for all) embraced. It is that simple. That is the way forward.

Lesson 2: Asia can gain from examining how Japan built up its technological supremacy—by consensus capitalism, not solely government-directed projects. The idea of the Ministry of Finance and the MITI being solely responsible for the rise of Japanese technology is completely wrong. Consensus capitalism fits well with Asian forms of business, which are more network-driven in any case. The trick will be for such networks to achieve contact with governments sufficient to result in funding and support for technological improvement, but to avoid excessive government influence or domination, which tends to hurt returns.

An issue of much debate has been that concerning total factor productivity (TFP), or the total residuals when all inputs from GDP growth are taken out. TFP residuals are most commonly seen as coming from technology and innovation processes, that is, those (gray) accelerating factors that cause growth to leap forward without any accompanying equal input. Given that this concept is a residual, it is notoriously difficult to quantify, and estimations of national TFP readings are quite frankly all over the map. The issue of TFP, in an Asian context, came to prominence when eminent MIT economist Paul Krugman argued in his groundbreaking 1994 article that Asia's "miracle" was in fact a myth, that it was simply due to rapidly increasing inputs that could not be sustained and thus would inevitably fall. The key, he argued, was that TFP readings were extremely small or even negative with regard to developing Asian countries and thus Asia's economic rise was bound to falter. As a predictive piece, it has profound resonance today. Whether or not all his assumptions regarding TFP are correct is quite another matter. Several equally eminent economists have taken issue with Krugman's findings. According to their calculations, Asian countries, notably Singapore, Japan, and Hong Kong, actually had extremely high TFP readings—this presumably confirming the anticipated longevity of their economic expansion.

For my part, I take the following view: TFP readings from anyone are imprecise, however valid the scholarly work supporting them, and thus should be taken with a grain of salt. Whether an economy possesses TFP is another matter. TFP is clearly a vitally important concept for continued economic development. Because the data are so unreliable, anecdotal evidence and common sense can play a greater role. Just looking at Singapore and Hong Kong as examples, it is incontestable that these economies have improved not just as a result of inputs—investment, most notably. Both have experienced major strides in terms of technological advancement, innovation, and education which cannot simply be explained by input or funding. In a sense, education itself is a TFP-oriented process given that you can get a lot more out of it than what you put in. In addition, standard measurements of TFP in Asian countries do not take account of the higher degree of active government intervention in Asian economies relative to those in the U.S. or Europe. After all, if TFP is the residual of growth after inputs are subtracted, the weight of the inputs is vital in attempting any measurement of the TFP residual. In other words, standard TFP measurements look at Asian economies as if they were Western-style economies, completely market-driven and free of government intervention. In short, they are not only inaccurate, they are not even on the right lines. Take out the government intervention within the economy—if you can measure it—and you get a much more accurate reading (relatively speaking) of the TFP concept that Western economists allude to. Not to do so is to allow inherent distortions within the reading. Do I have empirical evidence for this? No. It is just common sense. You are measuring apples and oranges if you do not take account of different types of inputs. Whatever the reading of TFP, it is a useful way of looking at the long-term growth potential of an economy. Possessing TFP, even if one cannot read or measure it accurately, is vital for countries to achieve the requisite accelerated development needed to compete in the global economy. A final point: Even leaving aside TFP and looking at the inputs, it would seem that those who say total inputs—investment, labor, capital, and production—cannot be maintained at such high levels in Asia as a whole do not take account of the massive pools of labor and capital potential still available in countries like China and India.

One of the most visible challenges Asia faces is the need to create infrastructure—reminding one vividly of Bangkok and its lack thereof (at least, that is completed). The World Bank in various publications has estimated that some USD1.5–2.0 trillion is needed over the next decade to fund the infrastructure a growing Asia region will require. Infrastructure, as proved beyond doubt by the highways and ports in the U.S. and Europe, is fundamental to the growth of advanced nations and indeed accelerates that growth. Could infrastructure itself be TFP-orientated? Why not? If you take out all the inputs to TFP, you still have a residual surrounding growth—businesses that did not receive one dollar, ringgit, or rupiah of funding from the infrastructure project, but that grew up to surround the infrastructure project just because it was there. Fine, but where is the funding going to come from? Asia is in the midst of a credit crunch, which makes infrastructure slightly tricky to achieve. The answer is that Asia needs two types of infrastructure. One type is the infrastructure that you can see, such as highways, roads, ports, power stations, public buildings, telephone equipment, and so on. The other is institutional infrastructure, such as capital markets, regulators, and institutional investors. Make no mistake about it: Both types are equally important. Indeed there is an argument to make that institutional infrastructure is more important, for it benefits the economy as a whole rather than just part of it.

This brings us to one of Asia's most glaring weaknesses, a weakness that of necessity will be eliminated over the next two years. Asia lacks a bond market. It has equity markets. It has a loan market. But it does not have a deep, domestic bond market. Why is this crucial? Because Asian companies need the broad spectrum of capital markets to provide their funding needs. To rely simply on the equity market distorts the latter's purpose (and trading activity). As for the loan market, this is not liquid enough. A bond market provides the requisite secondary market trading ability that ensures timely, inexpensive (in relative terms), long-term funding. In other words, it allows companies not only to grow but to invest for the future. Pretty basic stuff you might think, but Asia doesn't have it—yet. What Asia does have is a wealth of corporate foreign currency–denominated issues. Bond traders take heart! A domestic Asian currency–denominated bond market is coming! It has to, in order both to provide the funding long-term needs for the Asian corporate base and to more efficiently allocate Asia's huge savings surpluses. The events of 1997 and 1998 will, in retrospect, mark the birth of sustainable, liquid, and deep domestic bond markets in Asia.

The lack of developed domestic debt markets contributed in two ways to the Asian currency and economic crises. First, banks and companies were forced to focus on foreign currency–denominated bonds and loans that were inherently vulnerable to foreign exchange risk; this is a factor that most ignored (to their peril). Second, because banks were the only available lender of corporate finance, the discretionary decisions of local bankers took on much greater importance. The bankers in turn could be influenced by governments to invest in chosen financial and economic sectors. Financial bottlenecks were created inadvertently, the results of which could lead to distortion and inefficient allocation and usage of Asia's extremely high savings. Equally, the lack of a domestic bond market with the long-term funding that it provides caused companies to rely on short-term funding, through commercial paper, loans, and foreign currency–denominated bonds. Thus, in addition to foreign exchange risk, they faced principal and maturity risk, as did the banks that lent to them. Some Asian governments might take the view that it is not in their own interests to allow the development of domestic currency–denominated bond markets because this would entail a loss of political control over the financial sector. What they have yet to understand is that they have already lost control. The globalization process and the development of the global economy necessitate that capital gets priced efficiently and cheaply. If there are nations or regions that do not do so—either deliberately or inadvertently—the capital goes elsewhere. Despite the extraordinary wealth that Asia has created in a single generation, it cannot rely on its own government funding alone. Asia needs to utilize its high savings rates more efficiently in order to provide the financial fuel for its economic engine to power it out of its recession. That fuel is a domestic bond market.

In order to have one, a country needs to create a deep institutional investor base—the buyers of these bonds. Pension fund industries, which exist only in Singapore and Malaysia to any notable extent in the form of the national provident funds, need to be created and built up. Especially given that some Asian countries face demographic problems caused by a large aging population, pension funds need to be created in order to save for the future. Government budgets will not be sufficient to deal with the financial burden that the aging of Asia will represent, nor should they be. For a country to have a savings rate of 30 to 35% and not have a pension fund industry to better allocate the financial resources of that, for both the private individual and the economy, is almost criminal.

The creation of Asian national domestic bond markets is one of the most important tasks that face national governments. To have a domestic bond market, the institutional infrastructure needs to be created. Hong Kong and Singapore have strong and well-respected central banks and regulators. Other Asian countries need to create or improve their regulatory systems as well. In addition, there needs to be an efficient, transparent settlement and clearing system. The Hong Kong Monetary Authority has waxed lyrical about the need for an Asia clear settlement system and clearinghouse. Such infrastructure is vital. It is up to the governments and financial authorities of Asia, perhaps along with the aid of the IMF and the World Bank, to set up an Asian clearinghouse for domestic and foreign currency–denominated bond markets. Institutional investors, both domestic and foreign, will require that it is fully transparent and that it has strict regulations that are fully upheld, giving no favor to any. Once they have the institutional infrastructure—the pension funds, mutual funds, and life insurers plus the appropriate independent regulatory bodies—Asian governments and central banks, whatever their own financial situations, need to issue sovereign benchmark bond issues in order to establish a sovereign bond yield curve against which Asian companies can price off their own issues. In other words, whether or not Asian government financial situations require that they issue bonds for funding purposes, they should do so anyway. In this regard, the HKMA has led the way, creating a domestic yield curve despite the fact that Hong Kong runs a budget surplus and thus has no urgent need for funding.

In the past, Asian corporate finance directors have largely used internal cash flow, bank loans, and foreign currency–denominated bonds to meet their funding needs and have focused on securing and maintaining revenue growth. They will now have to change those mind-sets. In the wake of the massive corporate restructuring process that will take place over the next two years, they will have to take greater account of driving down costs, in both manufacturing and financial terms. From a funding perspective, this can best be achieved by issuing long-term debt. In the case of Hong Kong, it has developed government and sovereign yield curves; yet actual Hong Kong corporate bond issuance remains modest. Hong Kong has far greater ambitions. It wants to be the financial center for China. To date, this has resulted in Chinese companies—both domestic companies and the "red chips," Hong Kong companies whose assets are based in mainland China—making initial public offerings of stock in the Hong Kong stock market. For China to issue Hong Kong dollar–denominated bonds and then for Chinese companies to follow suit would be a major step along this path. Once these domestic bond markets are created, Asian governments and private sectors will be better placed to finance the development of "real" infrastructure—ports, highways, and so on. The latter has been proved incontestably to accelerate growth, despite its initial costs. Also, apart from anything else, Asian populations will and should demand the creation of infrastructure. Asian middle classes who look to achieve a better life now that their immediate financial needs have been secured are likely to be especially vocal in this regard. Once again, Hong Kong and Singapore are way ahead of the pack in terms of real economic infrastructure, a factor that will support their economic progress in the future.

A further challenge for Asian governments, in terms of improving their countries' relative competitiveness in a global context, is to improve their education systems. In most cases, strong primary and secondary schools have already been created, a factor that has indeed been beneficial to Asia's economic successes over the past two decades. However, the higher-education "infrastructure" remains scarce and inadequate—yet again, the exceptions being Hong Kong and Singapore. Universities and business and technology colleges need to be created, with the help of both government and private funding. The lack of higher education has been a further example of Asian external overreliance. Apart from being expensive, this is a hugely wasteful use of Asia's human capital. If these young men and women stayed at home (providing they got an equally good education in Asia), the transmission mechanism would be more efficient and also quicker. Asian banks and businesses are short of skilled, domestic manpower to service its needs. Indeed, the *Far Eastern Economic Review* estimates that Asia needs up to 3 million upper-level and middle-level managers.[5] The domestic, higher education systems have to be created to meet these needs. At present, Hong Kong and Singapore (again) top Asia (excluding Japan) for the highest percentage of managers in the workforce. Yet even they are still well below the OECD levels. To compete in the global economy, this disparity has to be eliminated.

Despite the many problems present in the Indian economy, Indian managers are to a certain extent already filling this gap throughout Asia left by British and American managers in terms of an entrepreneurial, English-speaking, highly educated skill base that is readily prepared to move across borders in search of opportunity and prosperity. Tapping the business needs of Chinese companies is a monumental task that involves the participation of the Overseas Chinese, in terms of both networks and countries such as Singapore and Hong Kong. Yet this puts a strain on the domestic needs of the countries involved. The answer in China's case is to set up business schools and put more people through universities, which China has already begun to do.

Transparency will continue to be an important issue. Out of the emerging markets of Latin America, Asia, and emerging Europe, Asia as a region has probably the worst corporate transparency. Once again, this situation in a global context is not tolerable. Family-run businesses that did not have to answer to anybody in the past will have to increasingly answer to shareholders and bond buyers if they want their funding needs to be met. Business networks will not be able to meet their funding needs entirely, forcing them to tap the financial markets in one way or another. Institutional investors, whether domestic or international, are increasingly demanding a level playing field for issues such as corporate transparency. Any country in the world which says no to this will simply be bypassed and thus will not be able to achieve the requisite funding. If "no man is an island," as John Donne would have us believe, the same is certainly true for countries. There are only two possible answers to globalization and the global economy: yes or no. Sitting on the fence is not possible, not an option. Though some elements within Asian countries still battle against globalization—and thus loss of control—Asian countries have already answered the question in the affirmative. It is up to the regulators to enforce greater corporate transparency, and thus indirectly to enforce global standards for their manufacturing and financial sectors.

Asia also faces a demographic challenge in regard to aging. As previously mentioned, many Asian countries, notably those of East Asia (including Japan) which are in fact emerged, mature economies, face the challenge of the financial burden that will result from the aging of their domestic populations. In Japan, the problems are the most obvious and most widely discussed, but "emerging Asia" also faces similar problems. Rising proportions of retirees will have a profound effect on savings rates and growth—hurting both.

How does this happen? Countries the world over go through what is called a "demographic transition." This is the crucial period of change that alters the makeup and structure of a country's population in terms of age dynamics. Changes in Asian demography have already had a profound effect on the Asian economies. Indeed they have been a major driving force for the explosive growth that Asia achieved up until 1997. The Asian Development Bank has estimated that demographic change has accounted for between 0.5 and 1.3 percentage points of annual GDP growth per person during the period 1965–1990. This represents about 15 to 40% (depending on how you measure it) of the average annual growth rate of 3.3% in that period.[6]

As countries increase their general wealth and thus personal income, demographic forces combine with improvements in living and medical conditions to result in high birth rates and rapid population growth. As children become adults and then join the labor force, this provides a major boost to the industrialization process and thus the economy as a whole. This is indeed what happened in Asia. However, as countries achieve a certain degree of wealth, birth rates start to fall back. The reasons for this can be twofold. One is that falling birth rates are frequently the result of government-oriented policies that encourage fewer births. The other is that improving living conditions serve to provide a lesser necessity and focus for procreation. As economies advance, women gain greater equality, freedom, and choice. This causes changes in the overall demographic makeup. From having lots of infants and a relatively small elderly population, there is a shift to a declining proportion of children, and a far higher one of adults who are then free (or not) to join the labor force. It is this that provides the demographic boost to the country's economy. This means that the country's government is able to gain greater tax revenues and businesses have access to a more available (and thus cheaper) workforce. In addition, there are less dependent elements—children and the elderly—within the economy, thus reducing any financial burden on the budget. This demographic change or transition not only benefits the budget and the economy but also serves as a boost to the savings rate—thus providing the necessary financial fuel for private and government investment. The high savings rate is not just the result of Asians saving more than Westerners, though this itself has some validity. It is also the result of the demographic transition that Asian countries have only relatively recently (in historical terms) experienced. The U.S. and Europe went through this demographic transition over a century ago.

All this is very well, but what happens when this significant increase in the adult labor force moves further down the line, becoming elderly? The financial burden on the economy becomes greater as the dependents take up a greater proportion of the population. This, however, does not fully take account of specifically Asian dynamics, where there is far less emphasis placed on social security systems and national health care and more on the family acting as the safety net rather than the government. It is possible, though, that this itself may change as the economies advance, similar to the experience of the Western nations and Japan. As countries become older, savings rates are bound to decline. The key is how investment performs while this is happening. If investment is maintained at high levels and savings rates fall, then the country will be condemning itself to having to import capital rather than export it. Investment rates have to be cut when this happens in order to ensure that external overreliance is avoided. This, however, in turn affects the growth rate, which as a consequence is bound to slow.

All this sounds quite gloomy, adding to Asia's economic woes. There are two reasons why this is not the case, however. First, the next wave of children will hit the labor market as the first (major) wave goes on to the elderly, dependent stage. While the second wave might be smaller in actual numbers, given declining birth rates, it will still act as a catalyst for future growth. In addition, attempts to improve TFP and education should mean that quality will more than make up for lack of quantity. The countries of the more developed East Asia will face this problem—and this opportunity—just as Japan does right now. The second reason to be optimistic is that there are countries that have yet to go through this demographic transition or at least have not yet fully experienced it. This is most notably the case in South Asia—in India, Pakistan, Bangladesh, and Sri Lanka. And to a certain extent it is also the case in Southeast Asia and China—though one could argue in China's case that it has excessive labor potential rather than a deficit given the massive corporate restructuring that is needed there. India and Pakistan in particular are only just starting to see the economic benefits of this demographic transition period. They have a lot further to go—and thus I am extremely bullish on their economic prospects (if they don't let politics or war interfere with economic progress, which admittedly is a very big if). Despite the aging that some Asian nations are experiencing, as a whole Asian birth rates remain considerably higher than those in Europe or the U.S.; thus Asia will continue to take up an increasing share of the global population. A new wave of "megacities"—cities with more than 10 million people—will sprout up. Though estimates vary, about twenty new megacities could sprout up in Asia over the next two decades. This has profound implications for two further challenges to Asia's future, energy and its by-product, pollution.

The effects of Asia's growing demand for energy have already begun to be felt on the world's financial markets. The leading buyers of commodities, for instance, are no longer (so much) the U.S. or Western European nations, but China. Chinese demand for metals, oil, and grain is one of the major market determinants for these commodity markets. It has come down to as simple an equation as this: if China is not buying copper, the price of copper goes down, no matter the other economic or financial variables. Greater China as a whole and India, which makes up around 12% of world gold consumption on its own, have a profound effect on the gold trading pits in London and New York. Given the relative paucity of available (and easily tapped) energy in Asia, Asia faces a number of energy shortages—and thus external overreliance—including oil, coal, and natural gas. Japan, China, and all the Southeast Asian nations, apart from Malaysia and Indonesia (notably the latter), which have their own resources in sufficient quantity, are thus forced to import their needs. Needless to say, this is costly and opens them up to foreign exchange and inflation risk. For instance, the Philippines imports 95% of its energy needs. As a result, the economy experiences major inflationary pressures when the dollar rises sharply against the Philippine peso, which then has to be offset by monetary and/or fiscal policy. Lack of immediately available energy resources causes countries to search elsewhere, or at least in areas that are not immediately obvious. This in turn can cause confrontation with other countries that dispute the land or sea claims as their own—witness the dispute between China and Vietnam over sea territory in the South China Sea, as well as the Diaoyu Islands dispute between China, Taiwan, and Japan. The latter is not only about political sensitivity but also (more importantly) about the billions of gallons of oil that could be underneath the seabed around those islands. Without tapping new sources of energy reserves elsewhere, such as those in the South China Sea, Asia's dependence (what I have termed external overreliance) not only will be maintained but will actually increase. At present, Asia consumes around a quarter of global energy production. The ongoing period of economic consolidation and recession notwithstanding, Asian demand is likely to continue to increase. Even in those countries that are largely self-sufficient in one or more energy forms, such as Indonesia, reserve levels are relatively low and falling fast.

A by-product of Asian demand for energy and Asia's ascendancy over the past two decades has been a proportional ascendancy in the levels of pollution in Asia. You can see it with your own eyes. It is everywhere, whether you are talking about the haze that affected Indonesia, Malaysia, and Singapore, the canals around Bangkok which are foul and polluted, or even the rivers in Beijing. A common joke in Hong Kong is that if you fell into Victoria Harbour at night, there would be no problem finding you because you would be glowing—and simultaneously being infected with a plethora of viruses and disease. As a whole Asian rivers are estimated to contain three to four times the world average of fecal pollutants. Over the last three decades, Asia has lost about 50% of its forests and 50% of its fish stocks.[7] Urban pollution will continue to increase because an ever-increasing proportion of Asian populations will migrate to the cities. If we look back, then extrapolate, and also add on for anticipated acceleration of this process, we can predict that around 50 to 55% of Asian populations could live in cities by about 2020. This is potentially good news for growth and productivity, but awful news in terms of pollution. Asia is not far away from seeing its pollution levels acting as a dampener on growth. In addition, the longer Asian countries wait to do something about the pollution levels being created, the more it will cost them to clean the mess up and thus the greater the financial burden on the government budget and on savings. Again, this all sounds pretty bearish, but hope is at hand. Japan was in a similar situation when it went through its own initial demographic transition phase in the 1960s and early 1970s. Eventually, popular demand for change resulted in the government acting. The hope is that the same will happen in Asia. If one examines how long it took the Japanese government to act, one might conclude, however, that the situation (and living conditions) in much of Southeast Asia and South Asia will continue to get worse before it gets better.

In the advanced East Asian nations, such as Korea and Taiwan, popular demand for such change is already on the rise. As I said, the longer governments dither and delay, the more it will cost them in the end. Of course, pollution exists not only in the cities. There is also significant pollution and environmental degradation in the countryside as well, resulting in destruction and reduction of natural resources. Something can be done about this, however—apart from the obvious. Much of agricultural pollution can in fact be linked to trade, or more specifically to trade-oriented government subsidies and protectionism. By its very nature, government interference leads to price distortion and price distortion feeds back into production distortion—that is, overproduction and oversupply. This is by no means a uniquely Asian phenomenon. Think of the European Common

Agriculture Policy (or rather don't. For most economists, it is a glaring warning of how the goal of a single European economy could fail badly). Anyway, back to production distortion. Trade protectionism leads to overproduction, the level of subsidies being often directly linked to the level of agricultural production. Thus, it leads to overfarming of available land. Agricultural policies lead to farmers using more inputs than are necessary or desirable. Thus farmers rely increasingly on chemicals, which in turn leads to chemical runoff and soil erosion—which in turn reduces the available land to be cultivated, which leads to over-farming of available land, and so on, a vicious circle.

The way to deal with this is to eliminate trade protectionism, eliminate agricultural subsidies (the U.S., which claims some-what dubiously to be completely open to free trade, take note), and allow the market to eliminate the need for overfarming by correcting the pricing mechanism, and thus the need for production. This is undoubtedly a painful process, leading to people losing their jobs and farms and so forth. But what is the alternative? To continue to let trade protectionism destroy the countryside? Not only agriculture but natural resources, such as forests, could benefit from this as well. One reason we saw the haze last year to such dramatic effect was that the Indonesian government did not sufficiently charge concession holders adequate fees for timber harvested. This in turn led to overforestation and field and forest burning on a massive scale. The elimination of agricultural and natural resource subsidies and trade protectionism leads to trade and environmental gains. Of course, that is not all that has to be done to save our environment, but it would be an excellent start.

The final medium-term challenge that Asia faces is to reduce poverty and make national income distribution more equitable. As the ADB notes, if poverty is defined as personal income of less than 1 U.S. dollar a day, poverty was estimated in 1993 to be the highest in the world in South Asia at 43.1% of the entire population, compared with 39.1% for sub-Saharan Africa and East Asia at 17.3%.[8] The absolute number of "poor" people (as defined by the above definition) in South Asia alone was 515 million people. Looking at the region as a whole, that's about 1 billion people. To be sure, there is recent progress in South Asia. Notably this has occurred in India after it decided (wisely) in 1991 to give up economic splendid isolationism, faced as it was with a fiscal and economic crisis, and started to open itself up for trade. However, considerably more effort is needed if this problem is ever going to be eradicated, for poverty has many nefarious by-products that hurt the economy (and of course the people concerned) such as lack of education, poor health and nutrition resources, and higher infant mortality.

After all, what is economic development about if it is not about improving people's standards and conditions of living, and thus in turn reducing poverty? Growth in India and Pakistan in particular, despite the improvements made to date and the consequent emergence of a substantial (powerful and vocal) middle class in both countries, continues to be felt by an insufficient number of people. The trickle-down effect does not trickle down. How can this be alleviated? As someone who believes profoundly in the benefits of the market—even though they are by no means perfect, they are the least worst option—my answer has to be to open up the economy more fully to market-driven forces. Government can aid the worst off, in the process not only giving them financial and social aid, but providing training and education so that they do not remain dependent and thus provide a greater contribution, both to themselves and the economy. The best examples of more broad-based economies are Singapore, Hong Kong, and Taiwan. Economies that face considerably greater poverty challenges are China, Indonesia, the Philippines, India, and Pakistan. The way to achieve this is distribution liberalization of education, land, and the labor market. To sum up this section, Asia faces the following medium-term challenges: achieving better integration within the global economy, changing to a new model of growth, creating institutional and "real" infrastructure, improving education and legal, government, and corporate transparency, dealing with changes in demography, solving energy and pollution problems, and reducing poverty.

Given the astounding successes that Asia has achieved over the past two decades, it is eminently capable of meeting these challenges and succeeding again in the future. This is not to understate their significance or the difficulty of achieving success. Pessimists talk of the possibility of a "lost decade" which Asia could see, similar to the experience of Latin America after the Latin American debt crisis of 1982. Asia could go the way of Japan, again losing almost a decade in wasted economic activity while the government and bureaucrats talked but did little to improve the situation. However, while the threat remains that Asia could go down that path—and if it does, it will be Asian governments that are to blame—the essential flexibility that Asia has developed over the past two decades would suggest to me that it will take the pragmatic route. Asia has shown great flexibility before and I believe will do so again. If anything, the example of Japan should serve as what not to do in times of crisis and should thus benefit Asian governments in the decisions they take over the next two years. If one takes that optimistic view, the present situation of economic and financial crisis in Asia potentially represents an opportunity of historic proportions. It is to this that I turn next.

(Long-Term) Opportunities

The long-term fundamentals of Asia remain unchanged—high savings rates, demographic advantage (for some), hard-working people, pro-growth and pro-business governments, and low tax rates. Despite the economic and financial problems that the region is currently undergoing, the rise of the Asian middle classes, and in such numbers, is a major global phenomenon that will not go away just because of the downturn in growth. This has implications for the way Asian countries will develop and grow—in just the same way that the rise of the middle classes in the U.S. and Europe impacted not only the quantity but the quality of growth. The interim period of slower growth—or recession for some, such as Thailand—notwithstanding, middle-class Asians will want a better life and will focus to an increasing extent on getting it rather than on the achievement of wealth. This is similar to the corporate restructuring that will occur, focusing on profit growth, and thus quality, rather than revenue growth, or quantity.

Anyone who is reading this section for specific stock recommendations would be advised to bypass it altogether. I am not a stock market analyst and therefore I am not the person to give specific stock market and company recommendations. What I can do, however, is to look at the general economic forces that prevail and in turn that are likely to emerge and develop.

As I said, quality of life will be a much more important factor in the future. Of course, to poorer Asians, like the poor anywhere, such considerations are an unaffordable luxury. The focus for them will remain first on survival and then on improving their living conditions if they can. As for the middle classes, leisure and saving activities will take on greater preeminence. Prior to the crisis, it was already starting to happen. After all, what industries focus on leisure? Airlines, the hotel industry, and sports and recreation companies, along with fashion and high-end autos. The mushrooming of domestic airlines and hotels all over Asia did not just represent external tourist and business interest in the region. It also reflected the rise of domestic Asian interest in travel and leisure activities. There can be little doubt that the economic downturn in Asia will put a dent in this process. In my view, this is not a bad thing. I admit it is a lot easier to say this from my perspective than from that of someone working or investing in these industries. Asia had after all become too expensive in both manufacturing and tourism. The days when Hong Kong was cheap are long gone. If this problem is not dealt with, it will mean the terminal decline of the territory. Pricing power was used to excess in many Asian countries as retailers and hoteliers reacted to significant increases in demand. That pricing power has to a great extent been lost in the wake of the economic crisis, and thus prices are bound to fall—either sooner or later, and if later then by a lot more. Cyclical industries such as chemicals, autos, metals, and other commodities will be hit the hardest by the downturn. Leisure industries will also be hit and be forced to cut their prices significantly. Long term, however, if one dismisses the possibility of war breaking out in Asia and anticipates continued peaceful coexistence, Asian reliance on and exposure to leisure-based industries can only increase. The rationalization that is likely to happen initially within these industries, given the harder times ahead, will only serve to make them more competitive and profitable. As an increasing proportion of Asians grow older, health care spending will increase markedly. Thus, businesses such as private hospitals, health care services, and pharmaceutical companies should stand to benefit.

In terms of financial market investments, I asked a few bankers and fund managers what they thought would be good investments over the next two years. A number were too shell-shocked by the events of the past year to wish to comment, though there were a few notable suggestions. SBC Warburg's Ogus, who given his extremely bearish outlook for the region as a whole, says he does not like equities as an asset class. He recommended buying gold, given the cheap price and its usefulness as a hedge against major financial asset declines:

> The opportunities available depend to a great extent on the time span you are looking at. Buying gold is a medium-term option given the underperformance you are likely to see in Asian financial asset markets. You could also look to buy long-dated Eurodollar call options (if you believe in a deflationary scenario for Asia and possibly the world as a whole). The best thing in this environment is to be cash rich. If you have to buy companies at all, buy low-geared ones.

In terms of national outperformance in Asia, Ogus expected China, Hong Kong, and Singapore to outperform.[9]

One Hong Kong–based bond fund manager was quite frank about the difficulty in picking worthwhile financial asset investments in the immediate term:

> *In terms of bonds, it's bloody tough to find anything we would want right now. You could go bottom-fishing in some of the more solid corporate names, but their bonds could also fall further before they stabilize. Sure these yields are great, but for a start there is no liquidity so you might not be able to get out again once you bought in and also that yield could get even better!*

The fund manager said that added value is the key going forward, not just for companies but also for countries.[10]

> *It comes down to what are you bringing to the table, what products you are giving to the world which have the most added value at the cheapest price. If I look at Asia, I say why should Thailand be there? What does Thailand make that no one else makes? Thailand depended on price, but that's a fool's game because someone somewhere is going to come along and produce something cheaper than you can. When that happens, you lose. Thailand has nothing to fall back on, unlike Japan in 1990–1991. Thailand is in pieces and its asset markets will continue to get hit near term by high interest rates and the financial sector collapse. Indonesia has some potentially global companies worth looking at which look cheap (in terms of stock and bond prices), but they could get even cheaper. In addition, social unrest could be a BIG issue in Indonesia in 1998. There is going to be a lot of economic pain and people are not going to take well to that. Malaysia in 1998 could be the next nightmare in terms of banking and finance company exposure to the stock and property markets.[11]*

The one area the fund manager thought worth looking at from a bond investment point of view was China sovereign bonds. Overall however, the outlook was extremely gloomy. As for me, I see Singapore and China outperforming near term. China, though, still faces massive challenges in the next few years, most notably restructuring its state-owned enterprises

(SOEs) and avoiding significant social unrest despite increasing unemployment.

My favorite country, is India. After all, the Indian political scene is one of complete chaos. Governments come and go and nothing appears to get done. The streets of New Delhi and Mumbai (Bombay) are clogged to overflowing, as anyone who has taken a business trip there knows. Pollution is appalling, and the poverty levels surpass those seen in sub-Saharan Africa. Yet India has a number of comparative advantages that make it look like a good long-term bet. First is education. At the university level, the Indian education system, both that created by the country since independence in 1948 and that left over from its colonial past, remains superior to that of, say, China. Education is a cornerstone of growth and prosperity, and such an advantage is a major positive regarding economic prospects. That said, on balance, the story of Indian education is a mixed one. Below the university level, it is no exaggeration to say that Indian education is appalling. Unlike the ASEAN countries which sought first to build up primary and secondary education, India placed its education emphasis at university level. The result has led to sharp education and economic disparity. Over half the country's adults are illiterate. Successive Indian governments have promised to raise spending on education; yet it remains mired at a paltry 4% of GDP, less than half that of many of its Asian neighbors. In the likes of Thailand and Indonesia, large, cheap, and moderately skilled workforces have been developed, but with the economy lacking the requisite number of higher-skilled workers and managers. In India, it is the other way around. This has one advantage in that the managers can theoretically solve the problem. Of course, putting theory into practice is no easy task in India, plagued as it is by a tortuous political system.

In addition, India should benefit from the demographic change described earlier. South Asia as a whole is just starting to go through its demographic transition, just starting to feel the benefits of a generation hitting the labor market. While East Asian populations age, India will outperform in demographic terms—as will Pakistan, Sri Lanka, and Bangladesh. The contribution to the economy from this will drive the Indian economy for a decade. Given the political chaos that is the norm in India, it is indeed incredible how far India has come and not least how fast the economy is growing. In the last three years, India has been averaging 7% growth. Just think what it could achieve if the politicians ever got their act together!

Given the huge uphill battle it has had to face as a result of the destructive socialist policies of Nehru and Indira Gandhi, look how far India has come already. From 1991, when it faced a balance of payments crisis and a fiscal crisis, to the present day, it has cut the average import-weighted tariff from just under 90% to around 20 to 25%. This is notable progress, but more has to be done, such average tariff levels being twice the average in the ASEAN. Sectors like telecoms, autos, and the power industry have been partially opened to foreign investment, the rupee has been made partially convertible, the capital markets have been partially liberalized with Indian companies being allowed to list on and borrow from foreign asset markets, and price controls on some commodities have been removed. This is not to say that it does not still have a long way to go. Perhaps the most pressing need is to develop infrastructure. India's roads and ports were not built for the amount of traffic that is flowing through them. The result is delays. These are frustrating for individuals but extremely costly for business, and thus for the country, because such delays act as a deterrent in terms of foreign investors coming to India in the first place.

Despite the recent Asian currency crisis, the rupee should be made fully convertible on the capital account as well as the current account. As well, the bond market should be fully liberalized in order to provide a fully transparent and efficient funding mechanism for Indian companies and for Indian government institutions that can then use this to finance the infrastructure that India so badly needs. Import tariffs need to be cut back further. As I said earlier, import tariffs, far from protecting the domestic export industry, actually damage it, since they act as an incentive for companies to simply sell goods at home rather than take the effort to export. India's overall trade balance would benefit greatly from its import tariffs being slashed. It is important that this occur, for export growth has been declining for the past two years. Averaging an annual rate of over 20% between 1993 and 1995, export growth fell to 13% in 1996 and is expected to have been around 4–5% in 1997. While exports make up only 10% of GDP, the same dynamics that affected the export sectors of the ASEAN and North Asia have also been present in India. Despite the restrictions present in the Indian foreign exchange market, the cure for this is the same—the rupee has to weaken. That is indeed what we saw in the fourth quarter of 1997. While trade should be further liberalized, the insurance sector also needs to be opened up to foreign investment and competition and state-owned banks need to be privatized.

With regard to the last two suggestions, there is considerable political opposition to these—and none of the suggestions are guaranteed to be put through. Yet what is the alternative? Continued political stagnation. It is the politicians who are holding India back from its rightful destiny, not the business community and certainly not the heads of the Finance Ministry and Reserve Bank of India, both of whom have been at the forefront of the reform movement. It is the politicians who need to change. Though India is rightly and fiercely proud of its status as the world's largest democracy, that does not mean to say it cannot learn from others. Thailand also faced political chaos. It took a crisis for the Thai politicians to realize that change was necessary and thus a new constitution should be enacted. India could undoubtedly benefit from a similar approach to altering its political makeup.

In regard to the economy, a number of concerns remain. One is the persistent fiscal deficit that lingers at a high 5.0% of GDP, despite improvements that reduced it from almost the 6% level. In addition, inadequate progress has been made on reforming and restructuring India's own state-owned enterprises. The ninth five-year plan which takes account of the period 1997–2001 aims for annual GDP growth of around 7 to 8%, with strong contributions from both industry and agriculture. In order to accomplish this, it will have to be financed. That can be achieved in two ways: through liberalizing and deregulating further and by seeking ways to raise the savings rate. This last may seem bizarre as India already has a high gross national savings rate of around 27%. Yet gross domestic investment is just shy of 29%, thus guaranteeing that India is attracting more capital than it is exporting—and thus has a persistent current account deficit. While "only" around 1.5% of GDP, the combination of this and the budget deficit is dangerous, as Thailand and others have discovered. Also, India's external debts outstanding are around USD96 billion.

These negatives together with the fall in the government in late November caused the rupee to slide in the foreign exchange markets. Though modest by comparison with the falls in other Asian currencies, this did cause concern. It prompted the Reserve Bank of India to retaliate by tightening liquidity and imposing market restrictions, limiting dollar forward contracts to commercial use. The Royal Bank of India also intervened heavily in the market to stabilize the rupee. Indian officials, before and after, expressed confidence that the situation would be stabilized. "One advantage we have is that we did not see the huge amount of capital flows in the first place which other Asian nations experienced, although investment in India has picked up. Our current account deficit is also very modest," explained the then Royal Bank of India Governor C. Rangarajan. He added that restrictions on rupee foreign exchange trading—not convertible yet on the capital account—would also lessen the impact on India of the recent market turbulence in India.[12]

Should India, despite such restrictions, experience a similar type of currency and economic crisis to that experienced by countries in Southeast and North Asia, that could actually be a blessing in disguise. Talking to people in the market who either trade the rupee or invest in Indian asset markets, the one common theme coming back was that a crisis could actually be beneficial because it could force change on the politicians. "It took a balance of payments crisis in 1991 for them to change direction. It might have to take another crisis for them to change again, but if that means opening up the Indian economy more and reforming and deregulating faster, it will be for the good, long term. I'm a buyer of India long term, but they have to work through a number of problems first," said one Hong Kong–based manager for a U.S. investment bank.[13] A key positive for the future, relative to 1991 when a state of crisis was apparent and there was little option but to reform, is that a critical mass of political consensus has developed in favor of reform. The link between political and economic stability is no longer so direct, with the technocrats getting on with the job, leaving the politicians to fight it out. The politicians themselves are coming round to the view that the process of reform is irreversible. Many have said so in exactly those words.

The analogy for many is to see India more as a lumbering elephant than a tiger, but given the events of the past year, that is not necessarily a bad thing. To continue this analogy a little further, India is pulling far too much weight. It needs to be set free from its man-made shackles. Then it can really start to outperform as is—and should be—its rightful destiny given the strengths self-evident within its economy. What about the rest of Asia? Where does it go from here?

In the last section of this chapter, I give a country-by-country breakdown of the fundamental outlook. Since the crisis started in Thailand, I start with Thailand first.

Thailand

While Thai officials no longer seem in denial, the full extent of the decay within the Thai banking and finance company sectors has yet to be seen or experienced. Rationalization in this and the construction and real estate sectors will persist for the next two years at the very least. In return for the IMF loan package, Thailand is forced to pursue a program of severe fiscal austerity. This will necessitate that Thailand shrink its current account deficit and produce a significant budget surplus of at least 1% of GDP. The result of this in turn will unquestionably be full-scale economic recession in Thailand. The Standard & Poor's MMS official forecasts for GDP growth for 1997 and 1998 are zero and

~2.0%. The risk is to the downside of those estimates, at least for 1997 and possibly 1998 as well. The depreciation in the baht will add markedly to Thai corporate foreign currency–denominated debt burdens and will also boost inflationary pressures, though the worst of inflation will not be seen until well into 1998.

The one positive is that exports will continue their rebound of the last quarter of 1997, helped by the baht devaluation that made them much more competitive in price terms. As a result, the current account deficit is likely to shrink from some 8% of GDP in 1995 and 1996 to 1.5% in 1997 and to a surplus of 3.5% in 1998. While most of the baht's devaluation has probably already been seen, the key factor that will keep it weak in the immediate term is foreign currency–denominated debt which has to be rolled over or refinanced. The scrapping of the two-tier foreign exchange system at the end of January was a major long-term positive, but in the short term the baht will continue to experience volatility and weakness given fundamental concerns. The USD-THB could well see 60 before this is all over. With regard to real economic data such as retail sales, consumption, and investment, Thailand will experience a similar collapse to that seen in Mexico in the first half of 1995.

Indonesia

The regional currency turmoil has served to uncover the fundamental economic weaknesses within the Indonesian economy, notably, the huge amounts of foreign currency–denominated, unhedged debt. Bank Indonesia said that of total external debt outstanding of around USD130 billion, about USD9.6 billion is due in March. Of this, it is estimated that fully half had been hedged by December 1997. In short, the biggest buyers of dollars remain Indonesian companies to hedge their dollar liabilities. The problem lies in the fact that when the rupiah falls as a result of this, the need arises to further rehedge positions. The extent to which economic growth will slow depends greatly on the extent of disruption to the corporate and banking sectors. With regard to the latter, the authorities took a necessary first step by announcing that 16 banks would be closed down. Note, however, that this is 16 out of 239 banks in Indonesia.

If the sickness within the Indonesian economy is to be cured, this must only be the beginning. The authorities have further decided to delay capital spending and infrastructure projects, a further positive. The sharply lower rupiah will aggravate inflationary pressures, which in turn will have to be offset by tighter monetary policy—which in turn will weigh further on the economy. The IMF package should go some way to stabilizing the financial and economic situations. However, two market concerns remain: The first is the degree to which elements within the regime seek to fight the necessary corporate and banking rationalization, thus delaying crucial reforms and exacerbating the gravity of the situation. The second is the potential for social unrest given the downturn in economic conditions. Though Indonesia has achieved massive economic strides in the past two decades in terms of improving the general standard of living, the number of people who have as yet seen little or no benefit remains far too high. Suharto is guaranteed to win this year's presidential election, all things being equal, for a seventh five-year term. Yet there remains potential for social unrest going into the election given the severity of economic downturn.

In terms of Bank Indonesia monetary policy, the central bank fought the collapse in the rupiah in the third quarter by more than doubling the one-month SBI rate to 30%. Since then, it has been gradually trying to ease policy in order to alleviate the pain to the banking and corporate sectors of such punitively high borrowing rates. Yet further easing in the fourth quarter was put off by the further collapse in the rupiah, driven by panicked distressed dollar buyers within the Indonesian corporate sector. The rise in domestic prices, notably in food, will limit the ability of Bank Indonesia to cut interest rates any further; and indeed it could actually have to increase them again in order to stop inflation from getting out of control. Unfortunately, the need to stabilize the currency and seek to tame inflationary pressures will necessitate higher interest rates and for longer, weighing further on the economy. The risk remains that Indonesia could see severe economic recession—i.e., sharply negative growth of 5% or more in 1998. As for the rupiah itself, the problem is not only domestic factors but weakness in other Asian currencies, such as the ringgit, Philippine peso, Korean won, and Taiwan dollar, which continue to trigger sympathetic selling in the rupiah. Bank Indonesia must continue to try and smooth out foreign exchange movements rather than to attempt to stop them. At the same time, with the government's blessing, it must further seek to rationalize the financial sector and strengthen the supervisory powers over the banking industry. Now that the 15,000 level has been breached in the USD-IDR, the market could even test 20,000 or 25,000, given the amount of dollars that unhedged companies and banks still need to buy. This could have major political and social implications.

Malaysia

The next six months will prove a critical period for the Malaysian economy and will likely show the full extent of the damage that the financial sector has incurred in particular as a result of the regional currency and economic crises and past lending and lever-aged practices. Economic data releases will be closely scrutinized for signs of the drastic slowdown in growth which the more bear-ish forecasters expect. At present, we at Standard & Poor's MMS look for Malaysia to achieve 1.5% GDP growth in 1998, down from around 7.4% in 1997. The key factors will be whether export growth manages to stabilize and rebound and what happens to the financial sector. With regard to the latter, the risk—if one takes the most bearish view—is that the government's apparent reluc-tance to deal with the banking and financial sector's exposure to the real estate and stock market collapses in any strong or mean-ingful way could lead to the same type of financial sector melt-down that Thailand experienced. In Malaysia, the problem is not external debts, but overleverage in domestic asset markets.

Instead of implementing structural reforms in the financial sector, the authorities appear to be attempting to inflate their way out of trouble. Interest rates remain quite low at 9% relative to monetary growth, even if it slows to 20%, which they estimate in the October budget. This threatens to create an inflationary spiral, to the extent that when interest rates are eventually raised, they will have to be raised further and faster than otherwise might have been the case. Bank Negara Malaysia is caught between the need to raise rates to stamp out inflationary pressures and the danger that such a policy could cause a protracted slowdown in growth and could endanger the health of the financial sector. As for the ringgit, the short-term outlook remains grim given the slowing economy, structural problems that have yet to be tackled, rising inflation, and battered confidence. The danger is that with an easy monetary policy relative to inflation and monetary growth levels, along with insufficient fiscal tightening, the ringgit will increasingly price in inflationary expectations—and thus fall. Though we have probably seen most of this priced in already—to take the optimistic view—the USD-MYR could hit 5.0 before it is all over.

Singapore

Singapore, by contrast, has vastly superior fundamentals. The slide in the Singapore dollar, allowed by the authorities, has improved Singapore's trade competitiveness. We already saw the beginnings of a rebound in the non-oil export sector in the fourth quarter, and this is likely to continue near term. In particular, the pickup in U.S. electronics demand, coupled with greater pricing competitiveness as a result of the 17% decline in the Sing dollar versus the U.S. dollar in 1997, boosted exports in electronics manufacturing. In addition, with financial, construction, and transport sectors in Singapore still performing creditably in 1997, Standard & Poor's MMS holds to its 1997 and 1998 forecasts for GDP growth of 7.1% and 4.8%, respectively, an impressive performance given the difficult circumstances. As far as monetary policy is concerned, while this will have to be kept relatively tight by historical terms in the near term, the MAS does not face the accompanying headaches of high nonperforming loans or large unhedged foreign currency debt that beset its regional neighbors. This is the result no doubt of the MAS's own strict (and prudent) regulatory standards. One factor that Singapore cannot alleviate is the ongoing weakness of its neighbor currencies, which in turn weighs on the Sing dollar. The USD-SGD, as a result, remains very firm, and could approach 1.90 traded before any major reversal.

The Philippines

The one major saving grace for the Philippines was that it wasn't growing nearly as fast as most of its regional neighbors, did not experience the same degree of FDI and portfolio inflow, and therefore is unlikely to suffer the same degree of withdrawal. GDP growth should be around 5.1% for 1997 and 3.0% for 1998. These are low by regional standards but in line with the country's recent performance. There are two dangers: One is the threat of inflation. Given that the Philippines imports 95% of its energy needs and continues to run a current account deficit of 3 to 4% of GDP, the fall in the value of the peso will have direct inflationary implications for the economy, which in turn will have to be countered by tighter monetary policy by the Philippine central bank, Bangko Sentral ng Pilipinas. This in turn will hurt domestic demand and growth. Traditionally, a fall in the peso has meant recession. However, we do not expect such a dire outcome this time because export growth remains firm and should accelerate in the first half of this year, thus providing a support for overall growth. The second danger is that the Philippine banking and financial sector remains exposed to the property market, though not to anywhere near the extent that is present in Thailand or Malaysia.

On the positive side, net foreign liabilities as a percentage of central bank foreign reserves were only 46% in 1996, compared with 269% for Thailand. The cause of deregulation was hurt when a court ruled against deregulation of the oil industry. However, the passage of the tax reform package was a major long-term positive, both for the cause of deregulation and for the economy. As for the peso, its fundamentals remain more stable than those of Indonesia (external liabilities), Thailand (financial-sector collapse and huge current account deficit), and Malaysia (overleveraged financial sector). Thus we have probably already seen most of the peso weakness against the dollar. What will the top be on the USD-PHP? The peso has already overshot fundamental fair value, given the general regional crisis. And much will depend on external, regional currency factors just as much as domestic ones. The risk/reward certainly seems to be gradually moving in favor of the peso rather than the dollar, and thus it could be said we are close to the top. Whether that is 45 or 50 is open to question—and dependent on what happens elsewhere in the region.

South Korea

The situation is potentially as bad as, if not actually worse than, that in Thailand. While the initial news of the USD57 billion IMF-led bailout package was positive on the assumption that it would help to stabilize the financial system, further news that Korea has some USD100 billion of foreign currency–denominated debt due on or before December 1998 is needless to say somewhat bearish. That figure was previously stated by the government at USD63 billion; thus the full extent of Korean indebtedness remains unclear. Officially, total foreign debt was USD119.7 billion as of December. However, given the aforementioned understatement of the figures, this too could be understated. The bottom line is that the Korean economy, which has some underlying positives such as the revival of the export sector (itself largely due to the fall in the value of the Korean won rather than to any increase in TFP-type improvements), is burdened by massive debts. These are the result of interest rates being kept too low for too long, targeted credit policies, and Korean companies taking on ridiculous amounts of debt due to overexpansion plans. Terms of the IMF package were extremely strict, including tightening of fiscal and monetary policy, access by foreign companies to higher-stake levels in Korean companies and banks, the elimination of trade tariffs, and the targeting of 1998 GDP growth at

3% and the current account deficit at 1%. Yet doubts remain about whether the government will carry through all the measures in light of the impact they will have on the economy. For a start, the 3% 1998 GDP target was ridiculously optimistic. The IMF had been pushing for 2.5%, but even this has been scaled down. It could well be negative as a result of a combination of factors: the contraction in demand that could occur as companies continue to go bankrupt under the massive debt burdens they face, the rise in unemployment that will result from such bankruptcies, and the corporate and banking rationalization that will occur sooner or later (better sooner; otherwise the whole system could fail). Unemployment could more than double this year, which could in turn cause significant social unrest. This is a country that has a violent history of social unrest. None of it bodes well on the basis of a two-year outlook, even supposing Korea follows the IMF bailout terms religiously. It remains to be seen just how Korea is going to pay its huge debt burden, despite the IMF bailout, given the depletion in Bank of Korea foreign exchange reserves.

Taiwan

The outlook in Taiwan is decidedly more upbeat, although it would be overstating the case to say that Taiwan will have it easy. Taiwanese exports will still be hit by reduced demand in the ASEAN, given slowing domestic growth there and higher import costs as a result of ASEAN currencies falling further than the Taiwan dollar. This, however, should be offset by a growing demand for Taiwanese exports from Western nations, particularly in light of the modest rebound in U.S. and European electronics sector demand. Though Taiwan remains to a certain extent dependent on Japanese technology, the benefits of which it then reexports, it has built up significant added-value of its own. This is a factor that has traditionally supported the Japanese trade balance itself, and the same should be the case for Taiwan, albeit to a lesser extent. Although the ASEAN countries and Korea have revised down their forecasts for GDP growth in 1998, Taiwan should still see growth of around 6.4%, following growth of around 6.6% in 1997, an excellent performance in relative terms. The weak stock market and very muted inflationary pressure should offset any upside potential in domestic interest rates. The one imponderable is, of course, the threat of further regional market tensions. Despite this, the top for the USD-TWD is likely to be around 35. Indeed the Taiwan dollar could outperform this year relative notably to the Korean won and ASEAN currencies, given the more solid fundamental base. The fact that Taiwan has a current account surplus exceeding 3% of GDP is a major positive. The Central Bank of China (Taiwan's central bank) will likely maintain its policy balance of "not too easy, not too tight."

Hong Kong

Though the economy of Hong Kong is increasingly becoming integrated into that of mainland China and therefore dependent on Chinese economic trends, domestic factors will also continue to play a sizable role. The currency crisis in the ASEAN in the second half of 1997 put a magnifying glass to the fundamentals of all of Asia. As a result, the market focused on the viability of the Hong Kong dollar "peg"—in reality a currency board system linked to the U.S. dollar—and attacked on two notable occasions. The HKMA's response at the time was unequivocal, allowing interest rates to spike, squeezing out the shorts (those who were long on dollars, short on Hong Kong dollars). Given the nature of a currency board, where every 7.8 Hong Kong dollars in the system is matched with (at least) one U.S. dollar of reserves, asset markets should take the brunt of an economic adjustment rather than the currency itself. The selling of Hong Kong dollars would automatically lead to less supply from the HKMA, which would cause interest rates to tighten and thus bring demand back for Hong Kong dollars. Thus in the case of an attack on the Hong dollar on the view it is overvalued, the asset markets bear the brunt of the higher interest rates. The process is immediate, as opposed to the usual case where there is a substantial delay between currency and interest rate movements and the effect on the real economy.

Indeed, this is exactly what happened in the fourth quarter, with stock and property market prices sliding to reflect the new economic environment. In short, Hong Kong was (rightly) seen as too expensive and the market corrected this overvaluation. In theory, there should be no problem with the peg because the currency board system should work automatically, thus dissuading the market from attacking the Hong Kong dollar. In practice, the HKMA has been adding or subtracting liquidity from the system. By doing this, it has acted more as a central bank in order to smooth out market imbalances rather than as the creator that would stand aside and let the system work. As a result, doubts remain about the conviction of the HKMA in holding the peg, given its proclivity for market participation and intervention. Though understandable, this seems unjust. The HKMA's activities have been precisely aimed at smoothing operations, not at changing the nature of the system. In addition, barring a merger with the Chinese renminbi—which will not happen for some time as China will not allow the renminbi to become convertible on the capital account for several years—what is the alternative? The nature of a currency board dictates an equitable distribution of dollars and Hong Kong dollars within the banking system. If the peg was (theoretically) let go, a huge chunk of the capital base within the Hong Kong banking system would be wiped out overnight. Needless to say, this should not and cannot be allowed to happen. The peg must be held at all costs because the alternative would be worse than Thailand or Korea. Holding the peg will occasionally be painful in the form of high interest rates, but this is nothing compared with what would happen if the peg were let go.

Hong Kong assets corrected to more reasonable valuations. The falloff in tourism late last year equally reflected a view that Hong Kong was no longer cheap. If the market is allowed to transmit this message seamlessly, the pain will be relatively brief. Nominal interest rate premiums over the U.S. dollar curve will mean slower growth than otherwise would have been the case. And this will remain so until the market is convinced Hong Kong's cost base has been sufficiently trimmed. One economic fear was that Hong Kong exports would be hit by the ASEAN and Taiwan currency devaluations, but exports make up only around 10% of the Hong Kong economy. In addition, of those exports, the vast majority are actually reexports from China, where labor costs are substantially cheaper than in the ASEAN, to the benefit of export competitiveness. Hong Kong's current account deficit, which is expected to expand sharply to over 5% of GDP in 1998 from 1.0% in 1996, is a major concern. Theoretically, this will put pressure on the currency. However, that pressure in practice will be felt in asset prices instead, with the clear emphasis on maintaining the peg. Both the Hang Seng and real estate prices have significant further downside potential. In a worst-case scenario—excluding a possibility of the peg being broken—1998 GDP would be around 2.0 to 2.5%. But Standard & Poor's MMS expect it to come out at around 4.2%. Hong Kong has adjusted before and it will do so again. The system itself is sound, as long as it is allowed to function properly.

". . . Hong Kong is taking the pain and allowing asset prices to correct," says Simon Pritchard, financial columnist at the *South China Morning Post* in Hong Kong. "It is a fundamentally efficient place, but just too expensive. Indeed, the Hong Kong government is almost encouraging this process so as to engineer the needed correction in prices. That correction cannot be too swift. Otherwise it will strain the banking system. But if gradual, it should go a long way towards restoring Hong Kong's competitiveness."[14]

The key will be to further improve the physical infrastructure, education, and the quality of the service-sector workforce, which remains the main engine of domestic Hong Kong growth. All this being so, Hong Kong is increasingly exposed to developments within China's economy. Indeed, despite the fact that Hong Kong continues to act as the international financial center for China, a more serious danger to Hong Kong's future than the speculators could actually come from China itself. It is this possibility and China's economy that I address in the final chapter. Before that happens, it is necessary to look at the general efforts that the region as a whole, and Indonesia and Korea in particular, is making.

10

The Rescue — The IMF,
Then Rubin, Then Soros

RESCUES CAN COME in many forms. In the case of the Asian crisis, there appear to have been three key stages to this rescue process. First, of course, there were the IMF-led loan packages for Thailand, Indonesia, and then Korea. Then came the move by Western national financial authorities to speed up the loan packages (in particular for Korea) and persuade Western and Japanese commercial and investment banks to roll over existing short-term debt obligations. The final stage began when Western portfolio investors began to at least contemplate moving back into the region, typified by the visit by George Soros to Korea in January. This chapter examines these three distinct stages of the rescue attempt for Asia and their likely ramifications for the various Asian economies.

Looking at the consequences of the IMF loan packages and their accompanying terms, it would be easy for the Asian nations involved to wish that they had rather avoided such form of rescue. Indeed, it appears that Thailand and Indonesia are not content with merely wishing this. The former is seeking publicly to renegotiate the economic and fiscal terms of its loan package with the IMF. And the latter, on January 6, with the announcement of the 1998–1999 budget, appeared to completely ignore the IMF stipulation for a budget surplus of 1% of GDP. The social consequences of the Asian crisis are likely to be considerable. In Thailand and Indonesia up to 3 million people may lose their jobs because of the crisis and the IMF-led move to right national balance sheets through severe fiscal austerity. It is hardly surprising, then, that some governments are wary of testing their populaces' tolerance for economic pain, particularly Indonesia with its history of social unrest.

The IMF came under significant criticism in the wake of the crisis for not warning of the dangers of economic imbalance. But as its 1998 *World Economic Outlook* points out, it did indeed warn of such an event. In particular, IMF officials repeatedly warned Thailand that the size of its current account deficit was becoming unsustainable and could cause economic dislocation. The fact that the IMF led the initial loan bailouts for Thailand, Indonesia, and Korea was crucial in attempting to provide at least an initial stabilizing platform for Asian currencies. Yet these continued to plunge well after the fact. Why so? Principally because, while the loans helped these countries to shore up their central banks' foreign exchange reserves, in turn helping to start the bad loan reduction process, the debt problem this time was largely corporate rather than at the national level. Huge corporate foreign currency–denominated debt in very short-term maturities meant that Asian corporates and banks had demand for dollars which exceeded the size of the loan packages and which was due to mature or roll over in short order. As the reversal of currency overappreciation continued, the amount of local currency these parties had to pay in order to buy the dollars to hedge, repay, or refinance their dollar debt continued to grow—a vicious circle.

This made the process of stabilizing the financial system infinitely more complex—and to a great extent subject to the whims of the individual creditors. And this was occurring against a backdrop of sharp economic slowdown, if not outright collapse. This in turn brings into question the idea behind the IMF packages. After all, Asian budgets had been in pretty good shape overall. The deterioration in national current account deficits had not been the result of overconsumption or fiscal irresponsibility. Rather, it was due to overinvestment relative to extremely high—yet for that, inadequate—savings rates. Thus, one could ask why the need for fiscal austerity to supposedly cure the economies of their illnesses? The truth was and is that these three Asian economies in particular had become significantly overleveraged. The response to such excessive credit expansion has to be a credit contraction. That will not be satisfactorily achieved if it is not led by the governments and financial authorities in question.

More immediately, there was a need to shore up greatly depleted central bank foreign exchange reserves. In addition there was a need to stabilize the current account deficits and then help to reverse them through fiscal austerity. Yet there remains a case to be argued that the terms of the IMF packages, in particular those that required significant budget surpluses as a percentage of GDP, added to the problem rather than curing it to the extent that they exacerbated the degree of economic pain. That said, with such huge current account deficits, the fiscal side had to offset this deficit via a rising budget surplus—yet Asian currency devaluations have done much already to turn around current account balances and will continue to do so in the near term. Was the IMF effort mistaken in its effort to reform and restructure Asian economies? No. The IMF-led loan packages were a vital first step in attempting to stabilize the situation.

Just the same, the severity of the IMF terms have clearly added to the economic fallout costs of the currency devaluations. In addition, while the IMF may talk confidently about the efficacy of its surveillance techniques and the fact that it warned Asian governments ahead of time, this really is not good enough by itself. Without global regulation—which seems far off at this juncture, and probably justifiably so—no country can be made to accept IMF advice or guidance. And heresy as it might be, who is to say the IMF is always right in its advice? Learned and experienced it might be. Infallible it most certainly is not. Despite that, there should be some form of formal and public report, submitted by the IMF on a regular basis to the various regional and financial bodies, citing economic and financial concerns if applicable. Not only would this be more appropriate than private discussions or warnings. It would be more effective than simply including such concerns within annual publications. The press and the market would thus look to such formal and public reports for the first warning signals of official discontent at economic imbalance. It would be in the interests of all emerging market countries to comply fully with the data necessities of such reports—though this by itself is no guarantee every country will agree.

While the blame for Asian currency and economic imbalance must rest fully with those whose job it was to run their economies, it is clearly not enough for global, transnational financial authorities to rest on their laurels and say: "I told you so." The response to that might well be: "Fine, but what did you do about it?" Again, it is not enough to say that it is not the job of such authorities to do anything. The real world and the political and economic consequences that result from such periods of turbulence and destruction do not accept such excuses. But what can be done exactly? Barring global regulation and a truly global central bank and treasury—even less likely than a fully successful EMU—the only viable alternative is peer pressure. This is where such formal and public reports, along with formal accords, might come in. Indeed, the agreement in Manila marks a major step in establishing inter-ASEAN peer pressure to secure and maintain economic stability.

A final point with regard to the IMF-led bailouts is that they resulted in national humiliation—and thus the potential for national rejection. It is easy for Westerners to say pride comes before a fall, but the concept of "face" plays a significant part in Asian political, social, and economic activity. To have to borrow on bended knee from the IMF (read, "from the West") was bad enough, but to be then further humiliated by seemingly punitive IMF terms and conditions on those loans has been too much for some. This is not to say that those terms should not have been strict, for a degree of fiscal austerity, together with market-opening reforms, was clearly needed in each case. Indeed, there is a counterargument (which also has merit) to say that those who have to beg for loans as a result of their own economic and financial failings do not have the right to seek the pleasing yet delusional sanctuary of national pride. This is particularly the case with Thailand. The time has come for openness and honesty, and a willingness to admit one's mistakes and move on—with the help of such a loan bailout. Otherwise, international investors will pass you by on the other side of the road. The example of Korea, however, could clearly have been better handled. No Korean candidate for the December 18 presidential elections could be seen to fully and unequivocally endorse the IMF loan terms. The result was that the voiced objections—or at the least, questions—to the said terms made by opposition leader Kim Dae Jung (who was subsequently to narrowly win the election over the ruling party candidate Lee Hoi Chang) caused significant financial market concern and distress. This was entirely unnecessary and could have been avoided if the IMF loan package had been made with no public conditions, said conditions to be made public only after the election.

The second stage of the rescue effort was that undertaken by the national financial authorities, led by the U.S. in the personage of U.S. Treasury Secretary Robert Rubin. As noted in Chapter 4, Rubin's first few days as the Treasury Secretary were a baptism under fire, having to deal with the Mexican currency and financial crisis and the international market repercussions. His already extensive experience notwithstanding, this period proved an ideal training ground for the task of leading the (decidedly more complex) international effort to speed up the loan packages, particularly to Korea, and to persuade commercial and investment banks to roll over debt obligations owed to them. On December 24, the Korean government announced a package of reforms designed to restructure the financial system, accelerate and deepen capital account liberalization, introduce market-based measures to stem the outflow of short-term capital, and speed up measures to open the real economy to foreign trade and investment. After the announcement, Rubin made the following statement:

We have supported a broad international effort to restore stability in Asia. This effort is critically important to U.S. economic and national security interests. We welcome the steps announced today by the Korean government to strengthen and accelerate its reform program. These important steps demonstrate the commitment to sustained reform that is essential to a successful program to restore confidence and return Korea to a path of growth and stability. . . . The G7 and other nations have announced today their support of action to advance by early January existing commitments of official finance, in the context of a sustained commitment by the Korean authorities to implement an intensified program and in the context of a significant voluntary extension of the maturities of the existing claims by international bank creditors on Korean financial institutions and adequate progress by Korea toward accessing new sources of private international finance. The United States is prepared to join with the G7 and other countries in this effort.[1]

The efforts by the U.S. financial authorities, in the form of the Treasury and the Federal Reserve, along with other Western nations have been crucial in seeking to avoid mass Asian corporate and banking defaults—and, for that matter, a consequent spike in Western bank loan write-offs. Indeed, without these efforts, the IMF loan packages would not have been enough. This is not to say that further significant corporate default will not occur, but to a far lesser degree than would have otherwise been the case. Such efforts will need to continue for at least the first half of the year given the amount of short-term debt that continues to come due—and thus must be repaid or rolled over every month. Korea is estimated to have over USD25 billion of such debt obligations coming due up to the end of March. Clearly, the IMF package and the turnaround in the current account balance will help, but further persuasive efforts by the Western authorities with banks will still be needed in the near term. Needless to say, one way of helping the overall situation would be for the Korean government to guarantee these corporate and bank credits.

The third and final stage of the rescue effort has been the gradual reemergence of international fund managers, typified by the visit of George Soros, chairman and president of Soros Fund Management, to Korea. In a press briefing following meetings with Korean President Kim Dae Jung and his senior financial advisors, Soros said that he was seeking to "increase significantly" the investment of his lead fund, the Quantum Fund, in Korean asset markets. However, he first wanted to see significant corporate restructuring—which would inevitably result in painful but necessary heavy layoffs—greater corporate balance sheet transparency through the consolidation of accounts, and labor market flexibility.[2] Such views are also widely held by other international institutional investors. While there may be some who presently feel hell will freeze over before they return to invest in Asia, many still see the long-term potential—as I do—and thus look to the various Asian governments to adopt the correct microeconomic strategies to allow these fund managers to unlock value in their economies. It should be noted that such investment would not be plunder as the more nationalist commentators in Korea, Thailand, and Indonesia would have it, but would be for the benefit of all concerned. These countries, having been freewheeling with credit, are how facing severe and painful credit crunches. To put it bluntly, they could use the money. It's better that their corporate bases restructure, allowing investment to return—and employment levels to consequently recover.

Particularly in Korea, given the massive sales figures generated by the chaebol—an estimated USD350 billion by the top four chaebol alone—there is certainly value to be had. It just has to be unlocked. That means a massive infusion of equity capital, to restore some greater degree of balance to debt-to-equity ratios, either through share offerings or through mergers and acquisition (financed by equity rather than debt). While there is indeed value to be had in the currencies and asset markets of the Asian countries that have already experienced the Asian crisis, equally there remains the danger of further fallout in one that has yet to feel the full brunt of it—China.

11

The Danger — China Unscathed or the Next Crisis?

Amid the carnage of the ASEAN and North Asian currencies in 1997, one country stood out as a sea—a veritable ocean—of stability, China. In many ways, up until October when the full force of speculative pressures buffeted Hong Kong, 1997 had been China's year. As a result of the fiscal austerity measures put in place in 1994, inflation had been brought sharply under control, the economy continued to grow strong at just short of 10% annual GDP growth, foreign exchange reserves continued to rise toward the year-end goal of USD140 billion—a crucial defense against unwanted financial and economic turbulence— and FDI, which was USD42.3 billion in 1996, hit another record in 1997 at around USD43 billion. So much for the apparent health of the economy. On the political side, President Jiang Zemin had skillfully stamped his authority as leader at the Fifteenth Chinese Communist Party Congress in mid-September when he unveiled the next stage of China's economic revolution which called for the wholesale restructuring of the state-owned enterprises. This was a move as bold as the initial reforms instituted in 1977–1978 by his predecessor, the late Deng Xiaoping. At the same time Jiang Zemin removed powerful opposition in the form of Qiao Shi, who was ousted from his positions as chairman of the National Peoples' Congress and member of the

Politburo Standing Committee. The events of the Fifteenth Party Congress had secured Jiang Zemin's domestic and even international legitimacy, and had gained him the requisite power base from which he was now able to delegate policy in much freer fashion.

Amid the turmoil in other parts of Asia, China had initially stood aloof, expressing sympathy and diplomatic support, lambasting speculators, and offering financial aid. Such a fraternal approach notwithstanding, there can be little doubt that to many in China's government, the events of the second half of 1997 were pleasing confirmation of the appropriateness of China's foreign exchange and investment policy that dictated that the Chinese renminbi was convertible on the current account but not the capital account—eliminating the possibility of short-term capital flight by foreign investors. While the market had ravaged ASEAN currencies and economists hastily downgraded their economic forecasts, China had stood out as the exception. It had managed to steer through the potentially troubled political waters of the death of leader Deng Xiaoping, the British handover of Hong Kong, and the Fifteenth Party Congress. Its economy was strong and its currency safe from the speculators. Not a question was raised about its near-term future—until, that is, when the typhoon blasted Hong Kong, causing asset markets to collapse. In their wake, falling Hong Kong stock prices also dragged down the stock indexes of Shanghai and Shenzhen, as well as Hong Kong's own "red-chip" stock sector. The message was clear. No one was totally immune.

While the storm of October was clearly distressing, China had calmly weathered it, confident in Hong Kong's ability to deal with the speculative pressures. Yet within the sell-off another more specific message was also becoming clear. In terms of exports, Hong Kong's economy would not be that badly affected by the turbulence, given its modest presence in exports as a percentage of total GDP. However, this was most certainly not true for Guangdong Province in China, where most of the Hong Kong (re)exports were actually manufactured. And if exports from southern China could be hit, why not those from the whole of China? After all, the devaluation of the renminbi in 1994, unifying the swap and official rates, had been a major factor in the ASEAN losing its economic competitiveness in subsequent years. The loss of competitiveness occurred particularly in relatively low-tech products such as textiles, garments, shoes, and home appliances where China competed directly against the likes of Thailand, Indonesia, and the Philippines. In that move, Chinese products had regained around 26% price competitiveness, even taking account of domestic inflation—which at the time was soaring. Now the currencies of the ASEAN had just lost some 40% or more against the dollar. Couldn't the same thing now happen to China? To Chinese exports? To ask the question at the time was to question the unquestionable—that China's fundamentals were sound, that China was different from the rest of Asia and did not (and more importantly would not) suffer the same financial and economic ills as had the ASEAN and Korea.

Yet such questions were and are needed, for as bold as the planned restructuring of the state-owned enterprise sector is, it comes not a minute too soon. At one time, China had looked upon the chaebol of Korea as a possible corporate model to follow, only to turn away from that idea when the government saw how many of these Korean conglomerates had deteriorated. Still, those who now see a valid comparison between the existing SOEs and the chaebol, and also between the Thai and Malaysian banking systems and that in China, do so with at least some validity. Take the SOEs. There are some 305,000 that have to be restructured in only three years if all goes according to plan. Together they make up about 42% of total national industrial output and employ around 110 million people—out of a total working population of 685 million as of the end of 1996 according to the ADB.[1] Given state-directed lending policies that in the past required that 85 to 90% of all loans go to SOEs, the banking system has been saddled with official bad loans of some RMB1 trillion, or around 25% of total loans. The real figure could be much higher. No one actually knows what the full debts are, and consequently what the banking system's full exposure really is.

Under China's economic chief, Vice Premier Zhu Rongji, the government has been gradually cutting off the credit flow to the SOEs, well aware both of the danger of maintaining the status quo and of going too far too fast and risking economic or even social instability. Both at the Ministry of Finance and at the Peoples' Bank of China (PBOC), the emphasis is one of maintaining financial and economic stability and guarding against potential risks. This would seem to be a continuation of the cautious approach to economic policy widely attributed to Deng Xiaoping—despite the reformist revolution he created—known as "feeling for rocks underfoot while crossing the river"—"Mo zhe shi tou guo he" in Putonghua. Yet there is an argument to be made which says the critical state of the banking system in China and the SOEs requires immediate and radical surgery, crossing the river with all due haste rather than bothering about where the rocks are. The counterargument is that such action might cause one to lose one's footing and drown.

In the end, the likely policy will be of seeming to maintain the rock-hopping approach, while attempting to do so with as much speed as is possible without falling—a fine balance in many ways. Whatever the approach, the challenges are significant. The SOEs basically act not just as huge companies but as entire social security systems, running hospitals and schools and providing (very modest) pensions. They have traditionally been looked on by their workforce as a job for life. And even in the case where there are not enough jobs to do, they keep workers on. It is thought there are some 25 million "workers" in SOEs who are not actually doing anything. Over half of the SOEs are loss making. If they had not been kept afloat by the banking system—which in the process has nearly bankrupted itself—their cumulative losses as a sector would be considerably more. The need is thus, as President Jiang Zemin stated, to significantly restructure them. For the most part, this is likely to be through mergers and acquisitions between SOEs, though there are also plans for a number of them to have a stock market shareholder structure and to be listed as A shares (Chinese citizens only, listed in Shanghai and Shenzhen), B shares (foreign participation allowed, listed on Shanghai and Shenzhen), and H shares (Hong Kong).

In announcing the plans for the SOEs, it was suggested that restructuring, through mergers and acquisitions and share listings, would occur with a trial group of 1000 of them—to see how it worked. Bearing in mind that China already has a "floating population"—emigrated from the countryside in search of work in the wealthy eastern coastal cities, but without official full-time work—of 100 million and a rapidly rising official unemployed population, the social costs of this will not be inconsiderable. There have already been demonstrations by people who have lost their livelihood due to the general restructuring process. This could accelerate that, and yet there is no choice. It sounds harsh to say it—and very easy from where I am sitting, I admit fully. Nevertheless one has to say that the restructuring process that the SOEs will go through as a result of the decision taken at the Fifteenth Party Congress is crucial for the short-term vitality of China's economy, let alone its long-term health. A major positive is that Chinese officials, saying they have learned the lessons of Korea and Japan, have stated that they will allow SOEs to go bankrupt if they cannot be saved. Japan faced this decision more than five years ago and tried to hang on and we all know the result. Korea also let systemic debt levels get to the crisis point before it even thought of dealing with the problem—and then only because the IMF demanded the corporate and banking sectors be cleansed one way or another of their massive debt loads as part of the terms of the IMF package. The choice for China is to endure more economic pain now to ensure a sounder future or seek to delay and therefore potentially threaten that future. In order to offset the social consequences from this—most obviously in the form of millions of job losses—a patchy welfare system will have to be greatly, and swiftly, improved. Yet who will pay for this? The answer has to be a balance of the state and the population.

As for the banks, speedy reform is needed there too—and it is taking place. The Asian crisis has forcefully brought home the message that a key factor in securing long-term economic viability is cleaning out and shoring up the banking system. Chinese officials have watched how in Thailand and elsewhere banking crises, fed by excessive and unproductive lending practices (like lending to the SOEs), have fueled currency crises, which in turn have exacerbated the original banking crises, causing both banking and corporate failure and massive general disruption to the system. If this happened in China, given the size of the SOEs and the consequent debt exposure of the banking system, it could hurt the economy severely. It is for this very reason that the Chinese government is prudently seeking to deal with the problem before it gets out of hand, by cutting off credit links between the commercial banks and SOEs, to improve asset quality by higher bad loan provisions and cost cutting within the banking system itself.[2]

Is this a banking crisis? No, not yet. The problems within the banking system were after all brought to light as a result of the stated plans for SOE-sector reform, not as a result of financial or economic difficulty. It is precisely because China has mapped out its intention to deal with the problems within the SOEs and the banks that the market has focused on them in such detail, much more of a preemptive strike than was the case in Thailand where it was definitely too little, too late. This is not to say that reforming the banking system, at the same time as carrying out the largest corporate restructuring in the history of capitalism, is guaranteed to succeed. The obstacles remain formidable; yet one could easily have said that about the last fifteen years in China. Such has been the economic performance to date, albeit with some underlying problems to be sure, that at least some degree of faith must be put in those who run the economy. Cynics will retort that faith is not nearly enough. Of course, that's true, but the performance of Zhu Rongji and those under him suggests a degree of competence and seriousness about the task in hand which is rarely found in Thailand or Korea. Ultimately, the goal must be for a wholesale recapitalization of the banking system. This can be achieved through similarly severe layoff policies, the write-off of bad loans, and government financing through bond issues. A key issue for the banks is overall liquidity—a factor also noted in Japan! China must keep growing at around the 8% level in order to provide that liquidity and to keep the reform process on track.[3]

At the end of 1997, China's fundamentals remained favorable to the rest of Asia. Growth appeared to have slowed in the fourth quarter; yet it was still superior to anywhere in the ASEAN or Korea on an annualized basis. And the trade surplus continued to improve, thus benefiting foreign exchange reserves. Inflation for its part remained muted or even negative. For a snapshot of China's fundamental picture, see Table 8.

Table 8

China's fundamentals

	1994	1995	1996	1997 E	1998 E
GDP (%)	11.8	10.2	9.7	9.0	8.8
Agriculture (%)	4.0	4.5	5.1	4.5	4.5
Industry (%)	17.4	13.6	12.3	11.1	9.2
Services (%)	8.2	8.0	8.2	8.0	8.0
Investment (% of GNP)	40.0	41.2	39.6	39.8	39.7
Savings (% of GNP)	41.5	39.0	39.3	38.6	38.8
RPI (%)	21.7	14.8	6.1	2.3	5.0
M2	35.1	29.5	26.8	19.0	24.0
Exports (% Y/Y change)	35.6	24.9	1.5	25.0	10.0
Imports (% Y/Y change)	10.4	15.5	5.1	3.5	15.0
C/A balance (% of GDP)	+1.3	+0.2	+0.2	+0.4	+0.2

Source: *ADB 1997 and 1998 Outlook,* Standard & Poor's MMS Economics Database.

Could this relatively solid picture change for the worse? Apart from the situation of the SOEs and the banks, there remain a number of fundamental concerns. First of all, toward the end of the year, RPI, the most closely watched figure for inflation before the changeover to CPI, started to actually decline year-on-year. While declining RPI growth was rightly taken as a positive sign that the effects of the antiinflationary measures taken in 1994 were working their way through the economy, actual Y/Y falls in the RPI rate are a valid concern. They are a potential sign not of lessening inflation pressures but of deflationary pressures. Notably, this was matched by declining M2 growth below the

20% level, shy of the official target of around 22% relative to almost 27% in 1996. Interestingly, despite the PBOC's vigilance against excessive speculation in the China asset markets and specific measures against stock market speculation in the A-share market, M1 continued at a healthy pace, markedly above the 20% level. The divergence between these two readings would appear due to persistent speculative pressures, following in the wake of the two interest rate cuts of 1996 and the 150-basis-point cut in lending rates on October 23.

Despite this, toward the end of the year, evident signs of economic slowdown in the third and fourth quarter and the lack of response from the real economy, notably production and the real estate market, to the October 23 rate cut added to the pressures for a further interest rate cut before year-end. Against an environment of high and rising real interest rates in China, serious reform of the SOEs and the banking system will add to job insecurity and thus further dampen incentives for private consumption. The PBOC is caught between seeking to avoid excessive loosening of monetary policy which might prompt renewed speculative flows into the asset markets and at the same time guarding against excessive slowdown in the real economy, which equally might do the weakened banking system no good at all. Regarding the labor market, fortunately job insecurity works to the benefit of the economy, as well as against it, encouraging precautionary savings that would otherwise leave for the asset markets. Hence, an easing in current real economic conditions should not cause the same degree of speculative excess as was witnessed in 1996.

A further positive for the economy is the persistently strong performance by the agricultural sector, benefiting from successive years of good harvests. But can this last? Given the reemphasis on reforming—or eliminating—the SOEs, the agriculture sector could suffer. This is important not only from an economic but also from a social point of view. The agriculture sector, having been an important driving force for growth from 1978 onward, is already feeling hard done by in the wake of the ascendancy of the coastal cities. In recent years, the emphasis has been on improving urban living conditions and productivity. As a result, farm yields have continued to deteriorate since 1993 despite a series of good harvests, with the consequence that the pace of poverty reduction in the rural sector has slowed markedly. By itself, from a purely macroeconomic point of view, this would not be a danger signal if it were not for the increasing disparity between the rural situation and that of the cities—which encourages further emigration to the cities, thus continuing to bleed the land dry of its human capital. While Shanghai in the short term appears to have reached its economic peak (looking at the long-term economic cycle, it is nowhere near peaking), average household income is approximately five times the national average and over ten times the average of the poorest province. The ADB notes that urban resident per capita income was RMB4380 as of 1996 (up 3.4% Y/Y), whereas rural resident income was RMB1900. Bridging the rural and urban sectors, the township and village enterprises (TVEs) were *the* font for growth in the early 1980s. Indeed, they continue to contribute significantly to growth—TVE output rising 23.9% Y/Y in 1996[4]—and yet they are simultaneously faced with oversupply concerns and the inability to upgrade their technological base sufficiently. While the TVEs have been much more market-oriented than other production centers and therefore are of necessity more efficient, their emphasis within the economy appears to be lessening as more overly capitalist and private business structures are given freer reign.

An emphasis for the Chinese government will be in continuing to build up the service sector. At present this is barely a quarter of the economy, compared with more than two-thirds in Hong Kong. The government is trying to boost this for two key reasons: The first is to increase the domestic skill base—and therefore the resource center for TFP-type productivity. The second is to seek to absorb "surplus" labor resulting from rationalizations within the agricultural and industrial sectors. This is a fine idea in theory, but harder to achieve in practice. It will certainly require a considerable degree of retraining—which brings us back to the idea of education. A fundamental weakness within the Chinese economy, one that the Chinese government is admittedly seeking to address, is the issue of education, or rather the lack of it. Given relative wages within northern and western China compared with those of the rest of China, the mainland will easily remain "the workshop" for the world, as some would have it. Yet those in the south who saw their role as that and nothing more—in other words, those who competed only on price—will over time see their margins squeezed and ultimately eliminated. It is happening already. To misquote: "If you live by the price only, you die by the price." Thus, to increase the absorption rate within the service sector, skill-base centers have to be developed and expanded. As part of this emphasis on the service sector, and in tandem with the government attempt to clean up the banking industry, efforts are gradually—the emphasis is always on gradualism in everything—being made to liberalize the finance sector. Tourism revenues continue to expand. This is the result not only of the government emphasis on tourism in the past few years but also of the liberalization of air travel within China.

China is traditionally—at least in recent years—known for fiscal prudence. In 1996, total expenditure as a percentage of GDP was officially around 11.0%, while total revenue was 10.8%, thus producing a minimal budget deficit of about 0.2% of GDP. Yet this figure does not tell the full story. Add in the effect to state spending of financing the SOEs, either through government-directed loans or through state bank–directed loans, take account of even a relatively conservative estimate for nonperforming loans within this, and the budget deficit could suddenly expand to over 5% of GDP. At first glance, this is undoubtedly alarming. But one has to take account of the fact that the SOEs, and the state banking system, are gradually being forced off the books of the state itself and thus compelled to compete in the marketplace. In addition, if one thinks of the situation of the SOEs and the banks prior to any attempt to clean them up, the situation was even worse—hardly an empirically based concept, but nonetheless valid. Make no mistake about it, the situation is serious, but it is not critical yet. And it need not get to that stage.

China is undergoing changes in a number of spheres. It is finally seeking to rationalize its bloated SOEs, and it is also seeking to alter the emphasis on export-driven growth to a more balanced economy, one supported by domestic demand in the form of private consumption just as much as manufacturing exports. Indeed, the pattern of FDI over the past two years appears to have reflected this, with the most recent cases of corporate FDI in 1996 and 1997 targeting domestic consumer-related industries. Many works have discussed the Chinese consumer boom at length, and it is not the purpose of this one to merely add to that list. That said, the basics are worth reemphasizing. Never in the history of the country has the youth of China, at least those in the urban centers, been able to enjoy the educational and economic freedoms as they do now. Though China appears to be further along the demographic transition path and thus the first wave of "capitalists" are aging fast, it still has a deeper well from which to draw managers, bankers, and officials then was ever the case before. This is not to say that they are not needed urgently, nor that the education system's skill base, particularly in terms of technology- and management-based skills, could not be further improved. However, it does offer an important support mechanism. Still, it is a double-edged sword. Many of this urban generation have not undergone the hardships of the past and thus in very Western fashion want more, faster than is available. Demand might exceed supply, which could be inflationary. They are also less willing than their predecessors to tolerate downturns in their economic or social fortunes.

Returning to the export sector, will China lose its trade competitiveness as a result of Asian currency devaluations and what implications can and does that have for the economies of China and Hong Kong? To answer this question, one first has to go back to the Chinese renminbi's real effective exchange rate (REER)—the trade-weighted exchange rate, adjusted for relative inflation levels. If one examines this on the basis that 1990 = 0, the Chinese renminbi's REER rose to 107.0 in 1991 and then 111.1 in 1992, jumped to 130.7 in 1993, and went into orbit in 1994, almost doubling to 231.3.[5] There can be little doubt that this was an incentive for China's policy of unifying the exchange rate and thus effectively devaluing against the dollar. A high REER simultaneously reflects a high degree of competitiveness—as a result of trade and/or capital and FDI flow—and the gradual loss of the competitiveness. The more the REER increases, the harder it is to compete on a relative basis. This is exactly what happened to many of the ASEAN countries as a result of the peg systems.

There is, however, a further variable: domestic price competitiveness. If wages in one country are a fraction of that in another, the first's REER has to rise that much more against the currency of the second before it starts to lose trade competitiveness. In 1995, China's REER fell back to around 214 and fell again in 1996. In 1997, it is likely to have risen and will do so again in 1998 as a direct result of the Asian currency devaluations. Logically, one might assume that Chinese exporters have as a result of this lost 40% of their trade competitiveness and that Chinese exports will collapse. It is not as simple as that. China has a far greater labor surplus than its Asian competitors. In addition, that labor surplus is growing and will grow as a result of the rationalization program mentioned before. That will help to drive down the exporters' cost base. Based on mid-1997 levels, average hourly wages in China (Shanghai) were USD0.90, relative to 1.80 in Jakarta, 4.60 in Kuala Lumpur, and 3.00 in Bangkok. The currency devaluations will certainly reduce China's wage-cost advantage, but it will not eliminate it. This is not to say that Chinese export growth will not slow (see Table 8), but a collapse is not likely. Rather, China will see a gradual slowing of its export growth—a pleasing result no doubt for U.S. and European politicians and bureaucrats who fret about a supposed avalanche of Chinese exported goods competing with domestic manufacturers on price. In addition, some ASEAN countries will experience imported inflation as a result of their currency devaluations, further adding to their own cost bases.

Further out, if one assumes a combination of rising wages in China coupled with prudent macroeconomic and fiscal policies in the ASEAN—neither assumptions being guaranteed—the ASEAN will regain much of the trade competitiveness it lost in

1994, events in the Japanese yen also allowing. Then, China will face a greater trade threat. Ahead of that, it has some time to tinker with and boost incentives for its export base. A major way of doing this is to seek to further lower the cost base for exporters by reducing import tariffs. As part of China's pledge to enter the World Trade Organization (WTO), China has reduced its tariffs to an average 17% from 23% and said it would cut them to 10% by 2005. Remember, the emphasis is always on the need to maintain the stability of the reform process, on the need for gradualism. The goal is long-term outperformance, not immediate quarterly returns. This specific measure lowers the cost to the exporters of imported goods and services, which they can then reexport at a more competitive price.

Of course, much depends on China's own foreign exchange policy. This, too, like everything else about Chinese economic and financial policy, reflects an emphasis of gradualism. As I said earlier, the renminbi has been made convertible on the current account, but not on the capital account. This is the first of a number of stages of both opening up China's economy and seeking to secure its place within the WTO. Any thoughts that the renminbi would be devalued in response to the ASEAN devaluations were quickly banished by Zhu Rongji, who twice in December eliminated any possibility of such an event, adding that China will continue to find ways of achieving price and trade competitiveness without having to resort to devaluation. Indeed, it would not be in China's own interests to devalue the renminbi for several reasons. For a start, such a move, without any pressure being put on its balance of payments on the current account, would effectively be seen as a "competitive devaluation." In economic terms, this is tantamount to an act of war and certainly would not be taken favorably with regard to China's (long-running) attempt to gain entry to the WTO. In addition, a devaluation of the renminbi would put further pressure on the Asian region as a whole, potentially inciting further regional asset and foreign exchange market turbulence. Finally, and perhaps even more importantly, it could put severe pressure on the Hong Kong dollar and on Hong Kong asset markets.

Potentially more important than the real economic effect would be the symbolic devaluation of the "parent" currency, leaving that of the offspring vulnerable to serious and major attack. Such an attack cannot be tolerated. The Hong Kong dollar peg is not only crucial to Hong Kong's economic future but also symbolic of China's commitment to the autonomy of the territory of Hong Kong and thus of the maintenance of "one country, two systems." This policy in turn is not only aimed at reassuring international investors in the future prosperity of Hong Kong, but also aimed squarely at Taiwan, as an example of the kind of economic and even political autonomy that Beijing would allow in return for Taiwan allowing itself to undergo its own diplomatic "handover" back to the mainland. China also has strong interests in holding the peg at all costs, and not only for Hong Kong's interests but for its own as well.

All this is theory. In practice, the renminbi has been gradually appreciating—rather than depreciating—against the dollar since the move to unify the currency rates in 1994. As a result, far from seeking a weaker renminbi, the PBOC has been buying dollars in the market to stop it from appreciating further. To try to aid this process, the PBOC revised certain foreign exchange regulations, allowing select mainland trading and manufacturing companies to hold up to 15% of their export earnings in foreign exchange rather than renminbi. This will have the added benefit of reducing domestic money supply growth, which will in turn allow the authorities greater policy flexibility given the lessened longer-term inflation threat.

At the end of Chapter 9, I said China was a potential threat to Hong Kong, as well as being a major economic supporter. Where specifically would this threat come from? After all, Hong Kong gets most of its own export competitiveness from the low Chinese manufacturing cost base which it simply passes on to the consumer. The answer is that Hong Kong will experience a long-term secular decline relative to the facilities available in China, notably in Shanghai, if it does not attempt to justify its extraordinarily high cost base by moving further up the added-value chain. Let's face it, in terms of property market competitiveness, Hong Kong is not competitive. It is that simple. Hong Kong is one of the most expensive cities in the world and is facing increasing competition as the region's preeminent international financial center outside of Japan. Hong Kong's place in the sun was guaranteed while China remained a closed economy, but as China opens up, its role as a middleman to China is threatened.

So goes the argument much propagated by numerous bearish economists and commentators on the territory, including the doom and gloom merchant of them all, Dr. Marc Faber. These arguments have some validity, but what they fail to recognize is that China's opening remains gradual. To threaten, directly or indirectly, the economic viability of Hong Kong so soon after it has been reunited with the mainland is politically inconceivable and China will do all it can to avoid that. Again, it is not in China's interests to do that. For one thing, it wants to maintain Hong Kong as its source to international financial markets, a vital link enabling it to seek the necessary investors and capital in order to allow it to restructure its industrial base in the coming years. For another, Hong Kong is China's attempt to show Taiwan how autonomous its future could be in the context of a political and diplomatic reunification. China will not threaten the goal of regaining Taiwan by allowing Hong Kong to fall apart through its inability to compete with the mainland. That is one (of many) key reasons why China's "opening up" of the economy remains so gradual. Full convertibility of the renminbi on the capital account will not be allowed until after equally full restructuring of the domestic SOEs and banking system. At the least, that will be five years away. We are probably talking about a decade or more in reality. The opening of China's asset markets will also remain gradual, in order not to allow economic—and therefore potentially political and social—instability, and also not to allow Hong Kong to be displaced as China's international financial center. If China opened up its economy tomorrow, first of all the economy would be in severe trouble because there would be savings and investor flight out of the banks and then out of the renminbi. This would cause a systemic banking crisis and also a renminbi devaluation that would devastate Hong Kong. Hong Kong would equally be devastated because it would not be able to compete with Shanghai as a financial center in that environment given its much higher cost base. China will not do this. The aim for Shanghai is to make it first into the preeminent *domestic* financial center. Long term, there is no doubt Hong Kong has peaked and it will be replaced by Shanghai, the political environment allowing. However, long term in this context means twenty years or so. China will not have fully restructured, and Taiwan will probably still not be willing to allow itself to be integrated into China before then.

All this is not to deny that there is already a threat from Shanghai and elsewhere in China. There is indeed a threat, and it concerns price. For instance, real estate prices and shipping handling fee prices are a tenth in Shanghai of what they are in Hong Kong. As China continues to open up, this will inevitably divert trade and investment away from Hong Kong and to Shanghai. Real estate in Hong Kong will continue to correct to reflect international and domestic (inter-China) competition. On a ten- to twenty-year basis, you buy Shanghai real estate and you sell Hong Kong. Inevitably the spread between the two in terms of pricing will increasingly favor Shanghai before a decade is out. The Hong Kong stock and bond markets will also face tough competition for available capital as China opens up, pressurizing prices there as well. Inevitably, this means that corporate and economic restructuring is necessary in Hong Kong, both to improve price competitiveness and more importantly to improve the skill base, that TFP-oriented component which Shanghai does not yet have in sufficient abundance to be able to really threaten Hong Kong. Technology, education, and added value are key. Maintaining Hong Kong's relative advantage in these areas over Shanghai and Shenzhen in terms of the services it provides will make or break Hong Kong. The territory can become a mature, Western-style economy, or it can sink back into oblivion, a barren rock of disillusion and lost hope. The choice is Hong Kong's. To fail to live up to that challenge would mean inevitably that the territory's economic indicators, in the form of the Hang

Seng stock index and real estate prices, would head significantly lower than even those levels achieved in the fourth quarter of 1997. To fail could mean Tokyo-style deflation. Given the unique abundance of dynamism that is present here, I am fully confident that Hong Kong will live up to both the challenge and the opportunity that present themselves in the coming decade. That said, in the long run, the future is in Shanghai.

Such considerations of price and trade competitiveness remain economic concerns not only for for China and Hong Kong, but for the region as a whole. The degree of alacrity, determination, and haste with which Asian nations address these concerns remains the key to Asia's future.

Conclusion

So, IS ASIA FALLING? Or is this just a temporary stumble in its long-term rise? Some analysts would suggest that Asia faces the prospect of a "lost decade." This is the fate that befell Mexico and subsequently much of Latin America after the debt crisis of 1982. The sheer immensity of the debt problems in much of Asia could well lead one to such a tempting conclusion.

Indeed, one could argue that at least the initial stage of the rescue effort, whereby the IMF attached draconian terms to the loan packages it led for Thailand, Indonesia, and Korea, added to the severity of the Asian currency and debt crisis rather than alleviating it. While, as I have said, it was crucial to provide some semblance of stability to the global financial system—let alone Asia—by organizing loan packages for these countries, the initial terms and implementation orchestrated by the IMF clearly added to the panic. In the process, the banking system of Indonesia in particular all but melted down as ordinary people in the street reacted predictably and understandably to the dubious prospect of widespread bank closures—by withdrawing all their money.

The closure of banks is of necessity a very delicate issue, requiring much care, with the need to make clear through public statements—in this case, from both the IMF and the national authorities—that the health of the overall banking system remains assured, but in isolated cases specific institutions have to be closed or merged. Even in that event, deposits, both in those institutions and within the system as a whole, would be guaranteed. Instead, the reality was that the closure of banks, while necessary, was handled in an appalling manner, producing widespread panic. In terms of trying not only to stabilize but also to calm the situation in Indonesia in particular, the first six months of the rescue attempt by the IMF were a disaster.

Subsequently, it appears that the IMF has learned a number of lessons, not least those concerning the different nature of the Asian crisis—involving corporate and banking debt rather than national debt. The focus by it, leading national authorities such as the U.S. government and the leading creditor banks, to bring creditors and debtors together in order to reach a level of agreement more appropriate to the specific needs of the Asian crisis, has represented a marked improvement in the way the overall rescue effort has been handled—and thus in its success. To date, this has resulted in one major achievement—the Korean debt rescheduling agreement in January for USD24 billion in short-term bank debt. This is an achievement that has gone some way to shoring up confidence in the Korean financial system as a whole, and thus in providing a base for further such negotiations as more debt comes due and has to be refinanced. Still, the task of achieving similar agreements for the remainder of the Korean debt burden remains considerable. The job is not over yet, not by a long shot, whatever the recovery in Korean asset markets might appear to suggest. The latter is driven by liquidity—lower domestic interest rates and foreign capital inflows—not a rerating to the upside of earnings' prospects. Such liquidity-driven rallies, as opposed to those supported by solid fundamentals, can be all too fleeting, as indeed we have seen before.

In Indonesia, the situation remains exceptionally precarious. While the "moratorium," or delay of corporate debt payments, has also provided a realistic base from which creditor-debtor talks can now take place, the fundamental issue of how Indonesia's massive corporate debt burden can ultimately be refinanced or repaid remains unresolved. Such is the damage done that much of Indonesia's corporate base is technically bankrupt. In addition, Indonesia's case is significantly more complex than that of Korea because the debt is owed by a substantially larger number of banks and companies. The dollar-rupiah (USD-IDR) rate has for now stabilized somewhat as Indonesian companies no longer have the immediate dollar buying needs of having to meet dollar-denominated debt payments. However, these will have to be paid eventually.

Meanwhile, as of this writing, there remains the possibility that President Suharto could implement a currency board system, around the 5000 rupiah rate to the dollar. While a currency board can help provide added stability to a financial system, it can only do so once a foundation for stability has been achieved. This is yet to be the case, with riots breaking out in parts of the country in response to rising food prices, the political issue over succession unresolved, and the debt issue still outstanding. In addition, a currency board might require no foreign exchange intervention, in which case interest rates would have to take the full burden. As a result, they would rise to levels that would be intolerable. Then either the currency board would break down or foreign exchange would be used to support it, and thus foreign exchange reserves would be quickly depleted. What is needed is for banking deposits to be guaranteed, for the banking industry to be further rationalized on a case-by-case basis, and for the creditors and debtors to agree on initial refinancing of the shortest maturity debt issues/loans which are coming due. This might help provide that much needed foundation from which further agreements could be made.

The Asian crisis appears to have gone through four stages: In the first, fundamental weakness was observed—primarily in Thailand and then subsequently elsewhere. In the second, financial instability and then panic took hold. The third occurred when initial debt rescheduling agreements were made and the financial crisis abated. In this stage, some degree of stability was achieved and the process of relative value investment—looking at specific investment options within Asia rather than looking at Asia as a whole—began to take place. The fourth stage has only just begun: the economic crisis. If 1997 was the year that saw the meltdown of Asian financial markets, 1998 and 1999 will be characterized by the sharp downturn in Asian real economies—collapsing growth rates, rising unemployment, increasing inflationary pressures in food prices, and resultant social strife. Thailand, Korea, and Indonesia will all see contractions in their economies (i.e., negative GDP growth) in 1998. Malaysia has yet to experience the full extent—or anything like it—of the internal debt problems from which its economy suffers. Its attempt to reflate its way out of danger on the monetary side, coupled with fiscal tightening, might just work. However, the danger remains that it could yet lead to a further collapse in the ringgit and subsequently asset values—the price of fueling an inflationary bubble of a second sort to try to escape the first. Hong Kong will see a marked slowdown relative to its growth of recent years, as the needs of the currency peg system force asset prices to bear the burden of economic adjustment in the new Asian economic environment of fierce price competitiveness. Throughout Asia, investment spending will fall dramatically. Private capital will no longer provide the base for economic growth, governments having to bear more of the burden, which will in turn pose challenges with regard to their ability to maintain fiscal discipline. There will be a few notable exceptions (Taiwan and China), but the regional trend is for sharply lower growth.

Within the Asian economies, the problem of dealing with nonperforming loans—which are already over 20% in Indonesia, Korea, Thailand, and China and rising—remains. Just looking at those financial institutions that have been officially closed down, little has been done as yet to liquidate and sell off their remaining and viable assets. Take Thailand, for example. In December, the Thai government finally agreed to close down fifty-six out of fifty-eight finance companies in question, but the real estate portfolios backing or owned by these companies' bad loans have yet to be sold off; indeed the process has barely started. Equally in Korea, it remains uncertain whether the merchant banks that have officially been closed down will in fact be liquidated or whether they will be allowed to reopen. There remains considerable reluctance on the part of some Asian authorities to allow for a fire sale of banking, finance company, and real estate assets because of the likely consequences on asset prices of otherwise "healthy" institutions. Yet to attempt to artificially support the market would equally be sheer and proven folly—just look at the case of Japan. The Thai government appears to be seeking to stagger the economic pain of this liquidation and sale process, but this merely extends the period for which the pain is felt—again, look at what happened in Japan. The U.S. method of saving and clearing up the savings and loan industry via the Resolution Trust Corporation would be an excellent example to follow. Indeed, seven years after the Japanese asset bubble burst, Japan is making the first tentative steps at doing just that through the Deposit Insurance Corporation. The danger is that instead of an Asian fire sale of assets, there will be no sale at all and the market for such assets will simply grind to a halt with no actual transactions taking place. Even if this occurs, however, through either government instigation or market forces, sales will eventually occur—and prices will fall further. The activity in Asian stock markets in 1997 reflects the market's anticipation of what will happen subsequently to real estate values and bank margins. It is better that this contraction happens in 1998 and 1999, allowing the rebound, when it comes, to take place that much sooner.

However reluctant to allow the liquidation and restructuring process certain elements within the administrations of Thailand, Korea, and Indonesia may be, the need to attract foreign capital and the conditions of the IMF-led loan packages will impose the necessary discipline either sooner or later—and sooner is better, however painful. Asian governments, whatever their rhetoric or feelings, have a good track record of pragmatism and flexibility. Indeed, the pronouncements emanating from the recent ASEAN and APEC meetings suggested a very realistic and level-headed approach in seeking to deal with the economic effects of the crisis. Yet, to be truthful, the challenges remain formidable, not least the bankruptcy codes of countries like Thailand, Korea, and Indonesia which are tortuous. The new Thai bankruptcy code to come into effect is a start, but greater emphasis needs to be put on speed. The faster you admit the full extent of the mess, and thus the full extent of nonperforming loans are declared, the faster you set up the appropriate organizations to buy distressed assets, and the faster you will be able to clear up the mess. If there is one lesson of the experience of Japan of the last seven years—and there are many—it is that financial illnesses fester and expand the longer they are not dealt with. It is a salutary lesson that many Asian governments would do well to take on board. The Asian go-go years of growth are no more, but they do not have to be replaced by the "lost decade," if—and only if—the problems are dealt with now. Hard decisions, involving the liquidation of companies and the resultant expansion of unemployment and other nefarious side effects, have to be taken now, or the risk is that when they are eventually taken, the "illness" will have become considerably more serious.

Either way, there is no getting away from the fact that Asia will experience severe economic pain in the short term. What of the effect on the rest of the world? The U.S. economy had, in the words of Alan Greenspan, an "exemplary" year in 1997, with high growth and low inflation, ending the year on a real GDP-chain-weighted growth rate of around 4% in the fourth quarter. Greenspan himself admitted that it would be hard for 1998 to replicate that performance, and indeed a slowdown seems likely. It is a question of the degree of slowdown, not whether or not it will happen. While domestic demand, in the form of consumption, remains relatively robust, the Asian crisis will act as a catalyst for even fiercer price competition in the domestic market. The threat of deflation is a real one when Korean car exporters, in one example, are selling brand new models for USD2000 straight off the factory floor. While the U.S. economy clearly remains strong enough to withstand such pressures and emerge in relatively healthy shape, the same cannot be said for corporate margins—and therefore trouble lies ahead for the stock market. If the U.S. economy is the Titanic—the largest, fastest, and supposedly most efficient ship of its time—the Asian crisis is clearly an iceberg. The only question is how big is that iceberg. What is under the waterline and therefore how much damage can it do? Needless to say, the correct macroeconomic response is to apply the breaks. It would appear that there is not sufficient stopping room to avoid a collision entirely. Why should this matter? Because the U.S. economy, while exceptionally strong on the surface, has a number of structural weaknesses—in the hull of the ship beneath the waterline, to use the same analogy.

For a start, despite the recent and notable fiscal improvements, it remains a net debtor. In addition, it has a large and structural current account deficit, due to overconsumption and insufficient saving. Finally, in this most recent expansive cycle, productivity has spiked due to a combination of technological, competitive (increasing international competition), and demographic changes. On the surface, such high productivity levels are excellent news, helping to temper the price pressure of asset and goods. Yet if the rate of productivity (the cost-effective rate of the production of goods) exceeds that of real wage growth (or the ability to pay for those goods, however cheap they are due to productivity improvements), the economy has a problem, a supply-demand imbalance. This problem can temporarily be offset by speculative demand—temporary consumption fueled by credit creation or capital gains, for instance in real estate and stock prices. Margin consumption, in other words. What happens when that margin is called? The structural weakness of overcapacity is revealed, resulting in accelerated asset—real and financial—price deflation. Imported deflation from Asia could add to this imbalance, or more accurately cause it to be revealed.

The United States might yet be able to stamp on the brakes sufficiently to limit the collision with the iceberg to a modest dent and grind and then steam swiftly by, but it will be close, with plenty of potential for wild gyrations in asset markets along the way. As for Europe, the latest Bank of International Settlement data suggest that European banks have a considerably higher loan exposure to the Asian crisis than do their U.S. counterparts. While this is unlikely to result in anything as severe as a credit crunch in Europe, it will impact banking earnings. Are markets presently pricing that in? If not, they soon will. The current rationalization of the European banking sector is an excellent liquidity play for investors, but it is not an earnings' play. Eventually, that will come home to roost. A final aspect of the Asian crisis, perhaps even the most important, which could impact both the U.S. and Europe, is trade. The Asian currency devaluations will cause not only deflationary pressures in the global economy but also substantial increases in the U.S. and European trade deficits with Asia. In the U.S., the protectionist elements within Congress are unlikely to take well to this. The trend for global deregulation of trade barriers—if such there is, and one could argue both sides—could potentially be derailed or threatened. There are indeed many alarming similarities between the situation in 1928 and 1998. What could be the harbinger of such nefarious effects of the Asian crisis as overcapacity and asset price deflation? A sharply falling dollar.

Amid such doom and gloom, there are, however, some hopeful signs back in Asia itself, most notably the turnaround in the first quarter in Asian trade and current account balances. This is likely to continue into the second half of the year as the Asian currency devaluations and consequent collapse in domestic demand in many countries combine to result in a similar collapse in imports and a sharp rise in export volumes. There will be sharply lower unit prices initially, resulting in exported deflation, although these will eventually stabilize. As a result of the improved current account situation, Asian currencies will themselves stabilize, which will in turn allow for liquidity-driven recoveries in many Asian stock markets. This is likely to be not so much a "dead cat bounce" as a false dawn, which will lead to subsequent corrections as earnings continue to get rerated lower to reflect the increasingly apparent real economic effects of the crisis. From there, the markets will watch to see how—or if—the fire sale of assets proceeds. The new administrations of Thailand and Korea have promised much. However, in light of the painful market consequences of past policies, international investors will remain cautious and hold them at their word—or not return.

Unlike the Latin American debt crisis of 1982 and the Mexican crisis of 1995, the present one in Asia principally involves corporate as opposed to national debt. This is potentially harder to cure, as it necessitates a more lengthy and complex process, particularly with regard to the legal aspects of dismembering defunct and liquidated companies. However, many of the core fundamentals that caused the rise of Asia—high savings and low tax rates, demographics, productivity enhancements, and strong primary and secondary education systems—remain in place. In addition, for the most part, Asian governments ran relatively tight fiscal ships prior to the crisis. That together with the turnaround in the current account balances will allow them greater flexibility to push through the necessary regulatory measures for the de-leveraging of much of the Asian corporate base and banking system. The economic situation in China still represents a danger (as noted in Chapter 11), not just to Asia, but to the entire financial system, as indeed does Japan. In my view, both, however, will be able to avoid falling into full economic crisis. For one thing, China is allowed greater breathing space to deal with its fundamental problems by the very restrictions it maintains on its financial system and specifically on the capital account.

In the end, as I have said, it is up to the Asian governments to decide whether or not to use the lessons of the Asian currency crisis of 1997 in order to restructure their economies along more long-term, sustainable lines. If the past is anything to go by, they will do just that. Among the many strengths of this region are its flexibility, its willingness to learn and adapt, and its dedication to the task in hand through sheer hard work. Such strengths are not found everywhere and will serve Asia well through its painful, yet necessary, restructuring process.

A major factor that could yet help the recovery of Asia is Japan. After the latest economic stimulus packages, the Japanese economy remains extremely fragile, verging on recession. The banking industry, after years of painfully slow attempts to clean up its balance sheet with respect to domestic Japanese (real estate) bad debt exposure, has been hit with the added gut-wrenching blow of bad debt exposure to the Asian crisis. Japanese banks have the highest exposure to Asia, relative to their U.S. and European counterparts. Given the subsequent falls in Asian currencies, against both the dollar and the yen, and the debt moratorium in Indonesia, this has further damaged Japanese bank balance sheets. To offset this, "assets"—loans—will have to be reduced, resulting in reduced lending even to healthy corporations in Asia and elsewhere; and equity will have to be boosted, most likely by preferred stock issues. The March 31 end of the fiscal year is the deadline for dealing with and achieving the agreed international capital adequacy ratios. All this may sound negative, but this is not necessarily the case. Remember that it took a crisis in Japan in the fourth quarter of 1997 for the Japanese authorities to act. The threat of further financial strife could well cause them to accelerate the much needed hollowing out and deregulation of the financial sector. This in turn will bring closer the day when Japanese institutions start to lend again—within Japan first of all and then elsewhere, notably in Asia.

Japan has a crucial role to play, not only to safeguard its own financial future but also to help secure a greater degree of financial stability for the Asian region as a whole. It remains to be seen whether the politicians and bureaucrats who have "supervised" the last seven years' worth of paltry growth and lack of meaningful deregulation are able—or willing—to change their ways. The best chance of this being achieved is if it is forced on them by a state of crisis. That crisis is here, as Japanese bank exposure to Indonesia, a country where debt payments have stopped for however long, attests to. Their response will be awaited around the world with interest.

Emerging Asia Chronological Developments

1997

MAY 14–15   Bank of Thailand intervenes to defend baht from attack by speculators. Singapore provides assistance to Bank of Thailand.

Philippines Central Bank raises overnight borrowing rate by 175 basis points to 13.0% to avoid spillover from baht onto peso.

JUNE 27   Bank of Thailand suspends operation of sixteen finance companies (in February it had named ten of these insolvent).

JUNE 30   Thai Prime Minister Chavalit assures the nation in a televised address that there will not be a devaluation of the baht.

JULY 2   Bank of Thailand abandons peg for the baht, which depreciates by 18% to about 30 to the dollar.

JULY 6   *Singapore Sunday Straits Times* quotes Philippine Financial Secretary de Campo that the peso "may devalue," triggering a new round of pressure when trading opens the next day. Philippine authorities insist they were misquoted.

JULY 8   Malaysia Central Bank intervenes aggressively to defend the ringgit, boosting the currency to high of 2.5100/10 after low of 2.5240/50.

JULY 11   Philippines Central Bank, Bangko Sentral, gives up defense of the peso. It had spent one-eighth of the international reserves in the first ten days of July and hiked overnight borrowing rate as high as 32%. The peso promptly depreciated by more than 10% to 29.45 to the greenback, its weakest rate in more than 3½ years.

Indonesia widens intervention band from 8% to 12%.

JULY 13   Creditor banks announce they will grant emergency support to help automaker Kia, Korea's eighth largest conglomerate, avoid bankruptcy. On July 23, S&P and Moody's place several Korean banks on a negative credit rating outlook.

JULY 14   Malaysia's Bank Negara gives up the defense of the ringgit after unsuccessfully defending it by jacking up interest rates to 50% and spending an estimated USD3 billion. The ringgit promptly plunges to a thirty-three-month low.

Philippines Bankers Association suspends its 1.5% volatility band used to limit fluctuations in peso on PDS trading.

JULY 21–23   Bank Indonesia intervenes to sell both dollar spot and forwards to resist the contagion that has spread from the Thai baht and Philippine peso to the rupiah.

JULY 22   Philippines draws down a portion of the $1 billion loan facility that the IMF is making available to help it replenish foreign reserves.

JULY 24   Currency meltdown. MYR hits thirty-eight-month low of 2.653 to USD, and Prime Minister Mahathir launches bitter attack on "rogue speculators." Hong Kong dollar steady, but authorities later reveal that they spent US$1 billion on intervention during two hours on unspecified day in July.

Moody's revises ratings outlook to negative on four Korean state banks (KDB, Housing & Commercial Bank of Korea, IBK, and Korea Ex-Im Bank), and says that it also reflects a negative outlook for sovereign A1 rating. This follows July 23 move by S&P to place five private South Korean banks (Hanil, KEB, Korea First, Korea LTCB, and Shinhan) on CreditWatch negative, in reaction to the heightened risk of default among heavily leveraged Korean chaebol.

JULY 26   Malaysian Prime Minister Mahathir names George Soros as the man responsible for the attack on the ringgit.

JULY 28   Thailand decides to seek assistance from IMF.

JULY 30   Philippine Central Bank hikes liquidity reserve requirement from 2% to 3%, tightening money market in support of peso (two days later, requirement hiked to 4%). Taiwan dollar falls to nine-year low.

Aug. 1   Standard & Poor's Ratings announces it is putting Thailand's $3 billion foreign currency debt (currently rated A) on negative CreditWatch.

Aug. 4   Malaysia imposes limit on noncommercial-related ringgit offer side swap transaction with foreign customers for USD 2 million.

Aug. 5   IMF unveils outlines of Thailand bailout package. Bank of Thailand announced it was suspending another forty-two finance companies, bringing total to fifty-eight.

Aug. 11   Agreement reached in Tokyo for IMF-led package of $16 billion in loans to Thailand, including contributions from IMF, Japan Ex-Im Bank, Singapore, Malaysia, Hong Kong, Australia, Indonesia, South Korea, ADB, World Bank, and China. (Total was soon enlarged to $17.2 billion, including funds from Brunei.)

Aug. 13   Rupiah comes under severe pressure, hitting historical low of 2682 versus USD, before ending at 2655 on active defense by Bank Indonesia.

Aug. 14   Bank Indonesia abolishes intervention trading band, effectively letting the rupiah float.

Aug. 18   Bank Indonesia hikes SBI intervention yields twofold to threefold on maturities of one week (20%) to three months (28%) to support rupiah.

          Standard & Poor's revises Malaysia's outlook from positive to stable.

Aug. 20   Philippine Central Bank closes its lending window as part of effort to drain liquidity in defense of peso.

          IMF formally approves its $3.9 portion of the assistance package for Thailand.

Aug. 21   Bank of Thailand reveals that it had $23.4 billion in outstanding forward sales of USD maturing within next year, thereby set to absorb much of their $30 billion in foreign reserve holdings as of the end of July.

          Standard & Poor's Ratings affirms long-term foreign currency and local currency ratings on Malaysia's Petrolium Nasional, Telekom, Tenaga.

Aug. 22   Moody's maintains banking outlook in face of Indonesian currency crisis.

Aug. 28   Malaysia imposes restriction on short selling of KLSE index–linked counters.

In attempt to bolster the peso, which weakened beyond 30 versus USD, Philippine Central Bank hikes liquidity reserve requirement from 5% to 8%, sending T-bill yields to five-year high at September 1 auction.

AUG. 29 Indonesia imposes swap restrictions on offer side for USD5 million.

SEPT. 3 Standard & Poor's Ratings revises Thailand long-term foreign exchange sovereign rating from A to A–; outlook is negative.

Philippine Central Bank announces two-step cut in liquidity reserve requirement from 8% to 6%, easing money market rates that had provoked concerns as a burden on the economy.

SEPT. 4 Indonesia unveils ten-point austerity measures. Bank Indonesia cuts one- and three-month SBI intervention yields by 3%.

Bank of Korea will lend 1 trillion KRW to troubled Korea First Bank, and government will boost its capital with purchase of 600 billion KRW in Korea First common shares.

Ringgit breaks through 3.0 versus USD. Malaysia delays several big construction projects.

SEPT. 5 Malaysia lifts ban on short selling of KLSE-linked stocks.

SEPT. 9 Bank Indonesia cuts SBI intervention yields on seven and fourteen days by 1%, one and three months by 2%.

Jinro, South Korea's largest liquor group and nineteenth-largest conglomerate, becomes third large Korean firm to go bankrupt this year, with debts of nearly $3 billion.

SEPT. 10 Moody's places Thailand sovereign long-term foreign currency debt under review for possible downgrade of current A-3 rating (already cut from A-2 in April). Also under review are long-term foreign currency and bank deposit ratings for Bangkok Bank, Ex-Im Bank, Government Housing Bank, HSBC Bangkok, IFCT, Krung Thai, Siam Commercial, and Thai Farmers.

SEPT. 11 Singapore's Monetary Authority of Singapore says it would prefer if the NYCE delays the launch of the Sing dollar futures contract on FINEX.

SEPT. 15 Malaysia corporate share buy-back scheme to start.

Bank Indonesia cuts bilateral SBI rates, lowering the one- and three-month rates by 200 basis points to 23% and 21%, respectively, along with 100-basis-point cuts on seven days (to 18%) and fourteen days (20%).

SEPT. 16   *South China Morning Post* reports that the IMF is dissatisfied with progress in Thailand, and threatens to withhold remainder of rescue loan package if Thailand does not move quickly to implement the necessary reforms.

Indonesia finance minister says will reschedule 3.28 trillion IDR in development and 39 trillion IDR in infrastructure projects in FY97–98 budget. Focus on those with high import content, in effort to limit current accounts deficit to 3% of GDP in next two years.

SEPT. 17   Citing recent regional currency turmoil, IMF *World Economic Outlook* lowers forecast 1997 GDP growth to 2.5% for Thailand (same figure cited when unveiled loan package), 7.0% for Indonesia, 7.5% for Malaysia, and 5.3% for the Philippines. While growth in Thailand will slow significantly in short term, "provided adequate measures are adopted to strengthen the financial sector and BOP, confidence should be restored relatively quickly" and growth return to "quite strong" long-term trend.

Standard & Poor's Ratings downgrade ratings on seven Thai financial institutions: Bangkok Bank (A– to BBB), Siam Commercial and Thai Farmers (both BBB+ to BBB–), IFCT (A– to BBB+), Bank of Ayudhya (BBB to BBB–), Bank of Asia (BB+ to BB), and Phatra Thanakit (BBB–). Outlook on the group is negative.

SEPT. 18   In press conference at IMF annual meeting, Managing Director Camdessus says that "so far we see (Thailand) complying pretty well with all the macroeconomic elements of the programme."

Khazanah, investment arm of Malaysian government, starts buying stocks with some of 794 million MYR in proceeds of recent bond issue.

SEPT. 19   Moody's says it will review Thailand's Prime-2 short-term foreign currency rating for possible downgrade, along with its review of long-term ratings announced last week. Also affected will be short-term ratings of several banks.

SEPT. 20   Addressing IMF conference separately over the weekend, Malaysia Prime Minister Mahathir declares foreign exchange trading should be illegal, while George Soros labels him a menace to his own country. After Mahathir quoted in *South China Morning Post* that foreign exchange dealing should be limited to the financing of trade, triggering a sell-off in the ringgit and stock market. Finance Minister Anwar subsequently attempts to allay market fears by saying that there was no intention to change currency trading rules.

SEPT. 21   Half million Filipinos march peacefully to warn President Ramos against attempting constitutional amendment to allow a second term. New pledge by Ramos to step down when his term ends next year. Manila markets surge upon Monday open on relief from political concerns, but peso and stocks give back early gains by end of day.

SEPT. 22   Ringgit is pummeled to as far as 3.12 versus USD, highest since at least 1971, and KLSE composite index plunges 3.5% as markets react to weekend remarks by Prime Minister Mahathir suggesting restrictions on foreign exchange trading.

Bank Indonesia cuts bilateral SBI rates for the fourth straight week, lowering rates by 200 basis points on one-month (to 21%) and 3-month (19%), and by 100 basis points on one-week (to 17%) and two-week (19%).

SEPT. 23   Philippine Central Bank will lower liquidity reserve requirement in two steps, from 6% to 5% effective October 15 and then to 4% on November 15. It extends cut from 8% implemented in early September, in reversal of hikes from 2% in late July to 8% at end of August implemented to bolster peso.

SEPT. 25   S&P Ratings revises outlook from stable to negative on both Malaysia's "A+" foreign currency long-term debt rating and its "AA+" long-term local currency rating. It cites the authorities' reluctance to curb rapid credit growth and the likelihood that bank asset quality will deteriorate next year. MYR plunges from 3.06 versus USD to a record 3.145 on news.

Philippine Central Bank approves requirement that banks set aside loan loss reserves equal to 2% of loan portfolio.

SEPT. 26   S&P Ratings affirms Republic of Philippines BB+ long-term foreign currency rating and B short-term foreign currency rating, and A– long-term and A-1 short-term local currency ratings, but revises outlook on these from positive to stable.

SEPT. 27   Thailand parliament votes overwhelming approval of reform constitution aimed at fairer and more effective political system. Prime Minister Chavalit survives no-confidence vote (coalition now jockeying over cabinet reshuffle).

SEPT. 29   Stock Exchange of Thailand (SET) suspends 48 listed companies (including 26 finance companies), more than 10% of the 455 companies listed on the exchange.

A number of Kia units, including Kia Motors, receive South Korean court order in past few days, freezing debt obligations and assets, but avoiding immediate bankruptcy until court places them under receivership or court protection. Two-month grace period expires.

OCT. 1   ASEAN regional currencies plunge to new lows versus USD, as traders essentially get out of the way of the virtual panic pervading the region. Malaysian ringgit drops nearly 5% in just a few hours, reaching a record 3.40 versus USD, before firming near 3.36. Indonesian rupiah weakens from opening of 3275 to beyond 3400 versus USD for first time, while Philippine peso reaches as low as 35.61 versus USD, before finishing at 34.65, off about 1% from Tuesday close.

Local press reports that Thai Finance Minister Thanong submitted his resignation Tuesday, frustrated as other cabinet ministers resisted efforts to cut the budget, but it was rejected by Prime Minister Chavalit. Officials deny the reports.

OCT. 2   Moody's lowers Thailand's long-term foreign currency country ceiling from A3 to Baa1, with negative outlook, and long-term foreign currency country ceiling for bank deposits lowered from A3 to Baa1, remaining on review for possible downgrade. The short-term foreign currency country ceilings for commercial paper and bank deposits are lowered from Prime-2 to Prime-3, both remaining on review for possible downgrade. Moody's cites erosion in credit fundamentals, cutting the rating for sovereign and ten banks.

Philippine money market rates soar as Central Bank drains reserves to meet IMF quarterly targets during ten-day test period, in part by hiking its overnight borrowing rate to 14% from 12%, where it had stood since late August.

S&P Ratings downgrade the long-term foreign exchange ratings for several Korean banks, while affirming several others (but outlook revised downward for some). Korea First Bank affirms BBB–/negative, and thus manages to avoid becoming the first speculative-grade Korean bank on the strength of government assistance (49% stake).

OCT. 3   Moody's puts debt and deposit ratings for Maybank and Public Bank of Malaysia under review for possible downgrade, citing growing problems in the Malaysian economy and increasing strains on its leading banks.

OCT. 6 Indonesia rupiah plunges for a second straight session to a record 3870 versus USD at Monday intraday low (down 12% from Thursday close), before rebounding on Bank Indonesia intervention to finish near 3700.

OCT. 7 Philippines Bankers Association implements new foreign exchange volatility band, whereby trading is temporarily suspended after breaching initial 2% band on either side of previous afternoon average, suspended a second time after moving an additional 1%, and then closed for the day upon moving another 1% to the third ceiling. Trading suspended twice on first day on peso depreciation.

Moody's downgrades Thailand's First Bangkok City Bank and Bank of Asia's long-term senior debt ratings to Ba1 (speculative grade), while lowering their financial strength rating from D to E+. It cuts Thai Military Bank's financial strength rating from E+ to E, but maintains its Baa3 investment-grade rating. Moody's cites vulnerability of weaker banks to asset quality and liquidity pressure. It places under review for possible downgrade financial strength rating for Krung Thai Bank, Thai Farmers Bank, and Bank of Ayudhya (also debt rating of latter).

OCT. 8 Indonesian government announces it will seek IMF assistance to bolster its foreign reserves and help stabilize its financial sector in the face of recent sharp depreciation of the rupiah. It would like to increase its access to standby loans, and is sounding out long-term support funds from international institutions. See IMF involvement as helping restore confidence in the rupiah, which has been battered in recent weeks.

OCT. 9 Philippine Central Bank reopens its lending window (closed since August 20). It sets several conditions, only allowing banks to borrow if they have reserve deficiency, are not net lenders in interbank market, and have a square foreign exchange position, and not buyers of USD on PDS of relatively large volume. Initial 15% overnight lending rate. It also lowers its overnight borrowing rate from 14% to 12% reversing previous week's hike.

OCT. 10 S&P cuts Indonesia's foreign exchange rating from BBB to BBB– and local currency rating from A+ to A–, citing concerns that steep rise in corporate external indebtedness (aggravated by fall in IDR) and slowing economic growth will prompt the government to bail out banks and corporations. S&P move effectively brings them into line with Moody's, and rating outlook is now stable.

OCT. 14   State Bank of Vietnam doubles the dong fluctuation band to +/– 10% either side of daily official rate from 5%. The move pushes VND to its new floor of 12,293 (as quoted by local banks), effectively implementing 5% devaluation, since VND had been stuck for weeks at previous 5% floor.

Singapore Prime Minister Goh says, "So the market has decided that for competitive reasons for Singapore, that should be the (dollar sing) level. We are quite happy to accept that." Dollar sing surges from 1.5310 to a high of 1.5455 on the remarks.

Thailand unveils plan for financial-sector restructuring, including creation of two new state agencies, Financial Sector Restructuring Authority (manage what is left of fifty-eight suspended finance companies, deciding within six weeks which will be allowed to continue, whether on own or through merger and assets of those that cannot continue). Will permit majority foreign ownership of banks or finance companies (current cap 25%), though a ten-year limit, after which not be allowed to add to equity holding. Government will cut 100 billion baht from FY98 budget (on top of cuts in August after inviting in IMF) and raise excise taxes by 40 billion (mostly on imported cars, oil, alcohol).

OCT. 15   ING Bank tentatively agrees to buy 10% of Siam City Bank for $35–40 million, and analysts expect more such purchases in the wake of relaxation of restrictions on foreign ownership announced to attact needed capital injections into weakened Thai financial sector.

OCT. 16   Taiwan Central Bank announces reduction in reserve requirements, effective immediately, by 1.5 percentage points on demand deposits and 0.5 percentage point on time deposits, to help boost sagging stock market.

OCT. 17   Malaysian Finance Minister Anwar unveils 1998 budget cutting state infrastructure spending, and includes increased import duties and breaks for exporters aimed at narrowing the current account deficit. Corporate tax rate cut from 30% to 28% to stimulate investment.

South Korea Finance Minister announces plans to establish 3.5 trillion won fund by late November aimed at buying bad loans at sharply discounted prices, and write off up to 4.5 trillion won worth of bad loans by year-end. Funding through state bonds.

OCT. 18   New Taiwan dollar falls to its weakest level in a decade, after Central Bank reverses course and stops defending currency, announcing it will let market forces set rates.

OCT. 20   Bank Indonesia cuts SBI intervention rates by 100 basis points on maturities overnight through three months, despite continued IDR weakness that had interrupted easing for almost a month. Overnight rate cut to 14%, two to six days to 15%, one week to 16%, one month to 20%, three months to 18%.

Thai Baht weakens to record 38.10 versus USD in offshore market, hurt by word that Finance Minister Thanong will leave his post when cabinet is reshuffled this week. His decision follows reversal of unpopular oil tax hike approved only last week.

South Korea KRW plows through previous support of 915 versus USD to record 924, as Central Bank gets out of the way.

OCT. 21   Bank Indonesia reopens SBPU lending facility, in move to help ease liquidity squeeze. It offers three-month SBPU at 20%.

OCT. 22   Doubts raised about maintaining the peg for Hong Kong dollar amid regional currency turmoil, though Financial Secretary Tsang said the Hong Kong dollar "remains rock solid" and there was no reason to consider delinking the currency from the USD. During four sessions, Hong Kong stock market loses nearly 25% of its value.

South Korea government announces that it will seek court receivership for the Kia group, effectively nationalizing the financially troubled automaker as the state-run Korea Development Bank converts its loans into the largest equity stake. Stocks rally 6% on the news.

China Central Bank cuts base lending rates by 150 basis points and deposit rates by 110 basis points. The surprise move appears aimed at boosting slowing economic growth, encouraging skeptical investors to support reform of state enterprises, and helping plunging stocks.

OCT. 23   Hong Kong stocks plunge to intraday lows off a record 16%, ending down 10.4% and bringing losses for week to 23. Overnight rates soar to 250—33%—amid doubts over sustainability of peg for Hong Kong dollar, though the high rates help Hong Kong dollar firm to 7.70 versus USD, briefly reaching 7.60. Other regional stock markets are off sharply in sympathy with Hong Kong, with Singapore STI down 4.7%, Kuala Lumpur Composite down 3.4%, Philippines down 5%, Jakarta down 2.2%.

Moody's places Thailand's Baa1 foreign exchange debt ceiling on review for possible downgrade, and cuts country ceiling for foreign exchange bank deposits to Ba2/Bot-Prime from Baa3/Prime-3. Little reaction in USD-THB, which firms in sympathy with regionals as domestic market is closed for holiday.

OCT. 24 After opening down another 2%, Hang Seng rebounds strongly to trade 4.5% higher mid-day, retracing part of its 23% decline during first four days this week, including 10% plunge Thursday that spilled over to stock markets worldwide. Overnight rate eases to 50% after Thursday high of 300%.

S&P Ratings downgrades Thailand long-term foreign currency rating from to BBB from A–, lowers long-term local currency rating to A from AA–, and lowers short-term foreign currency rating to A-3 from A-1. The outlook on long-term ratings remains negative. Separately, Prime Minister Chavelit to present list for reshuffled cabinet to Thai king this evening.

S&P Ratings downgrades South Korea foreign currency long-term rating to A≠ from AA–, and short-term rating to A+ from AA–. Also affects state-affiliated Korea Development Bank, Ex-Im Bank, Kepco, Korea Telecom. Downgrade reflects escalating cost of supporting ailing businesses.

OCT. 28 Moody's changes the outlook from stable to negative on its Baa3 foreign currency country ceiling for Indonesia. A negative outlook will also be attached to the Ba1 ceiling on foreign currency bank deposits. Moody's cites effects of recent depreciation of the IDR on government fiscal position and the potential for corporate and banking-sector financial difficulties.

Moody's also cuts Korea's short-term foreign currency rating to Prime-2 from Prime-1, and places the A1 long-term foreign currency ratings of three state-affiliated banks (KDB, IBK, and KEXIM) on review for possible downgrade.

Paced again by Hong Kong, where Hang Seng plunges 13.7%, regional stock markets are sharply lower Tuesday, in sympathy with the overnight 7% sell-off on Wall Street. Singapore STI finishes 7.6%, Malaysia KLSE 6.6%, Korea Composite 6.6%, Thailand SET 6.2%, Taiwan weighted index 5.9%, Philippines Composite 6.3%, Jakarta Composite 8.6%, though largely stabilizing after opening plunge.

OCT. 29   Strong rebound in Hong Kong, where Hang Seng soars 18.8%, paces a reversal of sharp drops the day before on stock markets across the region, in sympathy with overnight 4.7% rebound on Wall Street. Though giving back part of opening jump, Singapore STI finishes +3.0%, Malaysia KLSE +2.3%, Korea Composite +2.3%, Philippines Composite +4.3%, Jakarta Composite +5.4%, but Thailand SET −0.8%, Taiwan weighted index −1.7%.

OCT. 30   Moody's changes outlook from stable to negative for the credit ratings of eighteen Hong Kong banks, citing concerns over exposure to weakening real estate market. It also places under negative review the B financial strength rating of HSBC and Hang Seng Bank. The announcement contributes to a 3.7% drop in Hang Seng Stock Index.

Thai baht plunges past the 40.0 level versus USD, a new record level after new finance minister hinted that IMF target of FY98 budget surplus 1% of GDP is difficult.

OCT. 31   IMF-led assistance package for Indonesia is announced, including first-tier of $23 billion in loans ($10 billion IMF, $4.5 billion World Bank, $3.5 billion ADB), and with individual nations (including Japan, Singapore, Malaysia, Australia, U.S.) prepared to supplement this with over $10 billion in additional funds if necessary (potentially bringing the total package as high as $38 billion). Indonesia pledges financial sector reforms, announcing closure of sixteen troubled banks, and deregulatory moves including lifting monopoly of state commodities regulator, HULOG.

Moody's downgrades four Korean banks (Korea Exchange Bank, Korea First Bank, Commercial Bank of Korea, and Seoul Bank) that had been put on review on July 25. Senior debt and long-term deposit ratings of KEB cut to Baa2 from Baa1, while KFB, CBK, and Seoul Bank went from Baa2 to Baa3. Bank financial strength ratings of the latter trio were also lowered to E from E+. Short-term ratings of all four lowered from Prime-2 to Prime-3.

Standard & Poor's Ratings affirms Hong Kong's long-term foreign currency sovereign rating at A+ and long-term local currency at AA−. It cites government's strong net creditor position and a "well-capitalized and prudently-managed" financial sector.

NOV. 3   IDR strengthens 8% to below 3300 versus USD on heavy joint intervention by central banks of Indonesia, Singapore, and Japan (reportedly over $500 million, by some accounts $1 billion), to boost positive response to IMF plan.

Nov. 4	Markets react positively to announcement by Thailand Prime Minister Chavalit that he would resign later this week, after a long period of dissatisfaction with government handling of financial crisis. Baht firms beyond 39.00 versus USD from record levels near 41.00. SET stock index up 6.9%.
Nov. 5	Philippines Supreme Court overturns recent law deregulating oil prices, reversing a welcome reform.
Nov. 6	South Korea markets swirl with a spate of rumors, including talk that Korea would have to turn to IMF for assistance to bolster reserves (denied by MOF&E official) and that it was preparing to devalue the KRW (denied by Bank of Korea), and that Korea Development Bank was going to default (denied by KDB).
Nov. 7	A harsh turn in sentiment toward South Korea amid talk that the country is to seek IMF assistance, even though both sides deny help is needed right now. Stocks fall a record 6.9%, KRW weakens to 979.9 versus USD.
Nov. 8	Democratic Party leader Chuan Leekpai is appointed prime minister of Thailand after securing a parliamentary majority. On November 10 baht firms to 37.0 onshore for first time since mid-October.
Nov. 13	Chairman Greenspan tells congressional hearing that to date the direct impact from Asia's financial problems on U.S. economy "has been modest, but it can be expected not to be negligible," by hurting exports.
Nov. 14	Moody's says it will review ratings of Daegu Bank, Hanil Bank, and Shinhan Bank for possible downgrade, citing concern over asset quality deterioration from additional corporate failures.
Nov. 17	KRW weakens to a record 1008.60 versus USD, falling the 2.25% daily limit, as Bank of Korea unexpectedly abandons previous week's intervention in defense of the 1000 level. New Taiwan dollar weakened in sympathy with KRW, closing at 31.50 versus USD, its lowest in a decade.
Nov. 19	KRW trading halts after opening at a record 1035.5 versus USD, plunging 2.25% daily limit for third straight day. In perhaps last-ditch effort to avoid the rising pressure to approach IMF for assistance, government unveils financial stabilization package, including opening up corporate bond market to foreign investors, government raising short-term debt abroad, bailout fund capitalized at 10 trillion KRW ($10 billion) to help dispose of banking-sector nonperforming loans.

Plunging KRW again sets tone for weakness in emerging Asian currencies. Continued pressure on NTD, which penetrates 32.0 level versus USD to close at a new ten-year low of 32.753. Malaysian ringgit closes at record 3.48 versus USD, Thai baht weakens above the 40.0 level versus USD onshore, Singapore dollar tests its recent high at the 1.5970 level, rupiah tests the 3500 level versus USD.

Nov. 20   Trading band on KRW is widened from +/–2.25% to +/–10%, and within an hour after open it plunges daily limit to 1139 versus USD (three-month NDF 1260/90). Market apparently not overly impressed with stabilization package unveiled on November 19. Korea continues to resist pressure to seek IMF aid.

KLSE Composite Index plunges 30% November 18–20 to six-year low in response to controversial transaction in which UEM, Malaysia's largest construction firm, spent nearly $700 million to buy out influential shareholders in its debt-laden (and politically connected) parent company Renong. Minority shareholders in both companies saw their share prices plummet, as did many other cash-rich companies, amid suspicion that they might be coerced into a similar move.

Nov. 21   KRW rebounds on reports that South Korea has decided to seek IMF assistance, finishing at 1056 versus USD from Thursday's record 1139. After initially refusing to confirm the reports, Finance Minister Lim announces that night that Korea had decided to ask for IMF assistance in the form of standby credit, though saying that $20 billion would be sufficient, much lower than earlier estimates of $50–60 billion. Emerging Asian currencies rebound in sympathy with KRW, after many had weakened to recent lows earlier in week.

Nov. 25   S&P Ratings downgrades Korea.

Nov. 26   APEC Vancouver summit endorses the so-called Manila Framework, which gives the IMF the lending role in ensuring financial stability in Asia.

Citibank agrees to buy at least 50.1% of First Bangkok City Bank (Thailand's seventh largest), becoming first foreign bank to take majority interest in a Thai Bank.

South Korea bans eight merchant banks from borrowing overseas or lending foreign currency, effectively forcing them into takeovers by larger commercial banks.

Korea Finance Minister Lim reveals plans to expand money supply to lower interest rates. Government will redeem monetary stabilization bonds from trust companies and enable them to buy corporate bonds and commercial paper.

Halla Heavy Industry, fourth largest Korean shipbuilder, says it will cut half of its 6000 workers, in first big layoff since invited in IMF.

Nov. 28   Moody's downgrades foreign currency ratings for both Thailand and South Korea by two notches. It cuts Thailand foreign currency bond ceiling from Baa1 to Baa3, with a negative outlook, and foreign currency bank deposit ceiling from Ba2 to B1 (stable outlook), citing deteriorating credit and financial fundamentals. It lowers Korea long-term foreign currency ceiling from A1 to A3, short-term foreign currency ceiling from Prime-2 to Prime-3, and foreign currency bank deposits from A2 to Baa2, all stable outlook. It notes that performance of corporate sector has deteriorated because of underlying structural problems, a buildup of short-term external debt, and a weakening of the financial system.

Dec. 1   Taiwan stocks plunge 5% in response to poll defeat by ruling KMT party in local elections over the weekend.

Malaysian stocks slip another 3% after KLSE slapped trading restriction on five brokerages believed to have been stuck with huge losses run up by clients.

China Central Bank will restructure itself, setting up branch offices in some ten economic regions, to bolster oversight of banks.

Dec. 2   Halla Group, South Korea's twelfth largest conglomerate, seeks court protection after a unit failed to honor 400 billion KRW of notes. It is able to avoid default when merchant banks agree to roll over the bills at the last minute.

Dec. 3   South Korea and IMF reach agreement on bailout loan package totaling up to $57 billion, surpassing 1994 Mexico rescue as IMF's largest ever. It will include up to $21 billion from IMF over three years, along with contributions from World Bank (up to $10 billion), ADB (as much as $4 billion), and up to $22 billion from individual nations, disbursement of initial $5.5 billion to begin December 5. Korea agrees to trim its 1998 GDP growth target to 3.0%, to be achieved in part through budget cuts and higher taxes, monetary discipline. Other conditions involve restructuring of troubled financial system, and opening up of Korean financial markets to foreign investors, including foreign stakes in banks.

Before the agreement, uncertainty surrounding repeated delays in Korea/IMF accord had helped KRW, along with IDR, MYR, and THB, weaken to record lows versus USD.

DEC. 5   Divergent further Korean market reaction to IMF bailout package, with stock market matching 7% December 4 surge, but "sell-on-fact" weakening of KRW to 1230 versus USD, just short of Tuesday record close. Stock market rebound led by candidates for foreign investment after liberalized ceilings on foreign stakes under IMF plan.

Bank Indonesia repeatedly intervenes, struggling to defend 4000 level for USD-IDR (which hits a record 4020), as IDR pressured in sympathy with other currencies in the region, as well as on concern over President Suharto's health after he cancels trip to Iran conference.

Malaysia Finance Minister Anwar at Friday afternoon press conference cuts 1998 GDP growth forecast to 4.0–5.0% from previous 7.0%, and 1997 to 7.5–7.7% from prior 8.0%. Government spending will be trimmed to match slower revenue. His no-nonsense remarks help MYR firm from record 3.865 versus USD to close little-changed near 3.71, and stocks to finish +5.5% on late bounce.

NYCE's Finex resumes trading futures contracts on IDR, NYR, and THB. Contracts had been launched in July, but delisted within several months on slow volume. Contracts have been modified to be quoted in dollars.

DEC. 8   Taking a tougher line than expected, Thai government says that only two of fifty-eight finance companies suspended during June and August would be allowed to reopen. This was welcomed by IMF, which on December 9 approved disbursement of $810 million, second tranche in its $3.9 billion portion of $17.2 billion loan package. KRW plunges 10% daily limit amid panic-filled mood partly in reaction to failure over weekend of the Halla Group (twelfth largest Korean conglomerate). More significant were reports, apparently based on IMF leaks, that Korean "usable" foreign reserves fell to $6 billion by December 2, and that Korean short-term foreign currency debt (due within one year), earlier estimated at $63 billion, exceeds $100 billion if includes obligations of overseas units. Growing fears that unless Koreans can convince lenders to roll over debt, the $57 billion IMF loan package would be insufficient.

DEC. 9   IDR plunges over 10%, past 4600 level versus USD, on rumors that President Suharto was seriously ill.

DEC. 10   Korean government announces suspension through January 31 of five more merchant banks and plans sale of 24 trillion KRW in government bonds to help guarantee merchant bank deposits. Planned raising in ceiling on foreign investor stake in listed companies from 26% to 50% is moved forward to December 11.

DEC. 11   Within minutes after open of trading, KRW plunges the 10% daily limit for the fourth day in a row. Pressure aggravated by overnight move by Moody's downgrading Korean country ceiling on foreign currency long-term debt by two notches from A3 to Baa2, followed by S&P cutting long-term foreign currency rating by three notches from A– to BBB–. The turmoil induces KDB to postpone a $2 billion international bond issue it had hoped to launch this week. Dongsuh Securities, Korea's fourth largest broker, defaulted on debt (declared bankrupt December 12).

Spillover from the KRW helps THB, IDR, and PHP weaken to record lows versus USD, with MYR approaching last week's record low and SGD hitting 4-1/two-year low.

DEC. 12   KRW is quoted at 1891.4 versus USD immediately after open, down 10% daily limit for fifth day this week, but Bank of Korea intervention to halt the free fall enables it to finish session at 1710, slightly firmer for day, though off from 1230 a week earlier.

IDR plunges past 5000 level versus USD to new record, on word that President Suharto, on doctor's advice, would not be attending the ASEAN conference in Kuala Lumpur on December 15–16.

DEC. 16   Korean authorities allow KRW to float freely, abandoning previous daily trading limit of +/– 10%.

DEC. 17   Philippines Central Bank unveils measures to support the peso in collaboration with commercial banks. Starting December 18, banks would daily sell a minimum of $50 million directly to Central Banks, which would match these two for one with USD sales on PDS system. In addition, an NDF facility would be launched for hedging by borrowers of USD-denominated loans. Peso had weakened by 4% limit during four previous sessions, reaching record 41.60 in early trading, before rebounding to 39.77 close after the announcement.

IMF executive board adopts a new short-term loan program that will expedite disbursement of funds to countries facing immediate debt repayment problems or low foreign exchange reserves.

DEC. 18   Indonesia President Suharto makes appearance at military parade, helping calm concerns about his health. IDR strengthens past 5000 versus USD.

IMF approves second disbursement of $3.5 for South Korea under bailout package. Opposition candidate Kim Dae Jung is elected president of South Korea. Though he issues statement the next morning pledging to uphold IMF agreement, markets remain jittery about his past flip-flop on the subject and KRW and stocks each lose around 5% (but sustain a portion of rebound from their lows amid market panic the week before).

DEC. 22   Moody's cuts its foreign currency country ceilings for Indonesia, South Korea, and Thailand to Ba1 (junk status) and lowers rating for Malaysia to A2 (still investment grade). The agency cites the East Asian financial crisis as increasing the vulnerability of countries that had built up high levels of short-term liabilities. It affirms its foreign exchange country ceilings for China, Hong Kong, Taiwan, Japan, Philippines, Singapore, Taiwan, Vietnam, Macao.

IMF slashes projected 1998 growth rates for emerging Asian economies from October estimates, Forecasts Indonesia growth at 2.0% (previously 6.2%), Thailand 0.0% (3.5%), South Korea 3.5% (6.0%), Malaysia 2.5% (6.5%), Philippines 3.8% (5.0%).

DEC. 23   S&P Ratings cuts South Korea's foreign currency rating four notches from BBB– to B+, four notches below investment grade. S&P cites Korea's bank plan to be "inconsistent" with IMF program. South Korea joins Pakistan and Venezuela at B+ status. S&P also cuts rating on Malaysia long-term foreign currency debt to A from A+. Thomson BankWatch cuts its sovereign risk rating for Malaysia to A– from A+.

DEC. 24   IMF and thirteen individual nations agree to accelerate disbursement of $10 billion of the $57 billion bailout package. The IMF will provide $2 billion on December 30, while a group of thirteen nations will move forward to early January $8 billion in loans, about a third of their portion of the package that originally had been envisioned as "second tier" to await completion of disbursements by multilateral institutions. South Korea agrees to several new reforms, including quicker opening up of capital markets and allowing foreign

banks and security firms to open wholly-owned subsidiaries. It also hikes overnight call rate, at 25% since mid-
December, to 30% to support KRW. KRW surges upon
opening of trading December 26, and finishes at 1498 versus USD from 1836 December 24 close, after trading as
high as 1995 on December 23.

DEC. 26   Indo-Suez WI Carr Securities estimates that Indonesia may
have about $200 billion in total foreign debt (public and pri-
vate), almost double official estimate. The debt burden has
been made much heavier by sharp depreciation in rupiah.

DEC. 29   President Suharto's special economic advisor Radius Prawiro
attacks the Indosuez report as inaccurate, though he raises
government estimate of total Indonesian USD debt exposure
from $118 billion ($65 billion private) to $133.3 billion inclu-
sive of $15.3 billion in commercial paper and commercial
bonds. He concedes that 200 companies face problems
repaying USD-denominated debts, and asks foreign lenders
to come to Jakarta to negotiate repayment terms. On December 30 Indo-Suez WI Carr Securities disowns the report by its
acting head of research in Jakarta, calling it "erroneous."

South Korea legislature passes financial reform bills that
give Bank of Korea more independence in setting monetary
policy, unify financial regulatory bodies, improve transparency of corporate finance by forcing companies to issue
consolidated financial accounts. Will also eliminate by April
the ceiling on foreign ownership of stocks (now 50%), facil-
itating foreign takeovers. The 4% limit on individual ownership of banks will be lifted for all investors (though
regulatory approval will be needed when passes, 10%, 25%,
33%). Passage by December 30 is a condition of further disbursements by IMF.

Ten major Japanese banks agree to take an "accommodative
stance" on requests to roll over some $5 to $7 billion loans
to South Korean banks, while major U.S. lenders have
agreed in principle to roll over some of their existing loans
to Korean banks.

OCBC and UOB of Singapore, in second hike in less than a
month, raise their prime lending rate 50 basis points to six-
year high of 7%.

Major U.S. lenders agree in principle to roll over some of
existing loans to South Korean banks on case-by-case basis,
and are expected to iron out details at New York talks. In
addition to easing loan repayment terms, expected to address

possibility of new loans to sovereign which could total billions of additional USD.

DEC. 31   South Korea banks avoided year-end default on their international loans, as foreign banks agreed to roll over a certain portion for thirty days. Bankers still discussing arrangement for converting the short-term loans into longer-term credit, with banks reportedly demanding government guarantees.

Standard & Poor's Ratings downgrade Indonesia sovereign long-term foreign currency rating from BBB– to BB+ (junk status), with outlook remaining negative, citing its deteriorating economic condition. It also cuts local currency rating from A– to BBB+ (investment grade), while downgrading Bank Negara Indonesia and seven Indonesian corporations.

Indonesia announces planned merger of four state banks (Bapindo, Exim, DBN, and BBD) in July, and will open them to foreign investors.

1998

JAN. 5   South Korea exploring plans to borrow $35 billion in overseas funds during the first quarter. Under MOFE plan, state banks and companies would raise $20 billion in bank loans or bonds, in addition to the $10 billion in sovereign bonds already approved by parliament, and another $5 billion through syndication loan with U.S. banks. Government delegation will meet with bankers at JP Morgan Monday in New York, where expected to request new bank loans to government. MOFE estimates $21.6 billion in foreign loans fall due in the first quarter.

Concerns about Indonesian political stability reinforced when street vendors riot in the West Java city of Bandung, again targeting the ethnic Chinese minority.

JAN. 6   Indonesian President Suharto Tuesday night proposes a balanced 133.5 trillion IDR budget for FY 98/99, an increase of 32%, bigger than anticipated and raising doubts about whether the revenue assumptions are realistic. In backing off from earlier calls for a budget surplus and further austerity measures, it also raises questions whether it complies with the IMF agreement. Of interest following recent concerns over President Suharto's health, the leader reportedly appears in reasonable health.

JAN. 7   Central banks move to stem slide in regional currencies, with Malaysian Deputy Prime Minister Anwar confirming central bank intervention to support MYR, while the Monetary Authority of Singapore, as usual, declines to comment on intervention operations. MYR rebounds from record 4.88 versus USD to close at 4.565. Singapore dollar recovers from 1.795 to 1.75 close.

JAN. 8   Indonesian markets in free fall, with USD-IDR penetrating the psychological 10,000 level, after starting the new year around 5400. Latest plunge appears to have been triggered by disappointment with the budget for FY 98/99 presented January 5 by President Suharto. Reports that the IMF was dissatisfied, aggravated on the political front by rumblings of some of the first opposition to President Ramos's swirl of potential moratorium as foreign debt burden grows.

S&P Ratings downgrade Thailand long-term foreign currency sovereign rating one notch to BBB– (still investment grade, Moody's already cut it to junk status last month), negative outlook.

Next scheduled installment of $2 billion is approved for immediate disbursement by the IMF board, bringing cumulative lending from IMF to $13.1 billion out of its $21 billion portion of the $60 billion South Korea bailout package.

JAN. 9   Indonesian rupiah rebounds to 8000 versus USD, reversing its Thursday plunge that was extended past 11,000 shortly after Friday open. It apparently finds support from wire reports that say that IMF plans to disburse next $3 billion tranche in bailout package on schedule in March. Also, news that Treasury Secretary Summers will be visiting Jakarta increased hopes that United States has "taken note" of Asian crisis and may get involved.

S&P downgrades Indonesia long-term foreign currency rating from BB+ to BB, leaving it on CreditWatch with negative outlook, while cutting long-term local currency rating from BBB+ to BBB. On January 15 S&P downgrades fifteen Indonesian banks noting that sharp currency depreciation exacerbated asset-quality difficulties stemming from rising defaults and high interest rates.

JAN. 12   Senior IMF and U.S. government officials arrive in Indonesia to mount emergency effort to calm financial turmoil. IMF Deputy Managing Director Stanley Fisher terms meeting with President Suharto "constructive," though more work needed in coming days to hammer out specifics. He and U.S. Deputy Treasury Secretary Summers, who arrived in Jakarta today, are pressing Indonesian government to proceed with reforms agreed to in IMF package. Suharto also speaks on the telephone with Japanese Prime Minister Hashimoto, assuring him that Indonesia would honor its foreign debts and fully implement the IMF reforms.

Peregrine Investments, the Hong Kong–based investment bank, announces that it is effectively shut down and preparing to file for liquidation procedures. Planned purchase of stake by Zurich Group had fallen through last week.

IMF Managing Director Camdessus, in South Korea to meet with government officials, indicates that "so far" he is satisfied with implementation of conditions of IMF bailout.

Tat Lee & Keppel Bank, two smaller Singapore banks, agree to merge.

JAN. 13   Moody's places Hong Kong's prime-1 short-term foreign currency ceiling under review for possible downgrade, citing concern about recent market volatility. S&P has not yet put Hong Kong on CreditWatch with negative outlook.

Hong Kong Hang Seng index and Singapore's STI rebound over 7% Tuesday, following plunges of nearly 9% Monday, as traders are notably relieved when NYSE rebounded Monday following opening dip, after falling 2% Friday. Other regional markets also higher, paced by bounces in Indonesia (9%) and Malaysia (5.5%).

Philippines Central Bank raises overnight lending rate from 15.4% to 16%.

JAN. 15   Indonesia President Suharto and IMF Managing Director Camdessus sign agreement strengthening economic reforms. President Suharto indicates that government budget, much-criticized for unrealistic assumptions, will be revised to incorporate projected GDP growth at 0% and 20% inflation. Some government subsidies will be eliminated, along with scrapping monopolies by commodity regulators (except for rice), establishing a bank deposit insurance scheme, and ending tax benefits for national car program.

S&P Ratings downgrades fifteen Indonesian banks, citing rising borrower defaults aggravated.

JAN. 16   Moody's puts on negative review the ratings of four Thai banks: Malayan Bkg Bhd, Bank Bumiputra Malaysia Bhd, Public Bank Bhd, and Sime Bank Bhd amid.

JAN. 19   S&P Ratings revises South Korea sovereign CreditWatch status from "negative" to "developing" (though still on CreditWatch).

JAN. 20   Indonesian President Suharto confirms he will seek seventh five-year term in March, and hints that he will choose Research and Technology Minister Habibie for critical VP post. Nomination of Habibie would not please markets, in light of his past sponsorship of dubious projects (jet plane) and eccentric views (high interest rates raise inflation).

    Hong Kong brokerage CA Pacific goes into liquidation. The next day hundreds of investors take to the streets, demanding that the Securities & Futures Commission protect their interests, after their cash accounts have been transferred to margin accounts without their knowledge.

JAN. 21   In negotiations with foreign bankers in New York, South Korea reportedly proposes that short-term bank debt be swapped for one- to three-year loans with government guarantee, to apply to all foreign currency international debt by Korean banks maturing this year.

JAN. 22   Collapses in Indonesian rupiah continue, plunging to 16,000 level versus USD, before rebounding to 12,000 range on central bank intervention in thin trade. Downward spiral fueled by failure of authorities to take decisive action as the depreciating rupiah makes foreign currency private debt burden ever-more overwhelming.

JAN. 23   Little market reaction to release of the revised Indonesian 98/99 fiscal budget, which was mostly in line with what had been agreed upon with the IMF last week, including assumption of 0% GDP growth and 20% inflation rate.

JAN. 27   Head of Indonesian government team is set up to coordinate renegotiation of private foreign debt proposed voluntary, temporary three-month pause in servicing of foreign currency debt, beginning immediately (genuine trade credit would continue to be serviced) to allow for working out a new framework for restoring debt servicing. Separately, Bank Indonesia announced it will provide guarantees (for at least two years) on deposits and letters of credit issued by domestic banks, to rebuild confidence in banking system. It hikes interest rates, doubling overnight SBI rate from 14% to 30%.

    S&P Ratings cuts Indonesia's long-term foreign currency rating from BB to B and local currency rating from BBB to BB−, while leaving them on CreditWatch with negative implications. It cites debt servicing problems and growing risks of political instability.

JAN. 28   S&P Ratings lowers rating on eight Indonesian banks, including cutting long-term foreign currency rating for PT

Bank Internasional and Bank Negara to CCC– from B, for Bank Danamon and Bank Niaga to CC from B, and Bank Unum lowered four notches to CC.

JAN. 29   South Korea and foreign banks reach agreement on debt restructuring, in which $24 billion in short-term loans to Korean banks will have maturity extended to one to three years, with government guarantee. Loans will carry rates 225 basis points, 250 basis points and 275 basis points over six-month LIBOR, and South Korea will have option to pay back any time beyond six months if able to borrow on more favorable terms.

Moody's downgrades four Malaysian banks, cutting Public Bank Bhd long-term deposits to BAA2 from BAA1, Sime Bank BHD long-term deposits to BA1 from BAA2, Malayan Banking fin strength to D+ from C+ and Bumiputra Malaysia Bank financial strength to E+ from D. Cites heightened vulnerability of banks to asset quality and liquidity pressures.

Moody's changes its outlook for Singapore Aa1 foreign currency country ceiling to "stable" from "positive," citing effects of regional financial instability.

JAN. 30   MOFE says it will shut down ten of the thirty merchant banks, after in December having suspended operation of fourteen through end of January.

Bank of Thailand announces removal of certain currency restrictions that had made for "two-tier" foreign exchange market, with the movement now toward convergence of offshore and onshore spot rate.

FEB. 2   Regional stock markets surge, as many reopen following the Lunar New Year and Muslim Idil Fitri holidays. More optimistic mood. Perhaps we have seen worst of the crisis (bolstered by factors including agreement last week on restructuring of South Korean debt, Thai elimination of two-tier foreign exchange trading) that sent headline indexes soaring 10–14% in Hong Kong, Singapore, Thailand, Philippines, and Indonesia. Malaysian exchange, which remained closed, soars 23% upon reopening February 3.

Pitch IBCA upgrades South Korea long-term foreign currency rating from B– to BB+ in response to agreement reached last week with foreign bankers in restructuring $24 billion in short-term debt. Rating remains on positive rating watch.

FEB. 4   South Korea Finance Minister Lim reaches agreement in principle with IMF negotiator Hubert Neiss to allow gradual lowering of high interest rates, to be submitted to February 17 IMF board meeting for approval.

FEB. 6   Moody's cuts Malaysia's sovereign foreign currency ratings outlook to negative, citing potential problems in bank and corporate sectors, financial instability. Cuts outlook for Petronas, Telekom, Tenaga.

Notes

Notes for Introduction

1. Keynote speech given by Dr. Mahathir Mohammed at the Annual Meeting of the Board of Governors of the IMF and World Bank, at the Hong Kong Convention and Exhibition Centre, Hong Kong, September 20, 1997.
2. Televised press briefing given by George Soros, founder and president of Soros Fund Management, at the Annual Meeting of the Board of Governors of the IMF and World Bank, at the Hong Kong Convention and Exhibition Centre, Hong Kong, September 21, 1997.
3. Interview with a Boston-based U.S. mutual fund manager, Hong Kong.
4. Interview with a fund manager from the Quantum Fund, New York.

Notes for Chapter 1

1. Gary Fields, "Changing Labour Market Conditions and Economic Development in Hong Kong, Korea, Singapore and Taiwan," in *The East Asian Miracle: Economic Growth and Public Policy,* Oxford University Press and the World Bank, 1993.
2. Newswire reports.
3. *The East Asian Miracle,* p. 5.
4. *Asian Development Bank, 1996 and 1997,* Oxford University Press, 1996, p. 229.
5. Standard & Poor's MMS.
6. *The East Asian Miracle,* p. 41.

7. Walter Hatch and Kozo Yamamura, *Asia in Japan's Embrace: Building a Regional Production Alliance,* Cambridge University Press, 1996, p. 6.
8. Hatch and Yamamura, p. 175.
9. *The East Asian Miracle,* p. 2.
10. *The East Asian Miracle,* p. 37.
11. Newswire reports, February 13, 1993.
12. Comments made to me by senior officials of the Federal Reserve Bank of New York and the U.S. Department of the Treasury.

Notes for Chapter 2

1. World Bank, *Development in Practice—Managing Capital Flows in East Asia,* World Bank, 1996, pp. 4–8.
2. International Finance Corporation (member of the World Bank group), "Lessons of Experience—Foreign Direct Investment," IFC and Foreign Investment Advisory Service, 1997, p. 17.
3. International Finance Corporation, *Lessons of Experience.*
4. World Bank, *Development in Practice,* p. 7.
5. *Far East Economic Review,* October 12, 1996.
6. *Far East Economic Review,* July 18, 1996.
7. *The Economist,* January 6, 1996.
8. *Business Week,* December 25, 1995.

Notes for Chapter 3

1. Asian Development Bank, *Asian Development Outlook 1996 and 1997,* Oxford University Press, 1996, p. 233.
2. Asian Development Bank, *Asian Development Outlook 1996 and 1997,* p. 233.
3. Interview with a senior member of the Deutsche Bundesbank, 1995.
4. Newswire reports.
5. Federal Reserve Bank of New York, *Quarterly Foreign Exchange Report,* Q1, 1995.
6. Federal Reserve Bank of New York, *Quarterly Foreign Exchange Report.*
7. Interviews with foreign exchange dealers in New York and Asia.
8. Speech by Federal Reserve Bank of New York Executive Vice President Peter Fisher at the FOREX USA dinner at the Marriott Marquee Hotel, New York, 1995.
9. Speech by Peter Fisher and a Fisher press conference following the FRBNY's *Quarterly Foreign Exchange Report.*
10. Asian Development Bank, *Asian Development Outlook 1996 and 1997,* p. 233.

11. Eamonn Fingleton, *Blindside: Why Japan Is Still on Track to Overtake the U.S. by the Year 2000,* Simon & Schuster, 1995, p. 57.
12. Fingleton, *Blindside,* p. 60.
13. Fingleton, *Blindside,* pp. 68–70.
14. Asian Development Bank, *Asian Development Outlook 1997 and 1998,* Oxford University Press, 1997, p. 233.
15. Asian Development Bank, *Asian Development Outlook 1997 and 1998,* p. 223.
16. Asian Development Bank, *Asian Development Outlook 1997 and 1998,* p. 237.
17. *The Economist,* August 24, 1996.

Notes for Chapter 4

1. Miguel Savastano, Jorge Roldos, and Julio Santanella, "Factors behind the Financial Crisis in Mexico," International Monetary Fund, *World Economic Outlook,* May 1995.
2. Shahid Javed Burki and Sebastian Edwards, "Latin America after Mexico: Quickening the Pace," *The World Bank,* June 1995.
3. Burki and Edwards, "Latin America after Mexico."
4. John Ross, *Rebellion from the Roots—Indian Uprising in Chiapas,* Common Courage Press, 1995, pp. 7–17.
5. *Business Week,* February 13, 1995.
6. Burki and Edwards, "Latin America after Mexico."

Notes for Chapter 5

1. Pasuk Phongpaichit and Chris Baker, *Thailand: Economy and Politics.* Oxford University Press, 1998, pp. 60–61.
2. Phongpaichit and Baker, *Thailand's Economy and Politics.*
3. *South China Morning Post,* November 13, 1996.
4. Asian Development Bank, *Asian Development Outlook 1996 and 1997,* Oxford University Press, 1996, p. 242.
5. *Far Eastern Economic Review,* March 6, 1996.
6. *Far Eastern Economic Review.*
7. Alison Seng, "All Change in the Baht?" Standard & Poor's MMS, Emerging Asia Insight product, November 29, 1996.
8. Newswire reports.
9. *Bloomberg News* report, July 2, 1997.
10. Standard & Poor's MMS interview with Thailand Finance Minister Amnuay Viravan, February 24, 1997.

Notes for Chapter 6

1. Newswire reports.
2. *Bloomberg News* report, July 2, 1997.
3. Standard & Poor's MMS interview with Bangko Sentral ng Pilipinas Governor Gabriel Singson.
4. Interview with a foreign exchange dealer for a European bank in Singapore, September 1997.
5. Standard & Poor's MMS interview with Bank Indonesia Monetary Management Director Dr. C. Harinowo, July 15, 1997.
6. Comments made to me by Bank Indonesia Governor Soedradjad Djiwandono, September 20, 1997, at a Euromoney conference.
7. Comments made to me by Bank Indonesia Governor Djiwandono.
8. Interview with a treasurer for a European bank in Singapore, August 1997.
9. Interview with a senior dealer for a European bank in Hong Kong, September 1997.
10. Comments made to me by a senior dealer for a U.S. investment bank in New York, October 21, 1997.
11. Hong Kong–Special Administrative Region Financial Secretary Donald Tsang, speaking at a press conference.

Notes for Chapter 7

1. Interview with Dr. Mahathir Mohammed by the *South China Morning Post,* September 21, 1997.
2. Newswire reports, September 23, 1997.
3. Newswire reports, September 28, 1997.
4. Comments made to me by Bank Indonesia Governor Soedradjad Djiwandono, September 20, 1997, at a Euromoney conference.

Notes for Chapter 8

1. Interview with Simon Ogus, SBC Warburg Executive Director of Asian Economies, Hong Kong, November 1997.
2. Walter Hatch and Kozo Yamamura, *Asia in Japan's Embrace: Building a Regional Production Alliance,* Cambridge University Press, p. 348.
3. Eamonn Fingleton, *Blindside: Why Japan Is Still on Track to Overtake the U.S. by the Year 2000,* Simon & Schuster, 1995, pp. 14 and 18.
4. Hatch and Yamamura, pp. 36–37.
5. Satoshi Shimamoto, Standard & Poor's MMS, "Bond and Currency Outlook, Q3, 1997, Japanese Economic Outlook" research paper.

Notes for Chapter 9

1. Asian Development Bank, *Asian Development Outlook 1997 and 1998,* Oxford University Press, 1997, p. 234.
2. Interview with Simon Ogus, SBC Warburg Executive Director of Asian Economies, Hong Kong, November 1997.
3. Interview with Simon Ogus.
4. Newswire reports, November 26, 1997.
5. *Far Eastern Economic Review,* August 28, 1997.
6. Asian Development Bank, *Emerging Asia—Changes and Challenges,* Asian Development Bank, 1997, p. 159.
7. Asian Development Bank, *Emerging Asia,* p. 30.
8. Asian Development Bank, *Asian Development Outlook 1997 and 1998,* pages 20–21.
9. Interview with Simon Ogus.
10. Interview with a Hong Kong–based bond fund manager.
11. Interview with Hong Kong–based fund manager.
12. Comments by the then Reserve Bank of India Governor C. Rangarajan at a Euromoney conference and to me, Hong Kong, September 20, 1997.
13. Interview with a U.S. investment bank manager, Hong Kong, December 1997.
14. Interview with Simon Pritchard, financial columnist at the *South China Morning Post,* December 1997.

Notes for Chapter 10

1. Newswire reports, December 24 and 26, 1997.
2. Newswire reports, January 5, 1998.

Notes for Chapter 11

1. Asian Development Bank, *Asian Development Outlook 1997 and 1998,* Oxford University Press, 1997, pp. 47–54.
2. Meryl Phang, "China Banking System: An Asian Difference," Standard & Poor's MMS Emerging Asia Insight product, December 9, 1997.
3. Phang, "China Banking System."
4. Asian Development Bank, *Asian Development Outlook 1997 and 1998,* pp. 47–54.
5. Asian Development Bank, *Asian Development Outlook 1997 and 1998,* p. 242.

Bibliography

Books

Bello, Walden, and Stephanie Rosenfeld, *Dragons in Distress—Asia's Miracle Economies in Crisis,* Penguin Books, 1992.

Calder, Kent E., *Asia's Deadly Triangle—How Arms, Energy and Growth Threaten to Destabilize Asia-Pacific,* Nicholas Brealey Publishing, 1997.

Clifford, Mark, *Troubled Tiger—The Unauthorised Biography of Korea, Inc,* Butterworth-Heinemann Asia, 1997.

Fingleton, Eamonn, *Blindside—Why Japan Is Still on Track to Overtake the U.S. by the Year 2000,* Simon & Schuster, 1995.

Hatch, Walter, and Kozo Yamamura, *Asia in Japan's Embrace—Building a Regional Production Alliance,* Cambridge University Press, 1996.

Lingle, Christopher, *The Rise and Decline of the Asian Century: False Starts on the Path to the Global Millenium,* Editions Sirocco SL, Barcelona, 1997.

Naisbitt, John, *Megatrends Asia—The Eight Asian Megatrends That Are Changing the World,* Nicholas Brealey Publishing, 1997.

Phongpaichit, Pasuk, and Chris Baker, *Thailand's Boom!* Allen & Unwin, 1996.

Ross, John, *Rebellion from the Roots—Indian Uprising in Chiapas,* Common Courage Press, 1995.

Official Publications

Asian Development Bank, *Asian Development Outlook 1996 and 1997,* Oxford University Press, 1996.

Asian Development Bank, *Asian Development Outlook 1997 and 1998,* Oxford University Press, 1997.

Asian Development Bank, *Emerging Asia—Changes and Challenges,* Asian Development Bank, 1997.

Asian Development Bank, *Critical Issues in Asian Development—Theories, Experiences, Policies,* Oxford University Press, 1996.

Federal Reserve Bank of New York, *Quarterly Foreign Exchange Book,* Q1, 1995.

International Finance Corporation, *Foreign Direct Investment—Lessons of Experience,* International Finance Corporation and Foreign Investment Advisory Service, 1997.

International Monetary Fund, "Factors Behind the Financial Crisis in Mexico," research article by Miguel Savastano, Jorge Roldos, and Julia Santanella, *World Economic Outlook,* May 1995.

World Bank, *The East Asian Miracle—Economic Growth and Public Policy,* Oxford University Press, 1993.

World Bank, "Latin America After Mexico: Quickening the Pace," research article by Shahid Javed Burki and Sebastian Edwards, *World Economic Outlook,* June 1995.

World Bank, *Managing Capital Flows in East Asia,* World Bank, May 1996.

Newspapers/Magazines/Newswires

AFX News
Asiaweek
Business Week
Bloomberg News
Far East Economic Review
Korea Money
South China Morning Post
The Economist

Index